7/19/06

It's so wonderful to have parents who are also such good friends! I love you very much.

Kay

The Great Communicators

Royal Publishing, Inc.
P.O. Box 1120
18825 Hicrest Road
Glendora, California 91740

Library of Congress Cataloging in Publication Date in Progress

ISBN 0-934344-18-3

Printed in the United States of America

The Great Communicators

From **President Ronald Reagan's** letter to the
National Speakers Association

THE WHITE HOUSE

WASHINGTON

I am pleased to extend warm greetings to the
members of the National Speakers Association

Professional speaking is a rapidly growing field,
paralleling the information explosion we currently
face. It is not enough to keep abreast of new
information; we must also keep ahead in order to
make the future all that it can be.

As a CPAE since 1981, I feel a special kindred
spirit with the National Speakers Association --
a society deeply committed to the highest level
of professionalism.

Ronald Reagan

Reprinted with permission from the White House.

We dedicate this book to

The Great Communicator

PRESIDENT RONALD REAGAN

Official photograph, Pete Souza, The White House.

TY BOYD, C.P.A.E.
The Cullen Center
1727 Garden Terrace
Charlotte, NC 28203
(704) 333-9999

Cavett
Award

Ty Boyd

Ty Boyd, of Charlotte, North Carolina, is the recipient of the two highest awards in the speaking profession—the CPAE for Platform Excellence, *and the "Oscar" of the National Speakers Association, the coveted Cavett Award. He is a Businessman, Broadcaster, TV and Radio Personality/Spokesman, Salesman, Consultant and internationally-known Professional Speaker.*

As a Businessman, Ty Boyd is Chairman of Boyd, Kellen, Thomas & Cruse Marketing & Advertising, Inc., and President of Ty Boyd Enterprises, Inc.

As a Broadcaster, Ty Boyd has been seen and heard on nearly every television and radio station in America. He's the host of the new nationally-syndicated DAWN Show, a daily television series featuring motivational speakers and entrepreneurs.

On the Platform, Ty Boyd is an in-demand speaker for some 200 audiences every year, and is past president of the 3,000-member National Speakers Association. He is the featured star of numerous full-length management and sales films, and a Contributing Editor of QUOTE *magazine, the publication for speakers and leaders. He conducts THE EXECUTIVE SPEAKER INSTITUTE, a 3-day intensive workshop held in Charlotte six times each year, created the popular motivational and instructional cassette courses, THE SKILL BUILDER Series and is the narrator of the life-changing four-volume ENCYCLOPEDIA OF SELF IMPROVEMENT, written by M.R. Kopmeyer and distributed all over the world.*

Ty's exceptional experience and research give him an in-depth understanding of many of the challenges facing each of us, both personally and professionally.

Introduction
by Ty Boyd, C.P.A.E.

"The music that can deepest reach,
And cure all ill, is cordial speech."
—Emerson

I read somewhere the other day that "kindness is a language that the blind can see and the deaf can hear."

Each diploma we award in our *Executive Speaker Institute* in Charlotte is inscribed: "Words well spoken make of us giants." And it's true!

"I know the language—all the words—what else do I need?" That bit of rhetoric may have worked in days past. No more. Good communications is both an art <u>and</u> a science.

The SCIENCE of communications is complex and many faceted. Understanding Dr. David Merrill's concept called "Social-Style Awareness" is part science. Behavior may be described in terms of assertiveness and responsiveness. Each of us has learned certain behaviors in our attempts to influence or inform others. We discover the more assertive we are, the more we tend to *tell* others; the less assertive, the more we tend to *ask*. Likewise, the concept measures a person's need to emote or display his/her emotions on a responsive scale. We are measured on the scale all the way from "poker-faced" to a big, grinning "Golllleeee!"

The scientific aspects of this study conclude that people's behavior is truly different. The more ways we are different, the more difficult it is to communicate. The benefit of this study is that we can be aware that though our actions may be grossly dissimilar to a neighbor's, it is not necessarily a matter of "good/bad," "right/wrong"—but just "different." Being aware of those differences and adapting our behavior to accommodate another's style makes us *"versatile."* Versatility is the effort to please more people while keeping your own objective intact. It is a balanced concern for self, others, and the task at hand.

Now that's powerful communications!

It is as important for leaders to polish communications skills as it is to have market updates, economic forecasts, and research.

In today's constantly changing world, we receive a constant barrage of information. We are required to share explanations, changes, plans, information updates and attitudes with audiences of from one to one thousand and more. It is vital that we be able to communicate clearly and persuasively. Top achievers know that the ability to communicate well is essential to being an effective leader, team builder, front runner and excellence-aimer.

The ART of communications covers a world of subject matter. Our every action, or in-action, communicates. Touch communicates. Looks communicate. Smell communicates.

Many of the authors in this volume are members of the National Speakers Association. Our organization numbers many hundreds. Many of the speakers will actively practice professionally their speaking skills several times each month. And yet few of us have so mastered our craft that we are understood to say what we've actually verbalized. The practiced speaker is one who has learned over time just how to deliver a special phrase or story. The situation is not unlike the scripting of a Broadway play. And yet we err. I don't know a speaker who hasn't felt that he/she still could deliver the message a little more effectively. That's improving communications. If these professionals practice, practice, practice—and still have cause for improvement, doesn't it appear to make the case for all to remain students of both the art and the science?

On our daily syndicated TV show *Dawn,* some of our time's greatest communicators deliver their best twenty to twenty-two minutes of material. Almost every one is masterfully done. We recieve great and glowing tribute for their appearances. If only the audiences knew how long these "master communicators" labored to make their remarks seem "off-hand" and easy to understand.

When Dottie Walters asked me to write this introduction to a valuable volume, I realized how really near impossible it would be to capture the essence of the subject matter in a few words. I have not succeeded. Read on, however—there are masters among these pages, eager to lead you to a healthier skill level in your own quest to become a Master Communicator.

NIDO QUBEIN, C.P.A.E.
Creative Services, Inc.
P.O. Box 6008
High Point, NC 27262

Nido R. Qubein

Nido R. Qubein is one of America's leading professional speakers and sales consultants.

He is the author of many best selling books including Communicate Like A Pro, *the producer of numerous cassette learning systems, and the winner of all the awards given to speakers including the Cavett (the Oscar of the speaking profession), the CPAE (Council of Peers Award of Excellence), and the NSA's Distinguished Service Award.*

Nido is a past president of the National Speakers Association and the chairman of the Professional Speakers Benefit Fund. He also serves as a director on the boards of several corporations, financial institutions and colleges. In July 1972, he founded the Qubein Scholarship Fund which has granted college scholarships to over sixty deserving students in North Carolina.

Known widely for his many outstanding accomplishments, Nido is a very poular speaker and consultant among corporate giants including AT&T, General Electric, Dole, Wrangler, Mobil and hundreds more. In a recent article, MONEY *magazine boasted that "72% of Qubein's engagements are repeat invitations from clients who have utilized his services before . . ."*

Nido R. Qubein is indeed a living proof that America is still the land of opportunity!

Foreword
by Nido R. Qubein

"Misunderstandings don't exist;
only failure to communicate exists."
                    —Sengalese Proverb

You're in for a treat. This is a valuable book filled with practical ideas on the art of effective communication.

The principles for connecting with an audience are the same whether you are speaking to a loved one, addressing an audience of a thousand people, writing an article for publication, or negotiating an international arms reduction treaty.

I clearly remember when they all stood and applauded in appreciation for the address I had just given them. The 500 people in the audience brought to mind a flash-back of my early days when I first gave a speech out of desperation.

It was in 1966 that I came to the United States of America. I was to attend college here. I was alone and broke. But I had set my foot on the land where opportunity and success are alive and well.

Speaking very few words of the English language, and having been here for only a few months, it seemed that the end of the world had just hit me. How would I pay for school? How would I live? Discouragement began to set in and despair took over, but not for long.

Horace once said, "Adversity reveals genius, prosperity often hides it." My mother used to put it another way. She would say, "When things are bad, don't quit, shift gears. When things get tough, the tough get going."

I decided to do what many people throughout history have done when faced with difficult times. They made a plan. So I quickly began a roadmap for my life. I determined what my goals were. Essentially they were to continue college and to support myself. I must work for the money to pay for my education, so I planned the way to earn the money. And I read, time and again, good books on the subject of communication.

I learned that the process of communicating is basically sending and receiving images. We tend to think in images or pictures. To communicate those images to others we rely on vehicles such as words, pictures, sounds, and gestures. We use the same means whether we are trying to catch a waiter's attention to order another cup of coffee or trying to explain Einstein's theory of relativity to a group of college students.

Of course, the real challenge is to send accurate images to others, as well as receive accurate images from them: to convey things exactly as you see them, and to receive them exactly as others see them. Those tasks are complicated by our God-given abilities, as individuals, to send and receive very complex images, to relate them to other images we have captured in our memories, and to attach meanings to the images we receive and retain.

I like to think of communicating as mind-to-mind reorientation. In other words, when you communicate effectively you can change the way people think, feel, and act by enabling them to understand the way you think, feel and act. And if you are a good listener, you can reverse that process.

Now, believing that that process is the same in any country, or culture, or language, I set about to communicate as best I could with the people in my new land.

It was just before Christmas and I could hear the strains of "Oh Little Town of Bethlehem" coming over the radio. In my bag were slides of the Holy Land. Home! I took them out and arranged them together into a Christmas story. Then I wrote a letter to all the local churches. I offered them a "Meaningful Christmas Program" from a guy who was born in the Holy Land! They took me up on the offer. Soon I was doing several programs per month. They paid me five, ten and up to twenty-five dollars to come to a church, show my slide program, and tell them about the Holy Land.

Those years of adversity trained me well. They were tough years. They continued for all my undergraduate time in college. But through the power of believing, and by using some of the great techniques in this book, I was able to pull through from obscurity to a successful career in speaking and consulting.

When adversity comes, we cannot give up. Somehow when things are going fine and prosperity is upon us, the "comfort zone" begins to take over. We can so easily get into a rut, and the genius inside of us is not then revealed.

I stood on that stage and flashed back in my mind's eye to all those hard years. It has been a long time now since I've given one of those twenty-five dollar talks. But the twenty-five dollars meant more to me in those lean days than any amount I earn today. My college speeches to those small church audiences of fifteen, twenty or fifty people meant more because they were bringing forth all my drive and perseverance. In those struggling days it was tough to do even fifty talks a year and keep up my school work. Today, with an office staff to back me up, I do 200 presentations each year easily.

I believe that the thousands of salespeople, managers, and executives who attend my seminars each year can benefit enormously from the message in this book. So can you. Socrates said, "Know thyself." Yet, too many of us are blocked by communication when it comes to knowing who we really are—and who we can become.

We need to learn as many techniques of communication as we can, and practice all we can. The older I get, the more I admire the Norman Vincent Peales, the Earl Nightengales, and the Paul Harveys who have blazed the trail before me in the professional speaking field. If I can learn half of what they know, I can raise my effectiveness as a communicator to a level beyond my greatest dreams.

But they didn't become mature, effective communicators overnight. Nor will I; nor will you. It takes patience—the patience of giving it all you've got while waiting for what you acquire to mature.

You are unique. You deserve the best. You can achieve your dreams. But, first, you gotta master the art of effective communication.

The Great Communicators speaks to one of the most crucial aspects of human relationships— effective communication. Read, learn and enjoy. You're in for a treat!

—Nido R. Qubein
Author & Consultant

**Dottie Walters receives the
Certified Speaking Professional (CSP) designation
presented by Ty Boyd, past president of the
National Speakers Association.**

DOTTIE WALTERS, C.S.P.
Royal Publishing, Inc.
18825 Hicrest Road
P.O. Box 1120
Glendora, CA 91740
(818) 335-8069

Dorothy M. Walters, C.S.P.

Dottie Walters is unique. She began her long and illustrious career with no car, one rickety stroller, two babies and a borrowed typewriter and a high school education. There were no jobs. The country was in a recession when Dottie started down the long road. She put cardboard in her shoes and kicked the wheel back on the stroller each time it came off.

Today Dottie is a World Class Speaker, President of her International Speakers Bureau and Publisher of the largest newsmagazine in the world of Speakers. She has been honored three times by the National Speakers Association, with the Certified Speaking Professional designation, one of the first four United States women to receive it. She is a founding member of N.S.A., as well as the founding member and officer of the Greater Los Angeles N.S.A. Chapter. She has initiated and sold several businesses, all based on advertising and publishing.

She is president of four corporations, author, speaker, seminar leader, publisher (anthologies featuring outstanding speakers), poet, featured in many TV radio shows, newspaper and magazine articles, books and cassettes worldwide. Her first book, Never Underestimate the Selling Power of a Woman *is in its 14th edition.*

Dottie and Bob Walters have three children, an attorney, a drama teacher and the manager of their International Speakers Bureau. Dottie and Bob live in Glendora, California.

Prologue
by Dottie Walters, Publisher
Certified Speaking Professional

Great Communicators know the use of the "Gentle Question" to find out what their clients, family or prospects want. My friend of the mind Ben Franklin explains that we must "Put on the role of the humble inquirer."

But Ben would be the first to agree that we must first locate the prospect before we can ask those gentle, leading questions. Then the answers communicate to us just how to help our client solve problems.

What if the client will not speak to us? Ben Franklin hit just such a road block. He was sent to England as the official representative of the Colonies to try to get the hated stamp tax repealed. When Ben called on Lord Hillsborough, the Secretary of State who was in charge of colony affairs, he was coldly turned away. Ben could not even present his case. He might have just given up—sailed home to America a failure.

Ben Did Not Give Up

He figured out a plan. First he called personally on each of the members of Parliament. He began with those who were friends of the Colonies and got their signatures on a petition for repeal of the tax. Then he showed his list to those members who were lukewarm. Many of them added their names. Lastly Ben took his petition to those who had never been in harmony with America. Some of these, upon seeing how many others were backing Ben's repeal, took quill-pen in hand and added their names. He got the measure on the floor for a vote. On the day that the Stamp Act was repealed, Ben stood in the British Parliament. He said he was not revengeful in any way to Lord Hillsborough who had first treated him so badly. But he did wear the same suit of clothes he had worn upon that occasion. "Because the repeal made my American suit so happy!" Ben grinned.

Step Into My Office

If you could come into my publishing office to visit with me today, you would first see Ben Franklin's picture on my wall near one of Cowboy Bob, my husband. Then you might notice all across one side of the room a beautiful Spanish tile and mahogany soda fountain with nine leather covered stools. Unusual? Yes. But if those stools could speak, they would tell you a story.

Stool With a Story

This very same soda fountain was installed in the Rexall Drug Store of Baldwin Park, California, the most popular spot in town. Ruben Ahlman, the pharmacist, President of the Chamber of Commerce, was a king-pin of opinion. It was a recession period, after World War II. Jobs were scarce. My husband, Cowboy Bob, had purchased a small dry cleaning business. We had two darling babies, a tract home, car . . . the usual time payments. Then the bottom fell out. There was no money for the house payments or anything else.

I remembered my Alhambra High School English teacher in that time of desperation. She had inspired me to take journalism. She named me advertising manager and feature editor. I thought, "If I could buy space from the small weekly newspaper in the town and resell it for a bit more, maybe I could make that house payment." I had no car and no baby sitter. I pushed my two children before me in a rickety stroller with a big pillow in the back and a wheel that kept coming off. I hit it back on with my shoe and kept putting one foot in front of the other. The idea worked. I made enough money for the house payment and to buy an old used car Cowboy Bob found for me.

Then I hired a high school girl to work from 3 to 5 each afternoon, baby sitting. When the clock struck three I grabbed my newspaper samples and flew out the door to drive to my telephone-made appointments.

But Ruben Ahlman of that Rexall Drug Store

was my deadbolt. There was no communicating with him. Each time I came in he just shook his head from side to side, "No." He even refused to speak to me on the phone.

On this dark rainy afternoon, I thought I would try the Rexall Drug Store again. If Ruben Ahlman advertised with me, half of the other merchants in town would follow his lead. He was at the prescription counter in the back. I smiled my best smile and held up my newspaper with my shopper's column carefully marked in green ink. He emphatically shook his head in that negative gesture again. "No." He was my key, but I couldn't get a grip on his mind to turn him.

Tumbling the Lock

Suddenly all my vigor left me. I made it as far as the soda fountain at the front of the store with the feeling that I didn't have the strength to drive home. Mr. Ahlman's ad would have meant this month's house payment was covered. I pulled out my last dime and ordered a cherry coke, then put my head down on my hands and sighed. Would my babies lose their home, as I had so many times when I was growing up? My eyes filled with tears.

A soft voice beside me on the next soda fountain stool said, "You look so tired. What is the matter, dear?"

I looked up into the sympathetic face of a lovely lady. I poured out my story to her, ending with, "But Mr. Ahlman will not even let me speak to him!"

She took my marked issue of the newspaper in her hands and carefully read my shopper's column material. Then she stood up. In a commanding voice that could be heard down the block, she said, **"Ruben Ahlman, come here."** The lady was Mrs. Ahlman!

Turning Point

What made me turn back for a coke that dismal afternoon? Why did I tell my story to a stranger? Maybe it was the overwhelming desire within me to communicate. Perhaps my subconscious whispered, "Just one more effort. You can make it."

Ruben and Vivian Ahlman became our dearest friends, as well as steady advertising customers. My advertising business prospered and grew into four offices, with 225 employees serving 4,000 retail stores. That day on the soda fountain stool was a turning point. I learned that the key to a stalemate situation may be a third person endorsement!

Later when Mr. Ahlman removed the soda fountain from his drug store, Cowboy Bob, my dear husband, bought it and installed it in my office.

Come, Have a Soda Fountain Coke

If you could come and sit here at my soda fountain today, we would talk about communication. I'd pour you a cherry coke and sit beside you on a stool. I would remind you never to give up. Then I would tell you that if you can't communicate with a key person, try someone else. Try another path around. Maybe to someone who can communicate for you.

Perhaps you need two keys to open that lockbox with its treasures. Don't give up. **Someone is waiting for you to communicate.**

> "God has not given us the spirit of fear. But of **Power, and of Love, and of a Sound Mind.**"
>
> —*Apostle Paul, New Testament*

A speaker is a great person, who happens to speak well.

—Quintillian

The Great Communicators

C O N T E N T S

The Great Communicators

CAPTAIN GERALD L. COFFEE
United States Navy (Ret.)
98-1247 Kaahumanu Rm. 306-B
Aiea, HI 96701
(808) 488-1776

Gerald Coffee

Navy Captain Gerald Coffee is a native Californian. He graduated from UCLA in 1957, and was soon commissioned as a Naval Officer. He received his Navy Wings in 1959. His military flying was primarily in high performance reconnaissance jets, flying from the decks of aircraft carriers in oceans all over the world.

In early 1966, while flying combat missions over North Vietnam, Captain Coffee's aircraft was downed by enemy fire. He parachuted safely but was captured immediately. For the next seven years he served as a Prisoner of War in the Communist prisons of North Vietnam.

After his return in early 1973, he earned a Masters Degree in Political Science, graduated from the National War College, and commanded his own aircraft squadron. His last Naval assignment was in Public Affairs on the staff of the Commander in Chief of the U.S. Pacific Fleet in Hawaii.

Captain Coffee's military awards and decorations include the Silver Star, two awards of the Legion of Merit, the Distinguished Flying Cross, two awards of the Bronze Star, the Air Medal, two awards of the Purple Heart, the Combat Action Ribbon, two awards of the Navy Unit Commendation Medal, and the Vietnam Service Medal with 13 stars.

For his contribution to Americanism through public speaking, Captain Coffee has received numerous civilian awards, including the George Washington Honor Medal presented by Freedoms Foundation at Valley Forge.

1

I Am, Therefore I Communicate
by Captain Gerald Coffee

*"To speak his thoughts is every
freeman's right,
In peace and war, in council and in
fight."*

—Homer

"You must learn to communicate. You must learn the code. Everything depends upon it." The voice was unexpected; an urgent whisper. It was the first real English I had heard in over a month. "When the guard leaves the passageway between the cells we can clear it and whisper like this. But the rest of the time you must communicate by using the code."

And so, there in the musty gloom of a North Vietnamese prison in the winter of '66 came my first inkling of an entirely new form of communication; a form which would not only reveal new bounds of expression and understanding, but would also preserve the human linkages upon which my sanity and ultimate survival would depend.

As a Navy pilot flying reconnaissance missions over North Vietnam in February of 1966, my aircraft had been hit by anit-aircraft fire and crashed into the Tonkin Gulf. Just before the plane had disintegrated, my crewman and I had ejected at very high speed and completely out of control. In the fierce battle for our capture between North Vietnamese militiamen and attack aircraft from our own aircraft carrier, my crewman had been killed and I had been wounded and taken prisoner. After being exhibited in several villages and hamlets in the countryside where the people took out their anger and frustration upon me—the captured "U.S. Air Pirate"—I ended up in these dungeon-like cells of Hoa Lo prison in the heart of Hanoi; the capital of North Vietnam.

Medical care for my injuries had been cynically withheld. "You have a medical problem, and you have a political problem. When you are ready to do concrete deeds about your political problem, then we will talk about your medical problem." The interrogations had been painful and grueling. The physical reality of my plight had been readily acceptable; however, the psychological acceptance was coming more slowly.

Consistent with their overall policy, my captors had kept me in solitary confinement to "think about my crimes." I had known of several other American pilots being shot down and presumably captured before me. I had even seen some of their initials scratched in obscure corners of the cells in which I had shivered through February and some of March. They had left messages on these walls as well, "Smile, you're on candid camera," and
"God = strength."

But where were they now? The loneliness had been pervasive. It had begun to dominate my every conscious thought. Where were the others?

Tap Code

It was in this context that I had been moved to cell #6 in Heartbreak Hotel, so named because it was the cell block to which new prisoners were moved for the realization of their plight to really sink in.

"Man in cell #6 with broken arm. Can you hear me? Answer up." The unmistakably American voice—slightly southern—had made the hair on my neck stand out straight. I had sprung to the barred transom over the heavy wooden door, balancing precariously because of the need to cradle my broken right arm with the left. "You must learn to communicate."

The explanation was terse. "Somewhere on the walls of your cell you will find a little square matrix with twenty-five letters of the alphabet, five rows of five letters each, one row on top of the other. Leave out the letter K and use a C instead when you need to." My mind was scanning back over the walls of my cell. Yes. There were several of the alphabet squares scratched there. Most had been scratched out or white washed over, but one or two were discernable. The first five letters, A through E, were in the top row; below them, F through J in the second row, and so on. The result was five rows of five letters each, one row on top of the other. The rows were numbered top to bottom one through five. The vertical columns were numbered left to right, one through five.

	1	2	3	4	5
1	A	B	C	D	E
2	F	G	H	I	J
3	L	M	N	O	P
4	Q	R	S	T	U
5	V	W	X	Y	Z

The faceless whisper continued. "If you want

to communicate an A to the man on the other side of the wall, tap once for the row—row one, and once for the column—column one. A is one and one. If you want a B, tap once for the row—row one, and twice for the column—column two. B is one and two. For F tap twice for the row—row two, and once for the column—column one. So F is two and one, and so on. Call up the man next door with "Shave and a Haircut" tap—tap tap—tap—tap. My mentor tapped the inside of his door to demonstrate. I could now just see the tip of his nose. "He'll answer with six bits" tap-tap. "Then you can go on with your message." My mind strained to assimilate all I had just heard. Comprehension was overcome by the exhilaration of actual contact with another American. I was bursting with questions. "Who are you?" I blurted. "Shhhhh—not so loud. If they catch us communicating they'll torture us again just to extract an apology for breaking the prison regulations." Recollections of my last few weeks of interrogation flashed through my mind. "You must apologize to the American people who are against this dirty war." And on and on.

"OK, sorry," I whispered back, matching my new friend's volume as precisely as I could. Still my curiosity prevailed. "How many Americans are here in . . ." Thump! The fist thump on the other door had quickly followed the single phony cough at the entry end of the cell block. The guard entered and went slowly from cell to cell, sliding aside the little piece of rusty tin which covered the peephole in each door. As I sat there on the concrete slab of my bed I must have looked guilty as hell and my heart pounded loudly. I realized my first comm lesson was over.

It's probably just as well that I didn't realize that for much of the next seven years the tap code, with its many variations and applications, would be the only means of communicating with my fellow prisoners. It would become as natural as breathing. I would develop as much professional pride in my prison comm skills as I had in a near perfect carrier landing on a moonless night. Once the structure of the code was understood, the skill would be mastered through hours and days of practice. The motivation for proficiency would be very strong. And the callouses on my tapping knuckles would be with me forevermore.

Safety, Brevity, and Empathy

Once the structure of the code was understood, the skill was mastered through hours and days of practice. The motivation for proficiency was very strong.

All comm had to be covert to avoid certain punishment; usually several days in leg stocks with wrists cuffed or manacled tightly behind the back.

To comm safely we developed clearing systems which could be as simple as watching the changing shadows through the narrow slit beneath the door, or more complex, involving several men in various parts of a cell block, or even of the entire prison complex. Some clearing systems were ingenious. In some cell blocks the prisoner who portioned out the food for the cell block could ensure that a few grains of rice were dropped on the floor of the passageway between the cells. Later, as the men communicated among the cells, rats would gather around the spilled rice outside. If a roving guard tried to sneak quietly into the cell block the startled rats would scurry off squeaking loudly as they went. They provided a reliable danger alarm for the communicators who would have otherwise been caught. Except in emergencies, a reasonable clearing system was a prerequisite for any communication.

In order to maximize comm opportunities—to exchange as much information as possible in as short a time as possible—abbreviations and a sort of short-hand common to the unique environment were developed; or I should say evolved. Seldom was a full word ever spelled out. The single letter T was used for "the" and the letter N was used for "and." Most commonly used words were abbreviated in some way. The classic was the letter Q which meant "Quiz" which was short for "interrogation" in the first place. Obviously, there was no time for equivocation; no mincing of words. All information—essential or non-essential—was reduced down to its essence. The result was clarity.

Even with this condensation of information, most of us would spend hours communicating each day. You could learn all about the man next door; his childhood, his family, hometown, and hopes for the future when free again. Lasting friendships were bonded through the walls, sometimes without seeing one another, without a handshake or a hug until three or four years off in the future. "Conversation" became so natural that subtle nuances of feelings and emotions could be expressed and received, not only through the actual words but by the nature of the tapping itself. Even anger, despair, and excitement could be communicated. After many months of daily conversation, even laughter, or groans—perhaps in response to a joke or story—would evolve through little thumps or brushing noises transmitted with feeling. The tap code and all of its variations facilitated an incredibly effective support system; a system which in turn facilitated expressions of encouragement, compassion and sympathy, and the expiation of remorse when things hadn't gone well during a quiz or torture session.

Myriad Life Lines

Within the senses of sight, sound and touch, comm

possibilities through tap code were practically un-limited. Besides tapping on walls—or floors when there were no common walls, or there were empty cells between men—the code could be used by sweeping with a broom, by chopping wood, digging, or flapping wet clothing when hanging it out to dry. Ultimately, coughs, sniffs, hacking, throat clearing, and sneezing could replace the taps—one through five respectively—and a prisoner, while feigning pneumonia, could actually comm with men several cells away, or even in another cell block. The guards hardly noticed since they were always hacking and spitting anyway.

Tap code had many visual applications as well. On many occasions while waiting in a yard area for a quiz, or perhaps on a wood detail, I knew curious Americans were watching me through cracks or tiny holes they had drilled through their doors. Sometimes two coughs or sniffs would confirm my suspicion (two of anything meant yes, ok, go ahead, or positive, while one meant no, I don't understand, or danger). I would then simply drop my hand to my side and extend combinations of fingers to designate the number combinations of the tap code, silently passing news and information from my cell block to theirs. Other times, on a predetermined schedule, information could be passed from one prison compound to another by carefully "flashing" tap code along a common line of sight; making a white or easily seen object appear and disappear in the proper numerical combinations.

Note drops and pickups in common areas were very effective. However, since the jailers and guards were always on the alert for anything like that, the notes had to look innocuous, or like trash to blend in with the usual grubby surroundings. So, notes would often consist of thread extracted from clothing or a blanket, and with tiny knots tied in numerical groupings according to the tap code, i.e., four knots—space—five knots—space—four knots— space—three knots would equate to 4-5, 4-3, or US, etc. A knotted thread could be left for pick up anywhere because the knots were so tiny it attracted no attention. Another note alternative was to use a piece of wire sharpened like a needle to prick tiny holes in a piece of paper following the same pattern as the knots in the thread. The holes could only be seen when the paper was held up to light. Otherwise the note just looked like a piece of blank paper wadded up and discarded in the corner.

The tactile applications of tap code were especially ingenious. On one occasion, two men widened tiny chinks in the mortar of their cell walls near the floor. Since the openings were juxtaposed across a three foot void—designed that way to thwart communication—a thin wire was passed from one cell to the other. It was hardly noticeable running along the filthy corner of the void. Each day the men could comm by holding the ends of the wire and gently tugging in the numerical rhythm of the tap code. They had established a silent, almost invisible link in the comm chain that linked a senior officer to the men in his command.

Moves from prison to prison were fairly common, and would often involve several prisoners bunched together in the back of a covered army truck or other vehicle. In the dead of night we would be blindfolded and handcuffed, and guards— usually one for every two or three prisoners— would stand or sit among us to stop any attempts to communicate. They, of course, were listening for us to whisper. However, in the usual cramped quarter and darkness it was easy to carefully seek out another man's foot with your own and comm by gently exerting pressure from foot to foot, again in the rhythm of the tap code. Because this enabled us to trade news and information about different cell blocks, prisons and their living conditions, and about our captor's policies and purges, continuity and consistency of policy by our own senior officers was possible.

There were sometimes circumstances in the prison environment which made direct comm somewhat easier. If, for example, the entire cell block could be cleared by the man in the cell nearest the entryway, vocal conversations could take place through the cracks beneath the doors. Men could also converse through their walls by talking into their tin drinking cup against the wall, and listening through a cup against the other side. The tin cups transmitted sound through many inches of concrete or brick.

All of the prison communication based upon tap code and clearing systems required an incredible amount of ingenuity and persistence, and, of course, risk. Whenever the enemy threw up another barrier to our comm system, we would find a way around it. It became a matter of personal and professional pride to maintain those lines of communication throughout the prison system, and especially up and down our chains of command.

Why Is Normal Communication So Difficult?

So, what can we as business people, professionals, teachers, speakers, parents—communicators all—learn from those "Great Communicators" there in the Communist prisons of North Vietnam? How can the skills which evolved from nessity there be adapted to our own daily necessities where communicating with one another should be so much easier and efficient than we sometimes make it?

First of all, and most obvious, the disclaimer—usually uttered in exasperation—"I just can't seem to communicate with him/her/them" should take on an entirely new level of absurdity. Given the proper motivation and/or sense of urgency we should be able to communicate with anyone anytime about anything; especially within the context of our own normal working and social environment. Really, when was the last time you had to communicate with an associate, or a student, or a family member by furtively tapping away on the wall from office to office, or classroom to classroom or kitchen to bedroom. Why must face to face communications in relatively optimum conditions be so difficult? Especially when, as in the prison environment, our survival may be at stake; be it our professional or social survival, or that of our business or marriage.

The communication requirements of those American P.O.W.s in North Vietnam should also teach us more about our own specific comm skills. Although we seldom face such urgency of communication, and we surely risk no physical punishment for doing so, it is, nevertheless, imperative that we know how to be precise, concise, and directly to the point when the situation calls for it. Not only should our vocabularies contain the exact words for a specific situation, our comm discipline must dictate their use. Superficial verbiage can frequently obscure our intent and meaning. We become lazy in that respect because we are seldom faced with the need to express an urgent thought in the fewest words possible, and with no second chance to summarize, or reiterate, or clarify. Sometime in some instance, we may face that need.

Comprehension Beyond Words

If focusing upon the skill of precise expression has any merit, so too—perhaps more importantly—is the skill of precise listening. We constantly hear cliches and prescriptions for being a good listener. How frequently, however, do we really concentrate on the emotional inflection of the words we hear? Just as the men in those Hanoi cells learned to deduce the psychological state of their comrades through the brick and concrete of the walls that separated them, we too must concentrate to cut through the pretense of the words we hear; to correctly interpret the inflections and nuances, to comprehend beyond the words. Even with the obvious advantage of face to face or touch to touch dialogue, we frequently fail to hear what is really being said. The truly effective communicators listen as articulately as they speak. How else can the one exactly correct response be provided; the right words of understanding, condolence, love, or encouragement that may be needed; needed perhaps even desperately? Sometimes, if we've listened properly, the best response may simply be reflective silence. How often do the "great communicators" discipline out the articulate response and simply commune in silence?

Finally, we should occasionally pause to reflect upon the ease by which we maintain our interpersonal relationships through face to face communication. Consider how we offhandedly take for granted our personal, business, and social relationships; all the intensity and tears, the laughter and joy, and the gifts of empathy we share with one another. We should instead reflect upon and appreciate the wonder of what we are doing and what is really happening because of it. To communicate "greatly" is to communicate with love; with love of the process and love of the participants.

That's 3-1, 3-4, 5-1, 1-5!

Speech is the mirror of the soul:
As you are, so is your speech.
                              —Publius Syrus

JOE D. BATTEN
Batten, Batten, Hudson & Swab, Inc.
820 Keo Way
Des Moines, IA 50309
Bus. (515) 244-3176 • Res. (515) 285-7088

Joe Batten

In addition to his numerous honors in the field of management, Joe Batten is known throughout the world as the DEAN OF MANAGEMENT TRAINERS.

He is the founder and Chairman of the Board of Batten, Batten, Hudson & Swab, Inc., Des Moines, Iowa, a 28-year-old human resource firm engaged in creative management research, consulting, film production, and educational services. Joe is a renowned consultant, philosopher, speaker, trainer, film maker, and author. He is known world-wide as the author of Tough-Minded Management *and such films as* Keep Reaching, *and* Ask For The Order. *He has spoken over 2,000 times on motivation, selling, and management. He is a charter member of the National Speakers Association Hall of Fame (CPAE).*

Joe Batten is a renowned consultant and speaker in the United States and abroad. He has trained thousands in management, sales and human relationship skills. His teachings are acclaimed as the prototype for tomorrow's management. His philosophy advocates the development of the "Whole Person" and he and his colleagues have been heavily involved in counseling and speaking on "Whole Person Wellness" and stress management. He is generally considered to be the principal pioneer in the establishment of management philosophies, basic beliefs and values, as the basis of corporate cultures/climates. His book, Tough-Minded Management *is and has been the leadership Bible for several heads of state including some emerging African nations.*

He has written numerous articles for national publications and has appeared on network television and radio programs as well as local television and radio. As an author he has received wide acknowledge-ment from organizations thoughout the world.

2

Face-To-Face Communication
by Joe Batten

*"I have come that you might have life
and have it more abundantly."*
—John 10:10

Is face-to-face communication a science? Even more importantly—an ART? Can it be? Should it be? And—what's so important about it? In literally hundreds of seminars and workshops, as well as in hundreds of private "behind closed doors" counseling sessions with managers, my colleagues and I at BBH&S have sought to determine what is really at the core or center of key management jobs and sales transactions.

The results of surveys and innumerable discussions with our own staff have indicated that the total effectivenes of managers and sales people rises or falls directly in proportion to their "face-to-face" skills—their interpersonal insights and actions.

Nine tough elusive elements to be found in truly effective one-to-one relationships are as follows:

Vulnerability (emotional and mental)
Openness
Positive listening and, above all, HEARING
Kinesics
Excellent and stretching expectations
Forming conclusions and reactions
Reinforcement
Caring
Integrity

Let's examine these elements one by one, even though space will only permit a cursory—even simplistic—treatment here. And, let us remember throughout that communication does not simply mean dialogue (two or more people engaged in monologues). It means ". . . shared meaning—shared understanding."

Vulnerability—*"assailable, growing, responsive, resilient."* Real leaders, not those merely equipped with economic, political, or military power, have known for centuries that the courage to become and remain vulnerable in their relations with others will both require and develop strength and toughness. Most of us know, on careful reflection, that the defensive, invulnerable person plateaus early in life in terms of growth, vitality, and the capacity to obtain "followership" (without which a leader can't lead).

Such people cease to act. And when they begin to react to people, events, and circumstances, they become static and rigid rather than flexible, responsive, and in a state of flow. It is my belief that behavioral science research will increasingly prove that the confrontive requirements of vulnerability are vastly more developmental and effective than the avoidance expedient of invulnerability and defensiveness. Who grows when they flee? Who grows when they defend? A fundamental requirement for the person who seeks this kind of attitude is a high measure of self-esteem. Years ago, I wrote in the first edition of *Tough Minded Management* that real, sustaining self-confidence was the scarcest ingredient in managers. This still applies in full measure. It is the quintessential element of the fully functioning person.

It requires confidence, courage, and vulnerability to truly "open up" and feel and reflect real interest in what the other person is saying. It is when we "stick our neck out," when we rally from rebuffs, failures, and insufficiencies; when we take risks in the human enterprise; when we reach deep into our reservoir of physical, mental, and spiritual muscle, that we truly strengthen, toughen, and grow. If the baby chicken did not have to fight its way out of the shell, it would not have the strength to live.

Openness—". . . *available, exposed, to give access to, not covered.*" The capacity to achieve and maintain truly open relationships is a product—a bonus—of emotional vulnerability. In this way, we are able to *let the other person in and let ourselves out.* This is an essential requirement for face-to-face synergy—for true symbiosis.

Our capacity to interact openly, free of self-defeating defensiveness, increases steadily as we confront stretching objectives, testing obstacles and difficulties. A crucial requirement in such confrontation is that we must concurrently carry out a quest for new strengths—in *ourselves first*, and then in *others*. As individuals, *we are the sum of our strengths!*

As this strong self-awareness builds, we become increasingly able to reach out in a sensitive, caring, and truly interested way to others. We begin to develop more capacity to really listen—to really hear—to emphatically relate to what the other is saying and feeling. The tough-minded person learns to relish the growth, confrontation, and stimulation which occurs as a result of such openness.

Positive listening. We define negative listening as "...the tendency to hear the other person out and then say what you were going to say anyway." In other words, to listen and *not really hear at all*. Many people who have absorbed much literature and training in all other facets of communication then negate or void all such potentially valuable knowledge by this essentially phony practice—purporting to listen when they are only waiting for an opportunity to talk. And—phonies finish last!

Here's a quote from *The Confidence Chasm,* co-authored with my daughter, Gail Batten Pedersen:

> ". . . to establish true communication between these two, several meetings were, in fact, necessary. After hours of talk, Jim and his father were able to look at each other and converse frankly and openly. They began to realize that commenting with unsuppressed admiration and candor on one another's strengths was in no way effeminate or unbusinesslike, but in reality, took more courage than pointing out one another's weaknesses. In fact, they dis-

covered that this kind of open-minded listening—plus the courage to say 'I'm sorry' when necessary—was probably the only real and lasting way to cope properly with those supposed faults which had plagued each about the other."

Clearly this kind of interaction—shared meaning . . . shared understanding—requires vulnerability, openness, and confidence. It requires that we listen not only with the ear and the eye but also with the mind and the heart. Such listening can become positive instrumentation for building real substance into relationships. Here is another quote from *The Confidence Chasm:*

"Do we desperately try to 'rap'? Have 'dialogue'? Do our arms and minds falter as we attempt to reach one another across the void of the years? Do we continue to defer to weaknesses in order to mask our own?

or:

Do we confidently begin to fill—and to close—the chasm opened by anxieties, retreat, and invectives that can have no place in the world of today and tomorrow? Do we truly come together in mutually supportive confidence?

Kinesics. Much has been written recently

about "body English." The general subject is no doubt familiar to all of us. The important thing in face-to-face communication in this connection is that one should not judge the kinesics of another according to past biases or stereotypes. Such stereotypes close us in and close others out—precisely when we should be *opening up* and *stretching* for new insights. We must learn, for example, to really reach out to the persons with glacial, fixed facial expressions and seek to understand them rather than automatically concluding they are disinterested, resistive, or hostile. Such men and women are often thinking—and thinking seriously—about what we are saying. Frequently more real communication— the kind that will be retained—is happening in this situation than in the case of the person who seems to respond quickly and overtly to what is said. When such needless impasses build, it is the major responsibility of the stronger and more mature person to *reach out* rather than to expediently withdraw.

If a person is confident enough, secure enough, he or she can then reach out and project an attitude of genuine caring about others. When there is enough of this vital concern and caring, the kinesics will be the right ones.

Excellent and stretching expectations: Perhaps the quickest and most effective way to destroy effective communication is to create a vacuum of recognition, a situation where the other person feels ignored and insignificant. Fundamentally, we all know this but the failure to do much about it is one of the continuing weaknesses of too many people.

Upon reflection, the value of the reverse ought to be obvious. We show respect and care for the other person when we take the necessary actions to determine what their present and potential strengths are and then:

Speak to their uniqueness and individuality.

Expect full use of these strengths.

Expect accomplishment of stretching standards and objectives.

Base compensation and other forms of recognition on such accomplishments.

View them as walking bundles of present and potential strengths.

It is clear that we can denigrate and "turn off" people by expecting their second best or worst. It is equally true (although not attempted as often) that we can create synergistic communication and achievement when we *care* enough to *expect* much. In this way (and I believe it is the single best way) we help the other person to feel *significant.* To use one's best and most unique gifts and to be able to do so because someone cared enough to *discover* them, can be a truly significant experience. Central to all human needs is this one imperative—to feel in some way significant as a person. My colleagues and I teach our clients that, "Perhaps, the finest gift one can give another is the gift of an excellent and stretching expectation based on an assessment of the other person's present and potential strengths."

Forming conclusions. One definition of the word "conclude" is to make a final judgment of. This is not what I am recommending here. Rather, we should try to see the other person as being in a state of flow, of ongoing growth. In this way we can help avoid the tendency to build static, rigid, and relatively "closed" relationships—the tendency to "fix" on judgment of others in some permanent way.

When writing the original edition of *Tough-Minded Management*, I facetiously coined the phrase, "Batten's Law of Communication" which says . . . "When the communicatee does not understand what the communicator intended, the responsibility remains that of the communicator." I am not being facetious when I say that real "pros" scrupulously evaluate themselves before they evaluate others.

Daily face-to-face communication becomes and remains challenging, fresh, and often delightful if we avoid judgments per se (which are usually based on a preoccupation with the weaknesses of others.)

Instead of making judgments which close us in and close others out, we should constantly draw on our face-to-face relations—on the liberating power of on-going dynamic evaluations (which means an assessment of strengths). We must rigorously resist the temptation to label, box, or categorize others. Such rigid tendencies are not only counter-productive in managerial and sales situations, but they also take the challenge and joy out of face-to-face relationships in other dimensions of life.

There is a subtle but important difference between judgment and evaluation. Judgment in the usual sense involves looking for and relating to the other person's weaknesses. Evaluation on the other hand stems from a search for an assessment of the value of the person. In short, his strengths.

Reinforcement. Here I hope to accomplish a common recognition that "positive reinforcement" and our term "build on strengths" mean one and the same thing. One definition of the word reinforcement is "to strengthen with new force" and it is crucial to perceive that the only stuff from which synergistic communication can be built is the combined strength emphasis of the individuals. *A weakness is only the absence of strength!!* Strong, effective communication cannot be wrought from "absences, zeros, chasms, faults, or voids." Each of us is defined or profiled by our strengths. They and they alone comprise what we are.

Thus, we must start a never-ending quest for strengths in us and to seek further to build the strengths of the other person. Ergo, *real* communication!

"Positive reinforcement" can be, and often is, only a fatuous phrase unless it derives its nourishment from real self-confidence. And real self-confidence can only be etched out and made fully functional in relationship to and with other people.

Caring. We can only care enough about other people if we care much *about* and *for* the one we see in the mirror.

The need for these tough-minded insights is everywhere and I hope personnel executives by the thousands, and millions, will lead the way in their organizations, homes, and communities. Excellent face-to-face communication can accomplish wonders in coping with the major problems of our time. Indeed, it is the most crucial requirement of all.

We must care enough to really listen positively. We must care enough to reexamine every policy, program, principle, practice, procedure, and person. I assure you, the world is looking for the kind of person who makes this happen. It is vital, however, to go beyond listening and really *hear*. If I "listen" to you, I will perceive the words you are using. If I "hear" you, I'll *understand* what you *mean*.

Integrity—*". . . the state of being entire, wholeness, probity, honesty . . ."* Although Webster has not said so, I believe the words "integrity" and "strength" to be synonymous in meaning. Without one you cannot have a full measure of the other. No material (plastic, wood, iron, paper, etc.) has strength without integrity of structure and vice versa.

Please note that none of the foregoing single subject areas will insure excellent communication per se. Nor will the combination of them all be consistently effective if one ingredient is missing. That ingredient is integrity. It is needed for the crucial melding or meshing of these elements. It is not only consistent with practicality and desirability —it is necessary. Without credibility, no true communication can happen and, without integrity, there is not credibility.

In the beginning, I asked if face-to-face communication is or can be a science. The answer, happily, is no, because a science is only a science when its chief elements are constants which can be quantified and measured. People are skinsful of variables and to seek to reduce these relationships to a science would be stifling and deadening. There would be no heart. And without heart, there is no art.

Such communication can be an *art!* And the

mastery of art is usually a lifelong quest, a tough, difficult, and frequently delightful quest. Do you care enough?

This is a noble challenge and I would be remiss if I ignored the advice of Aristotle who said:

"Before you can do the noble you must first do the useful."

In order to insure that we're confronting useful, hands-on steps to prepare to *apply* the foregoing nine principles, I ask you to carefully address the following specifics.

How do you become an effective communicator? Here is what I recommend:

1. Know Yourself

a. Think about yourself.

What do you believe in?

In your estimation, what is your potential? What are your objectives? What do you want to achieve during the next 5, 10, 15 years? During your lifetime?

How long do you plan on living?

Why do you want to achieve anything?

Are you afraid to fail?

Are you afraid to succeed?

Are you truly happy?

Have you developed a basic philosophy and understanding of the meaning of life?

Are you giving yourself the best chance to use your physical, mental, and spiritual strengths?

What limits have you placed on achieving your full potential?

What particular habits and traits are most characteristic of you?

b. Objectively measure your strengths and beliefs.

(1) Consider the feasibility of consulting with a professional counselor and taking a battery of psychological tests and interest and skill inventories. Develop a comprehensive inventory of your strengths.

(2) Audit your physical condition by having a complete physical examination.

c. Obtain feedback on yourself from your associates and colleagues.

(1) Ask them to tell you about yourself candidly.

(2) Discuss your answers to the questions under "a" to get their opinion of them.

(3) Think back to any advice they may have

tried to communicate to you previously.

d. Put in writing the picture you have gained of yourself through self-appraisal. This will be helpful for comparison purposes in the future.

Developing a Tough-Minded Climate

2. Improve Your Knowledge of People

a. Review your conversations with associates in relation to Step 1c of your self-analysis and determine what their answers to the questions you asked yourself would be.

b. Ask a close associate to write an independent appraisal of a person you both know well and whom you too have appraised. Compare the appraisals and discuss their similarities and differences.

c. Ask people with whom you come in contact plenty of questions to determine why they do what they do and say what they say.

d. Pick up a simple, practical book on human motivation, read it, and discuss its contents with acquaintances. Try out its ideas in practical business situations. Many have used my book *Expectations and Possibilities* for this purpose.

3. Broaden Your Knowledge Through Reading

a. Set aside a few minutes each day to read. At this point it isn't important what you read; the object is to get into the habit of reading.

b. After each session, think about what you have read.

c. Discuss what you have read with others to achieve a better understanding of it.

d. Obtain three books you have been meaning to read but haven't found time for—or a book you wouldn't ordinarily be attracted to. Read them one at a time. Think about them and discuss them with others.

e. Gradually broaden your reading to include books that stretch your thinking, especially on topics with which you are *not* especially familiar or comfortable.

4. Develop Yourself as a Listener—Learn to HEAR

a. In daily conversation, purposely concentrate on what the other person has to say, not on what you plan to say in return. If what you have to say is worthwhile, you will remember it and it will fit in naturally when the time comes for you to speak.

b. Ask plenty of questions beginning with who, what, why, when, where and how. Don't be afraid of silence. Learn to relish it. Let the other person express himself fully before you comment.

c. Practice the habit of thinking comfortably during lags in conversation. It will most likely improve the quality of what you ultimately say. In other words, think before you speak.

5. Practice Developing an Emotional Context in Your Contacts with People.

a. Ask questions (and make statements) and observe the reactions to them.

b. Practice phrasing your questions and statements carefully so as to arouse emotions progressively on the part of those with whom you talk.

c. Take an unpopular position and advance its merits in conversation. Think, listen, observe, grow.

d. Develop a keen awareness of the visible signs of emotional involvement in people. Do they appear fidgety or nervous? Do they look away?

e. Whenever you have participated in or have observed a situation in which emotions have risen to the surface, think back and try to identify the physical reactions that preceded your actual recognition that a person had become emotionally involved.

From this point on you need practice. To judge from attitude surveys in hundreds of companies, employees badly want to know what is expected of them and how well they are doing. This is fertile ground for practice even if you have just completed your periodic appraisal sessions.

Does this outline sound too juvenile? Then please read it again. Remember that topnotch people in every type of endeavor find it necessary to revitalize themselves from time to time by going back to the basics of their professions. Review the principles of counseling and appraisal when you encounter problems and keep in mind that truly big people learn from their mistakes.

The very future of our world depends on shared meaning and shared understanding. I challenge you to keep your mind focused on the noble as you consistently seek to master the useful.

Will you do it?

DOROTHY DeBOLT, C.P.A.E.
and
ROBERT DeBOLT
DeBolt Family Productions
P.O. Box 11211
Oakland, CA 94611
(415) 547-4190 • (415) 658-8458

Dorothy DeBolt, C.P.A.E., and Robert DeBolt

Dorothy and Robert DeBolt have risen to international prominence based upon their humanitarian concerns. They are called miracle workers and America's foremost pioneers in their field of endeavor. Fourteen of their twenty children are adopted and most people would refer to them as handicapped. The DeBolts call them "challenged."

The DeBolts, speaking individually or together, transcend the issue of physical handicaps to speak to the very heart of everyone's family challenges and relationships. The Academy Award winning television special, Who Are the DeBolts? *has been seen by millions, and is frequently used in conjunction with their keynotes, workshops, and seminars, as are their books and cassette programs. All are available through DeBolt Family Productions.*

Dorothy and Robert have been interviewed on over 1000 TV and radio programs, and their story has been featured in publications throughout the world. They are in great demand as speakers and are active members of the National Speakers Association. Dorothy is one of the few women to have received the distinguished CPAE Award for speaking excellence.

The DeBolts founded AASK America, a non-profit program which leads the nation in adoptive placement of special needs children. Their work and their lives have been heralded with a staggering number of honors and accolades, including personal commendations from three U.S. Presidents.

3

To Communicate:
Stop, Look and Listen!
by Dorothy Atwood DeBolt, C.P.A.E.

*"To see things in the seed: this is
Genius."*

—Lao Tze

In the spring of 1969 a slight, wiry 14-year-old named Tich was swimming in a canal outside his home in South Vietnam. Suddenly artillery fire opened, and the boy was almost cut in two. Spinal cord severed, he was brought here near death.

Fourteen-year-old Anh, carrying a bag of rice to his mother in another Vietnamese village, stepped on a mine, with the same results. Both boys were brought to the U.S. for medical care unavailable to them in Vietnam.

In 1969 I was a widow struggling to raise seven children. I was teaching music, and speaking, and seemingly filling every moment. In the midst of all this a woman called and asked me to help recruit families for the two war wounded paraplegic boys from Vietnam.

"They've had their most intensive medical care," she said, "but they need to be in families until they can be returned to Vietnam. That might be years," she continued, "and I'm afraid the only thing we could help with would be medical expenses."

I assured her that I would try to find families, and hung up the phone. I had been off the phone about five minutes when God said, "What about you, Dorothy?"

It seems that every time I think I have my whole life planned, the good Lord steps in with one of these crazy, seemingly impractical ideas, with no answers, and every time I have had the good sense to listen, my life has been incredibly enriched!

Listen to That "Feeling in Your Stomach," Because That Message Comes From the Greatest Communicator of Them All!

My Swedish mother used to say to me when I was a girl, "Dorothy, you have to learn to listen to God, not through your ears, but through your stomach!"

What she meant, of course, is that when something deep inside you, some inner voice is telling you, "This is right, this is proper, this is good, do it," then *do it!*

My husband Bob, and I are privileged to be called great communicators, but if we are, it is because of what our remarkable children have communicated to us. It is *that* message which I want to share with you in this book, the same basic message which Bob and I, and some of our children, share with audiences everywhere.

I want to tell you about some very special children who have taught Bob and me so much about the human spirit, and about living life to the fullest. I want to help you improve *your* family relationships, enhance *your* self image, and tap the enormous resources within yourself.

I do not offer any specific techniques. That is not my approach. My method is to encourage you to think for yourself, to reach down within yourself. I want you to hear your own inner voice, as you hear my message.

After that phone call about Tich and Anh in 1969, I definitely had that "feeling in my stomach," and I thank God daily that I listened to it. Those boys came into my life and changed it more drastically and more beautifully than almost anyone who has ever entered it. It was Tich and Anh who first taught us the amazing capacity for renewal which lies within the human spirit.

Those two boys will never walk or run or make love as you and I, or do so many of the things we take for granted. I found myself washing diapers again because both boys were incontinent. Their problems were constant. Their urological equipment would fail with embarrassing results, Tich's hip bone would pop out of its socket, requiring resetting, they struggled to use braces and crutches, falling more often than standing, and their horrendous bedsores required frequent plastic surgery.

Tich and Anh Are Not "Handicapped." They Are "Challenged!"

Yet it was *they* who would comfort *me* when I would occasionally weep at their struggles. "You no cry, ma," they would say in their broken English, "we can no walk, but we can do many things, ma. You no cry . . ."

Today Tich and Anh, walking masterfully with braces and crutches, are totally self sufficient, fiercely independent, living in their own apartment, going to college. One is studying to be an engineer, the other an architect. I stand in complete awe of both of them.

"Who Are the DeBolts?"

Renowned film-maker John Korty, who created the multi-award winning documentary film on our family, "Who are the DeBolts?" says, "It is a measure of our conceit that we have invented the word, "handicapped" and applied it only to the physical aspect of people. Since we are finally realizing the ecological balance between our environment and ourselves, perhaps we also have a chance to understand more about the balance between body and spirit. Perhaps the images of the DeBolt Family can allow other families to find new meaning in *their* relationships, to exercise the weakened part of themselves, and to become more complete as human beings."

Those images of our family continue to be shown in the DeBolt films throughout the world. Those images are also what Bob and I project as we communicate, not only through film, but through our speeches, seminars, books and cassettes.

When Bob DeBolt and I married in June of 1970 I was a widow with nine children, and Bob brought his daughter from a previous marriage. That brought our family to ten. Then came our first adoption together, Sunee, a five-year-old Korean Caucasian girl, polio-paralyzed in both legs. Sunee quickly taught us some perils of communication.

Bob had just told Sunee goodnight and was sitting on the edge of her bed. He decided it would be a good opportunity to tell her how precious she was to all of us. He told her how pretty she was, how smart, how much we all loved her, and he really waxed eloquent. Sunee kept staring at him intently, and he went on and on, pouring his heart out to that little girl. Finally he ran out of words, and he looked down at her and said, "Honey, is there anything you want to say?"

Sunee, continuing to stare up at her father with rapt attention, said, "Yes, daddy . . . Why do you have hair in your nose?"

Now you might think *that* communication failed . . . but did it, really?

Sunee may not have said so, but she was conscious of what her father was saying. She heard the love he was communicating. A communication of love is never a failure!

Communicate Your Love.
The Only Failed Communication
Is That Which Is Not Attempted

When you sincerely say, "I love you" to any angry

or seemingly unresponsive child or spouse, that person hears you. That message is getting through whether he shows it or not. Whether his response to you is hostile or silent makes no difference. What is important is that YOU have communicated YOUR message of love.

I am reminded of our adoption program, AASK America (Aid to Adoption of Special Kids). Some social workers are devastated if a child they have placed for adoption is given back by the adoptive family. The workers feel that they have failed. Bob and I constantly point out that the only failure would be in not even *attempting* to place that child, for fear of possible disruption. *That* is failure.

When we, as members of a family, do not even *attempt* to communicate, for fear it might not work, *that* is failure.

A Joyous Spirit

In 1972 Bob and I adopted a beautiful five-year-old Black girl from New York, a quadruple amputee, born with stumps of arms and no legs. Without her artificial arms with hooks for hands, and her prosthetic legs, Karen was little more than a torso. But her intelligence, determination, and joyous spirit made her irresistible. Henry Winkler, in his narration of one of our documentary films, states, "To know Karen DeBolt is to know a truly whole person!"

When we adopted Karen she was the first child of that multi-handicap ever to be adopted in this country, but not the last. AASK America, the national non-profit adoption organization which Bob and I founded in 1973, has placed thousands of American children with special needs into permanent, loving, adoptive families, and many of them are amputee children.

Karen brought her special magic into our family. She breathes life into those steel hooks. She puts them under the hot water faucet and says, "Ouch, that's hot!" She slammed her hook in the door one day, and little Sunee came hobbling up on her crutches, "Ooh! Karen! Is it bleeding?"

Karen was five when she joined us, and when she had her sixth birthday, one of her siblings gave her a ring, and another gave her nail polish!

We don't see hooks, braces, color, crutches; all those manifestations are nothing, because what the children have taught us to see is that magnificent human spirit which resides within every person if one will just take the time to look for it!

*****

Please pause in your reading at this point, and make these two lists:

1. List everything you feel is wrong with your mate.

2. List everything you feel is right about your mate.

You might want to make the same lists about other family members.

Just write what comes naturally. You're not trying to impress or depress anybody. The lists are for your eyes only. Write what you really feel. And, please do not resume your reading here until you have finished.

*****

Now, then, how did your lists work out? Which was the longer of the two? Which came easier and faster?

Did you find that your spontaneous focus was more on the wrongs than on the rights? If so, you're not unusual. There is a very strong tendency in all of us to see what is wrong, and ignore what is right. When our children do something naughty, we immediately call it to their attention, but when they are quietly behaving themselves, we just as quietly take it for granted. We are inclined to do the same with all our family members. We focus on their negatives rather than their positives. If you are willing·to make the effort, however, you can turn that completely around.

Look Past What Is Wrong, and Focus on What Is Right, in Yourself, and in Others. You Will Discover Hidden Treasures!

We have a system which we use with our children, one which we have shared with many people in our "Family Team" seminars and cassettes.

We ask our children to make a list of what they like about themselves and bring it to the dinner table to be read aloud. The first time Karen tried it. She really didn't know that much about herself. The page was almost empty. Some years later she came to the table with a script THREE pages long. On the bottom of it she had written in huge black letters, "I LIKE MYSELF BECAUSE I CAN DO ANYTHING!"

Well, it is obvious that there are things this quadruple amputee cannot do. You know that. We know that. And she knows that. *But that is not where she places her focus!*

We also ask the children to bring lists on what they like about *each other*. In the beginning they all found that a real challenge. They laughingly admitted that it was easier to think of what they *didn't* like about each other.

The negative attitude began to change only when they made a *concentrated effort* to look for the good things in their siblings. Once they did so, it became more and more natural. Their later lists have been considerably longer and filled with truly insightful compliments.

Learn To Laugh

Karen had learned to feed, clothe and toilet herself before we adopted her, but when she first joined us she was a very little girl. She didn't have legs to straddle a regular toilet seat, so we got one of those little plastic types used for training toddlers.

She hadn't been with us very long when one day one of our children came running and said, "Mom, you'd better go see what's happening. Tich took Karen to the bathroom downstairs and I can hear all this racket going on . . ." I immediately ran downstairs, knowing we didn't have that little plastic seat down there. When I arrived, there stood Tich, propped up on one crutch against the back of the toilet, trying desperately to fish his sister, Karen, out of the toilet. All I could see of Karen was this beautiful black wooly head, her white eyeballs staring up her brother, and her mouth going, "Just don't flush, man! Don't flush!"

It took those two kids a while to forgive their mother for standing there roaring with laughter as they were going through their "terrible trauma," but pretty soon they began to think it was funny too, and Karen, who is today a beautiful 18-year-old senior in public high school, thinks it's hilarious.

She tells the story to anyone and everyone who will listen to it . . . "Hey, wait till I tell you about the time I almost got flushed down the John," she laughs.

Laugh at Yourself. The Ability to Laugh at Life's Foibles and Our Own Frailties Is a Key to Human Survival

Amputees and other severely disabled veterans in hospital wards are often accused of "sick humor" as they poke fun at themselves and each other. Rather than "sick," it is the most healthy healing process they could find. And so it is for all of us. Author Norman Cousins, in his well documented case, admits readily that it was his self-prescribed doses of laughter which allowed him to overcome serious illness.

Use it! Revel in it! Karen does!

Wendy Never Smiled

In 1973, a tiny four year old girl was found abandoned on a street corner in Seoul, Korea. She had been badly beaten, deliberately-inflicted burn scars were all over her body, and she was blind in both eyes. She was taken to an orphanage where she was called, "The Child Who Never Smiles." In that orphanage was a nurse with whom I had corresponded for years. I had been able to help find adoptive families for some of the children in her charge. She wrote, telling us about little Wendy. The child had been sent to the military hospital in Seoul to have one eye removed because it was so badly damaged. The doctors had determined that she might be able to see with the one eye she had left, if she could have a corneal transplant. The eye was deteriorating rapidly, however, and time was running out. The nurse asked if we could find an adoptive family in the U.S. to adopt Wendy and provide the corneal transplant.

At that time we didn't have the thousands of prospective adoptive families now listed in our adoption agency files, and we were unable to find new parents for Wendy. So, when God once again asked, "Why not you?" we listened, and we told the nurse we would take Wendy.

I'll never forget the day she arrived at San Francisco Airport. Here came this little girl, frail, frightened, bewildered, unable to see our faces, unable to speak our language, and yet, despite all she had been through, that little child put her tiny hand in ours, in an act of literal blind faith.

We brought Wendy home. Within one month, with the financial assistance of Crippled Children's Services, she was able to have a corneal transplant in that one eye she had left. AND IT WAS SUCCESSFUL!

The day before Thanksgiving, 1973, Wendy came home from the hospital with a clear plastic shield covering her one cornea. She went darting about the house, cupping the chins of her brothers and sisters in her hands, and laughing out loud at the sheer joy of seeing!

When is the last time you thought about the fact that you can see? That your children can see? That your grandchildren can see?

We never used to think about such things until these special children came into our family and made us aware of all we had been taking for granted.

Count Your Blessings, For They Are Many

After I finished telling the story of Wendy in one of my speeches, a woman came up with tears streaming down her face. She said, "I think I, too, am seeing for the first time. I'm seeing how blessed I really am."

After Wendy gained her sight, the "child who never smiles" became the child who never stopped smiling, or laughing, or jumping, or running. Indeed she became quite hyperactive. That's why we were amazed one day to see her sitting quietly in the backyard. "Wendy?" we asked. "Are you okay? What are you doing?"

She looked at us in some surprise, and said,

"Oh, I was just watching the leaves fall off the tree . . ."

And for the first time in a long time, my husband and I took the time to see the swirling, fluttering golden beauty of a leaf falling from a tree.

Stop and Smell the Roses
While You Can, For Neither They Nor You
Will Live Forever

After we adopted Wendy, came Vietnamese orphan boys, Phong, Dat, and Trang. Then came Vietnamese girls, Thuy and Ly (one blind, one polio-paralyzed) and a blind paraplegic boy from New York, J.R. (not the Dallas fellow!)

All these adoptions took place between 1973 and 1976. During that same time period Bob and I wrote a book, founded our adoption program in our garage office, and the first documentary film was made on our family. The film crew practically lived with us for 2½ years. We learned to look both ways before coming out of the shower. But that was only one of our survival techniques for those frantically busy years. Ever so often, Bob and I would escape to the wine country of Northern California for a weekend. There would eat, drink, make mad love, and pretend we were sterile and raised poodles.

It worked miracles!

*Stop, and take a break. Noses stuck to
grindstones become ugly, and so do their
owners' dispositions.*

Look At What Is Right—Focus On It

When we adopted J.R., our blind, paraplegic son, he
was 10 years old. The doctors told us that he would
never see, never walk, never get out of a wheel
chair. Negatives, negatives, negatives! Implicit in
what they said was that J.R. would never amount
to anything, and why would anyone want to adopt
him!

People looked only at what was *wrong* with J.R.,
and they had plenty to choose from. He was
paralyzed from the waist down, incontinent, and
totally, irreversibly blind. At age 10 he was obese,
with 30 pounds excess weight. He could neither tie
his own shoes, nor cut his own food. He was
vegetable-like in both demeanor and self image. Self
motivation was non existent, and his remarkable
intelligence was buried under layers of apathy.

That was ten years ago.

This year J.R. graduated from a public high
school, with honors. He alternates between braces,
crutches, and occasional wheelchair use, and takes
total care of his own urological equipment and
personal hygiene. He is very self sufficient, is an
active participant in household chores and activities,
and will enter college in the fall to study law. His

dream and his goal is to become a full fledged attorney. AND HE WILL DO IT!

J.R. got turned around when we, *and* he, stopped looking at what was wrong with him, and started focusing on what was right with him. That was when J.R. first started to visualize his own future with hope, with a dream, and with a goal.

Someone once said to Helen Keller that probably the worst tragedy that could befall anyone would be to be born blind. Miss Keller disagreed. She said, "No, the worst thing is to be born sighted, but to lack vision."

J.R. has vision. Do you?

Do you stop, look and listen? Or are you just sleepwalking your way through life?

Let Us Stop, Look and Listen Again . . .

1. LISTEN TO THAT "FEELING IN YOUR STOMACH" BECAUSE THAT MESSAGE COMES FROM THE GREATEST COMMUNI-CATOR OF THEM ALL.
2. COMMUNICATE YOUR LOVE. THE ONLY FAILED COMMUNICATION IS THAT WHICH IS NOT ATTEMPTED.
3. LOOK PAST WHAT IS WRONG, AND FOCUS ON WHAT IS RIGHT, IN YOURSELF, AND IN OTHERS. YOU WILL DISCOVER HIDDEN TREASURES.

4. LAUGH AT YOURSELF. THE ABILITY TO LAUGH AT LIFE'S FOIBLES, AND OUR OWN FRAILTIES, IS A KEY TO HUMAN SURVIVAL.
5. COUNT YOUR BLESSINGS, FOR THEY ARE MANY.
6. STOP AND SMELL THE ROSES WHILE YOU CAN. NEITHER YOU NOR THEY WILL LIVE FOREVER.
7. TAKE A BREAK. NOSES STUCK TO GRIND-STONES BECOME UGLY, AND SO DO THEIR OWNERS' DISPOSITIONS.

I told you that I wanted to share with you what our children have taught Bob and me about the human spirit, and living life to the fullest. I have barely scratched the surface of the stories we can and do tell, but I hope these "scratches" will help bring new meaning and awareness into your life.

May I ask one last favor? As you think about what you have read here with a mind that can reason, look at each page with eyes that can see, listen to loved ones with ears that can hear, and get up and walk on legs that can function, will you please say, "Thank you, God!"? But don't just say it. **ACT UPON IT!**

"What a man thinks of himself, that is what determines, or rather indicates, his fate."
—**Henry David Thoreau**

BRIAN TAYLOR
Speaker Training Programs
Suite 188-122 Gulf Canada Square
401 9th Ave., S.W.
Calgary, Alberta, Canada T2P 3C5
(403) 278-8463 • Res. (403) 271-5465

Brian Taylor

Brian Taylor has practised public relations for more than 25 years, specializing in corporate communication for senior executives.

An award-winning speaker and writer, he coaches business leaders in public speaking, and for media appearances.

His custom-designed workshops on "Executive Speaking," and his seminars on "Communicating for Profit" have been acknowledged in Canada, the United States, and Great Britain, by requests for repeat performances.

Mr. Taylor is also a speechwriting consultant, with a background of writing for national and international audiences.

He is a frequent keynote speaker at conferences and conventions where his humor, and his keen insight into human foibles, keeps his services in demand.

When asked his secret for repeat business, he simply says that education shouldn't be dull or boring— learning should be fun—and he proves it with his high- energy workshops and motivational presentations to top businesses on the continent. His seminars provide the individual and the organization with practical techniques for achieving greater productivity and personal fulfillment.

Mr. Taylor is president, and a charter member of the Alberta Speakers Association, a member of the National Speakers Association, the American Society for Training and Development, and Toastmasters International.

For many years he's been active with the International Association of Business Communicators and the Canadian Public Relations Society.

In 1978, at its annual conference, the Canadian Public Relations Society awarded Mr. Taylor the prestigious Shield of Public Service for "distinguished and dedicated service in the public interest."

4

A Crash Course on Vocal Communications
by Brian Taylor

"If all my possessions and powers were taken from me—with but one exception—I would choose to keep the power of speech . . . for by it I could soon recover all the rest."
—Daniel Webster

Recognizing The Leader's "Edge"

You can spot them right away, in almost any kind of situation: the stand-outs.

They are the centre of attention drawing a

crowd of people who hang onto every word they say.

Who are these people who seem to know just the right word?

They are good verbal communicators.

They are the perceptive people who know effective speech is the hallmark of today's business leader.

They are the people who have discovered that sharing ideas, exchanging views and encouraging awareness—is good business.

And they recognize that this basic management tool is also good for their careers. In fact it's crucial for individual growth. Because it's how we measure acceptance, achievement, and personal success in the workplace, and on the social scene today.

Unfortunately, people assume you either have it—or you don't; much like a sense of humor, or a sunny disposition.

But this is a false assumption, and as Daniel Webster observed earlier, speaking effectively can make a difference . . . *and it's never too late to start.*

Regardless of where you work, or what you do, being able to communicate well, to reach out and touch people in a meaningful way, can turn around your career, your business, or your social life.

Why? Because there are so few "effective" communicators.

It seems many people are reluctant to express

themselves in word or print because they feel inadequate, or simply don't know where to begin. Still others are fearful because of past experiences, usually bad.

And yet the rewards for effective communicators—the stand-outs—are immense.

In fact, the future belongs to them.

The stand-outs overcame the poor habits or conditioning that led to yesterday's limitations. You can do the same.

Suggestion:

Clear and effective communication is a process of exchanging information to build awareness and acceptance. It is rapidly becoming a business requirement, particularly if you want to climb the corporate ladder. And good communicators are well rewarded by their companies.

The Competitive Advantage

Who needs clear Communication?

We all do!

The success of any project, service, or idea depends on somebody's ability to communicate the benefits successfully.

We are all in the business of persuading others to think, believe and act in a certain manner. In other words, *we communicate to get results.* And speaking is a vital part of this process.

We speak to sway, or change an opinion; or to encourage an action. We speak to persuade or convince members of the audience to act, or react, in a certain way.

In essence, *we speak to make things happen.*

And in the process we find that people who make things happen, who develop the ability to exchange ideas, build awareness, and develop acceptance, gain the competitive edge on their competition.

But, more importantly, from a career standpoint, as the need for clear and effective communication grows, business and society will start to choose good communicators over those who lack the skills.

The good news for those lacking in this area is—the techniques can be learned. *It's an acquired skill.*

There's nothing magical or mystical about learning how to get up on your feet and express your point of view. Admittedly it takes effort and work. But the rewards far outweigh the investment in time, energy and thought, and like compound interest at the bank, it grows on a daily basis.

Suggestion:

Accept that good communicators are not born, they are made. Persuasive communication skills and techniques are acquired, or learned, and anybody can do it—including you. Best of all, you can start now.

"O.K. Where Do I Begin?"

How do you organize your thoughts to speak more effectively?

First and foremost, *talk about something you know.*

The fear speakers dread most is the thought that audiences know more than they do about the topic. They often counter this by resorting to occupational language to establish their expertise.

The result can be murky, technical jargon that's confusing to the layman, and not much clearer to the expert.

I once heard this syndrome described as "polysyllabic profundity," and that's exactly what it is—a message written to impress, rather than to express.

You and I have heard countless eloquent speeches that really had no purpose. Why? The objective had become obscured by the speaker's need to impress the audience.

Churchill said it best when he noted, "Big men use little words; little men use big words."

If your objective is to let the audience know how much you know, why not just send an indexed bibliography. Better still, dump your file cabinets in the centre of the stage. However, if your objective is to gain acceptance, and friendly agreement, then in simple language let the audience know you want to share some ideas that will benefit them.

Suggestion:

Two brief commandments: 1) Stay with the subjects you know; 2) Talk in language the audience knows.

Help people to understand your message by using simple and conversational language.

Decide on Your Objective

If speakers want things to happen, then they must stimulate the audience either mentally or physically. Having an objective can help by applying common-sense to speaking opportunities.

Your objective is to get the audience to do something— agree with you, support your decisions, or decide on a direction to take.

With an objective embedded in your mind you know where you're going, and can lead the audience.

It's the difference between going on vacation with a roadmap; and leaving it at home. With the map you can measure your progress—know how much further it is to your destination.

Similarly, when you share your roadmap with the audience, they can travel along with you, and understand the reason you're traveling in that direction.

Suggestion:

The result you require from your vocal communications must be fixed clearly in your mind, before you start preparing your presentation.

Analyze the Audience

Across North America at any given moment, scores of highly-paid people spend long hours huddled around film projectors. They do it to learn about people—their opponents.

These boggle-eyed film critics are sports coaches, and by careful study they can pinpoint the strengths and weaknesses of their opposition. This knowledge lets them develop a game plan and helps them prepare the appropriate moves and counter-moves.

In speaking it's much the same, only we call it audience analysis. It simply means assessing the audience, and anticipating their moves—or their needs and wants.

Perhaps the key phrase here is, *"What's in it for them?"* If we can answer that question adequately, then our presentation can be geared towards giving them what they need.

Here's a sample of the questions speakers should ask themselves:

- Does the audience know something about the subject?
- Are they interested in the subject?

- How deep is their level of understanding?
- Do they have attitudes about the subject?
- What are their real needs?
- Will they be open-minded?
- What is special about this audience?
- What benefits will they get?

These are just a few of the several questions you should ask so you can satisfy the needs of your audience.

We're searching for shared interests and mutual needs—a common ground where you and the audience can meet, and perhaps agree. And which will help you—as a speaker—reach your objective.

The old adage holds true; *"don't start talking until you've started thinking"*. Fuzzy thinking doesn't lead to fuzzy actions, it leads invariably to no action, because people don't know how to respond to confusing signals.

And remember—unlike automobiles, spoken words cannot be recalled for adjustments or replacements.

So you must keep uppermost in your mind the true purpose of your communication. Keep asking yourself, will this topic help me accomplish my objective? Will it move the audience, and persuade them to take the action I want them to follow? Is it specific enough to show what's in it for them?

Suggestion:

Satisfying the audience is the first step towards accomplishing your objective. You do this by talking in terms of their needs and wants. This means you must clarify your thoughts and ideas. Above all, show the benefits to be gained by the audience.

Collecting Ideas!

Once you have a feel for who the audience is, and what they may want to know, then you can give free rein to your creative process. Let the juices course through your veins. We can get organized later!

Accept any and all thoughts about your topic at this stage—you can weed out the inappropriate ones afterwards. Let your mind soar in that flight of fancy, awaiting the moment when the light bulb goes on, signalling the great idea that can set your presentation apart.

Where do ideas come from? From everywhere!

They come at inconvenient times, and when they're least expected. And for many people this creates a problem.

It's not the lack of ideas that stymies most speakers, but failure to record them as they occur.

Here's how to solve that problem.

Capture your thoughts on 3"×5" "idea" cards. The cards can easily be carried in purse or pocket.

Just jot down one idea per card—no more.

If a related thought crops up on the same subject put it down as a sub-head. But be careful to have no more than two sub-heads per card.

Collect as many ideas as you can. Don't worry about having too many. The greater the selection— the better the final choice. The key is to capture the idea before it evaporates, and the cards are the ideal way to do it.

When you have eight or nine cards with a single idea per card—*then* you can become organized.

Suggestion:
Don't open up the spigot if there's nothing in the barrel.

Likewise, don't start trying to write your presentation without an inventory of ideas and thoughts on your topic. Collect your ideas the easy way—on idea cards.

Organize Your Material

In the thousands of years that speakers have faced audiences nobody has devised a better formula for organizing a talk than the very ordinary *opening, body and close.*

It's simple, but very effective. A saying among professional speakers refers to these three basic presentation segments this way.

In the *opening,* you tell them what you are going to tell them.

In the *body,* you tell them.

In the *conclusion,* you tell them what you've told them.

Like many of the simpler things in life—it works. The audience can follow you, they can understand what you're saying, and they can grasp your meaning. And this is the first step that can lead to acceptance.

And yet, organization is one area frequently overlooked.   Here's what I find works well for me. It's so simple—it's sinful. But it is effective.

Set aside some quiet time, possibly a Sunday afternoon, and spread the idea cards on a coffee table.

Shuffle them around until the subjects start to form a logical sequence. At some point you may want to add an extra item, or possibly delete an item or two.

When you've decided on the sequence, number the cards, and presto!—you have a skeleton, or the beginning of an outline.

Try These Ideas

One very effective way of sequencing is in chronological order. This can be by date, such as *"last year, this year, next year."* Or, *"past, present and future."* Or it could be by order of importance starting with the most important and then moving to items of lesser importance.

Another very effective method is *"problem, cause and solution."*

There are numerous others. The trick is to select the one most likely to help you achieve your objective with this particular audience.

Putting the "Pieces" Together

Now you have a sequence in mind you can start to "flesh-out" your skeleton.

I prefer to write my conclusion first, because I want to know exactly how I'm going to end.

To me the ending is the most important part of the communication. It's the last chance to drive home the essential points, and this is important because the ending is the part of the presentation the audience will recall with the most clarity.

Once I'm satisfied with the conclusion, I move to the opening, making sure the opening contains the same message, and much of the same thrust as the ending, so the benefits of repetition are established at the outset.

Most speakers agree the opening is the second most important part of a talk. A speaker has about 45 seconds to get the attention and interest of an audience.

The "body," or major portion of the presentation can be worked on in segments—each idea card representing a segment. The key here is tying them in and making sure all the separate segments flow easily into one another. And we do this by bridging or using transitions.

While the change in subject matter takes your listeners in a different direction the transitional words such as "now let me move the focus from interest rates to inflation," will ease them into the turn.

Suggestion:

Organize your presentation, so the audience can organize its thoughts. If you're attempting to persuade them, make it easier for them by presenting your thoughts logically. Develop a sequence that "calls for order," and it will help you when it's time to "ask for the order."

Practice With Feeling

To communicate with impact means somewhere along the line the thinking, writing and arranging must end, and the practice must begin. And for some, this is the toughest part.

All kinds of reasons for avoiding practice can be manufactured . . . time constraints, travel, business pressures, you name it! And yet the success of your objective hinges on your ability to "come across."

Most professional speakers make sure they come across by ensuring adequate time for rehearsal. It's one of life's travesties that poise and polish can only be acquired—they cannot be inherited, or picked out from a mail order catalogue.

Professionals in every endeavor are quick to point out that any success they enjoy is due to continual hours of repetitive practice.

Yet prominent people in business are surprised when their well-designed, well-planned and well-crafted presentations founder through lack of practice.

Without adequate rehearsal a speaker will fall into one of these traps.

1. Be forced to read word for word from a script. The result: a dirge delivered in a monotone.
2. Try to "wing-it," straying far from the theme. The result: a disoriented and dozy audience which cannot be revived in the time remaining.

Here's how I recommend you practice.

First, read the speech aloud.

This helps you iron out the kinks. You can find the location of the difficult words and the awkward sentences that make you hiss, splutter and stumble.

Alliteration makes the novice speaker tongue-tied. Words you know intimately suddenly pop up as strangers. What appears soothingly correct when read visually, can grate on the ear when vocalized.

In addition, you could find you're running out of breath because the sentences are too long.

Next, get it on tape. No matter how resonant the bathroom, nor how complimentary the family comments—get your voice on tape! Then you can listen to yourself objectively. Tune-in carefully because this is the way you'll sound to your audience.

Roll the words around your tongue and taste them. Shout them, and then whisper them, trying to put the emphasis on different parts of the words each time. Above all, try to put feeling and color into the words—making the phrases come alive.

Let your body, and your arms, help express the meanings conveyed by the words.

Try to avoid rehearsing only parts of your speech, because you won't develop the overall rhythm and flow necessary to keep the audience's interest.

Suggestion:

The place to find all the glitches is in your living room—not at the lectern. Practice allows you to become familiar with what you want to say, and you won't get better without it.

Try to be as natural and relaxed as you can. Adopt the attitude that you're speaking one-on-one, not one to 100.

Extend the courtesy of giving the audience your best. Your best comes through practice.

Deliver With Style

When most aspiring speakers think of style they usually think in terms of Winston Churchill, or John F. Kennedy. And the fear of being compared to such luminaries is enough to kick the adrenal gland into overdrive.

Fear not! Style should not be imitated. It should not be borrowed, or copied, but should come from within.

In fact, good communication is expressing on the outside . . . what's happening inside. It is developed from the natural abilities already present, and polished through practice.

The worst mistake any speaker could make is to try and be "somebody else." It just doesn't work.

Why? Because a speaker has enough to contend with without trying to remember "a role" that they've adopted.

Trying to recall how your hero would make a gesture means you're not concentrating on the message—and the message will suffer. So, eventually, will the audience.

Keep your thoughts on what you want to say, and not how you want it said. This way your body language and gestures will be natural. It will be "you" who is coming across, with your personal message, not some poorly rehearsed imitation with a wooden presentation.

Remember, people have come to see you. If they're looking for caricatures they'll visit a theatre, or take in a movie.

They're listening to you because they've come for "your" message. *So make it your message, delivered in your style.*

By being yourself you are increasing the credibility of your message.

Suggestion:

Be yourself. A genuine and enthused "you" is much better than a pale shadow of Churchill.

Grasp every opportunity to speak, and use those opportunities to experiment with different presentation techniques. If you're serious about taking a greater interest in your "career development," it will pay off in prestige, performance—and, dollars and cents.

> *"Give me the right word, and I'll move the world"*   —**Joseph Conrad,** *Novelist*

Mend your speech a little,
lest it may mar your fortunes.

—**Shakespeare**

Judge LEE SHAPIRO
Lee Shapiro & Associates
128 Seventh Street
Del Mar, CA 92014
(619) 481-0493 • Res. (619) 481-0869

Judge Lee Shapiro

He's popularly known as The Hugging Judge because that's what everyone feels like doing after hearing him speak. People feel good about themselves and the people around them. They're eager to get on with their challenges.

Judge Shapiro says:

I can see it now:

Feuding former friends call and say, 'You know, I've never told you some of the things I really like about you.'

Parents who are getting too busy with the busyness of life suddenly stop what they are doing, look at their kids and say, 'Let's sit down together. I want to hear what you have to say.'

The Arabs and Israelis are having a huge party at the border. They're hugging, because they just discovered they have much in common. They all want the same things in their lives. Bagles and baklava. Why not?

At the workplace, managers and employees are sneaking around catching each other doing something right, or even almost right, a la Ken Blanchard.

In divorce court, the gladiators suddenly remember what brought them together in the first place. Case dismissed for lack of negative evidence. The judge doesn't know what to do with his gavel because the bailiff is saying something nice to him.

People are communicating with openness, honesty, and clarity. All over the world, stress and pain diminish. Everyone is getting along better at the workplace and at home. The letters to Dear Abby and Ann Landers take a turn for the positive. Production is up, hassle is down.

We can each help make it happen.

I rest my case."

5

Veritatus Simplex Oratio Est*
by Lee S. Shapiro, J.D.

*"Ships that pass in the night, and speak
each other in passing,
Only a signal shown, and a distant voice
in the darkness.
So in the ocean of life we pass and
speak one another . . ."*
—Henry Wadsworth Longfellow
"Tales of a Wayside Inn"

I s there anything more frustrating than feeling
unable to get your message across to another
person? To know exactly what you want to say, and
someone, maybe a loved one, a boss, a child, an

*The Language of Truth Is Simple.

employee, just isn't getting the point?

I started my life dealing with a real tough customer—my father. From the time I was a little kid, I can remember trying to get through to him. Many years later, I was still trying when he passed away. I was in my early 40's then, and I hadn't done much better than when I started. That didn't make much sense, because by then I was a highly skilled, successful trial attorney. My business, my life, was COMMUNICATING—to clients, judges, juries, and opposing counsel.

Later, I became a judge. I had a grandstand seat to what doesn't work in the people business! You've probably noticed that people don't usually go to court unless things aren't working. Most of the time, they are there because of poor communication. Divorces, custody fights, contract disputes, assault and battery, juvenile delinquency—you name it, I saw and heard it. After too many years of watching people devastate each other, and their children, I actually started to hear a voice in my head that said: "THERE'S GOT TO BE A BETTER WAY!"

Transition

That voice in my head led me to my friend the psychiatrist. I thought that I was flipping out. There I was, Mr. Big Shot Have It All Together, hearing a voice. No one would have believed it. I couldn't believe it myself. I'd sent many disturbed clients for counseling to help ease them through their pain. Now it was my turn.

My friend, the counselor, said, "What's up, Lee?" I took a deep breath, swallowed hard, and choked out, "I'm hearing a voice in my head, Scott, and I think I'm in real trouble." He calmly replied, "What's the voice saying, Lee?" "The voice is saying, 'There's got to be a better way.'" The Good Doctor chuckled (I was offended by that) and said, "Lee, you just don't want to do what you're doing anymore."

Being a master of the snappy response, I said, with great feeling, "Scott, you must be nuts." He was no slouch with the rejoinders either, and said, "I thought I was giving the diagnosis here. The fact is, that even though you have your airplane, Jeannie has her show horses, the home on the lake, sailboats, speedboat, fishing boat, etc. etc., you want to be doing something else." I left, convinced that he was really out of his mind. I'd worked most of my life to get to where I was—senior member of the law firm that I'd founded, a judgeship, respect, prosperity, power. And I truly believed that I was rendering a valuable and necessary service to my clients, and to society. I'd worked my way through eight years of school to earn the right to practice law. I couldn't afford to quit because of the fringe benefits.

But two years later, I put my judicial robes in mothballs. I was out of the law business. We sold the airplane, the horses, the home on the lake, everything. Jeannie, Lee, Teri, and Steve Shapiro were on the way to California, including Sammy the dog and Mushie the cat. That was a strong voice I was hearing, because I learned that the real power wasn't in wielding a gavel, or having all those goodies. They're nice, and I dearly love them, but they didn't help the ache in the gut every morning, or that voice in my head.

The Search for Better Ways

I found answers in unexpected places. I became a professional speaker and seminar leader, specializing in interpersonal skills and human relations—how to have more success in the people business (what else?). This was the time in my life to learn about, and teach, the flip side of everything I used to see and hear in the courtroom.

What would it take to:

1. Have better relationships at the workplace?
2. At home?
3. With our friends?
4. Get through to "difficult" people?
5. Have quick and easy conflict resolution?
6. Deal with that sense of frustration and

futility when that other person isn't listening?

Better Ways to Communicate

At the risk of appearing simplistic, I must say this:

**ALL THE GOOD STUFF IS SIMPLE.
THE CHALLENGE IS IN THE EXECUTION.**

The first goal is to let go of what isn't working—if a certain behavior doesn't get us what we want, then it's obsolete. It's usually behavior that we don't like in ourselves, and in other people. The hard part is to *do something different.* Hard, but not impossible.

**IF YOU KEEP ON DOIN' WHAT YOU'VE
ALWAYS DONE,
YOU KEEP ON GETTIN' WHAT YOU'VE
ALWAYS GOT.**
Cha Cha Cha

First, **WHAT DO YOU WANT?** If you've read this far, I know you're interested. Interested in what? That's the real question. What do you want? Better leadership skills, crystal clear communication, better listeners, higher quality relationships, less fuss, all of the above? Some hot answers are forthcoming, I promise.

Second, **WE LEARN FROM EACH OTHER,** including each other's mistakes. We can't live long enough to make them all ourselves, anyway.

Third, **YOU DON'T HAVE TO BE PERFECT.**
Excellence in any endeavor doesn't mean that we have to BE perfect, and we don't have to DO something perfectly, especially in the beginning. After all, at one time we didn't know how to do anything, and we've lived to tell the tale. I think that the less we worry about being perfect, the more we'll do things perfectly.

Fourth, **GIVE AWAY WHAT YOU WANT THE MOST.** Sometimes I give talks at homes for the elderly. Most of these people are lonely, and starved for affection. I ask them what sounds like a cruel question: "How many of you want more hugs in your life?" They all raise their hands, and some of them sob and cry. Then I say to them, "Find someone who needs a hug more than you do, and give one away. You can't give a hug away without getting one back." You should see what happens after that. It's beautiful.

Proof

I've found that the best time to give away what we want the most, such as hugs, affection, good listening, and understanding, is when we least feel like it. You want proof? (Judges, even former judges, love proof.) Try it, and see what happens. Results guaranteed. And if you don't get it the first time, do it again, and again, and again. You'll get what you want, sometimes from unexpected places.

Not only do we get what we want, but we set the example for others to follow. That's the only way we can "fix" someone else anyway.

Anyone Can Be Reached

I used to believe that there were some people that we just couldn't reach. I saw them on juries, on the witness stand, in my opponents in and out of the courtroom. We've all seen them. They're out there. Sometimes at home, at the workplace, driving in traffic, in our everyday lives. I'm not suggesting that we should want to reach everyone, but when it really counts, there's always a way. If I'd learned a few of the methods I'm about to relate, my father and I would have had a clear, open line of communication. But was it also too late with another loved one; my wife, Jeannie, the love of my life?

Case #1001

After handling over a thousand divorces, custody fights, disputes and conflicts of every description, I thought I had a pretty good handle on what not to do in the people business. But knowing, and doing, are two different things. Jeannie and I split up after 22 years of love, warmth, and intimacy. Love is not enough. The toughest cases I ever handled were between people who loved each other the most. My world came crashing down, and I couldn't believe it. The impossible had happened.

It's a terrible thing to realize that one is talking the talk and not walking the walk. I spent a long and bitter year learning, growing, and finally realizing that I had to let go of what wasn't working for me. Actually, the concept was simple, like all the good stuff. Having to be right didn't work. It didn't get me what I wanted, except for short term ego gratification. It doesn't work for anyone.

Ah, the pain of awareness. Abraham Maslow said it well, and I love and hate him for his clarity and perception:

"SEEING IS BETTER THAN BEING BLIND, EVEN WHEN IT HURTS."

Letting Go

That doesn't sound too tough, does it? It was. Judges are trained to be right. Who was better qualified, after all? And besides, I had all the training and education and experience in observing the human condition. Furthermore, I *KNEW I WAS RIGHT!* No question about it. How many times in your life have you *KNOWN* you were right, but you weren't getting what you wanted? It's a sweet thing to be right. You can roll it around on your tongue and savor the sweetness of it and love it and cherish it and KNOW it, and so what? Who cares? Only our own egos, that's who.

I never saw a case in court where people didn't think they were right. That's what brought them there, and that's why some cases went on and on and on, long after the trials were over. Judgment: Wasteful, destructive, and boring.

I'm Right!

I don't know of anything more harmful to clear communication than HAVING TO BE RIGHT. I couldn't figure out why Jeannie didn't agree with me. I was crystal clear. So was she. We were both right. What an incredible coincidence!

What will some people do to be right? To what lengths do people actually go because they *have* to be right? They lie, cheat, steal, commit violence, even kill. Most murders are committed by family members. They had to be right. What do countries do when they have to be right? They go to war. So much for having to be right. Suggestion: SUBSTITUTE LIKING TO BE RIGHT FOR HAVING TO BE RIGHT. The rewards are tremendous.

Understanding vs. Agreement

My son Steve taught me a big one: when it comes to human relations and communication, seek understanding rather than agreement. Agreement follows understanding the other person's point of view, not the other way around. Give away what you want the most—understanding. It will save you an enormous amount of hassle, frustration, and disappointment. It will get you agreement, friendship, respect, hugs, and more.

Winter Is Over

Somebody said, "Cherish the good times, forget the other." So Jeannie did, and I did. She came back from her one-year cameo appearance in Missouri. The emotional icicles melted, and all that was left was love, and a clear idea of what we wanted.

We both let go of having to be right. It worked.

We substituted understanding for agreement. It worked.

We are together.

Sailing on the bay.

Eating pralines and cream in bed.

Living and loving together.

It works for us.

It will work for you, in any area of your life.

Howard

There was a person in my life with whom I could never have understanding or agreement. He was known to be the toughest prosecutor in the state, and he had a track record to prove it. His favorite story was that he'd had his own son busted. This guy made "tough" look like sissy stuff.

I'd seen too often how an overextension of a strength could become a weakness. Sometimes "justice" worked that way. Howard's case was a classic, and tragic, example. He was my guitar teacher and friend. A gentle and kind man. I once saw him carefully pick a moth off the drape and release it out the door.

Howard was prosecuted by Mr. Tough Guy, and, on a relatively minor charge, the first offense of his life, he was sentenced to 15 years in one of the worst penitentiaries in the nation! His appeal was denied, and he was on his way to the end of his life. There was no way that Howard, the Gentle Man, could survive being caged with men of violence—rapists, murderers, child molesters, thieves.

Futility

Have you ever known, beyond a shadow of doubt, that there was no way to reach a person? I think we've all been there many times in our lives, but I saw Mr. Tough Guy Prosecutor as my Waterloo. He reminded me of my father.

I was standing outside his inner sanctum, drenched with a sense of futility and despair. Howard had asked me to help him, but since his appeal had been denied, his only hope was parole.

I'd been told by the Parole Board that Howard could not be considered for parole for at least five years. I knew that Howard would be ruined or dead by then, and something drove me on through the hopelessness to seek his release before it was too late. Each day Howard wrote to me, and each day he sank deeper into the despair that we both shared.

I had lots of character references and job offers for Howard, and many people were willing to help him, but I kept running into the bureaucratic brick wall—5 years, 5 years, 5 years.

Finally, in a burst of desperation, I said to the head of the Parole Board, "What if I get a supportive letter from the toughest prosecutor in the state? Will that do it?" The first faint glimmer of hope hit me in the gut. He said, "Maybe."

So there I was. How could I reach the Prosecutor? What would it take to penetrate that thick skin? I had no idea, and even less hope. How many times have you felt the same way in trying to reach one of your children, or a manager, an employee, a spouse or lover?

I kept repeating to myself, "Anybody can be reached, and I'm going to reach this guy," as I walked into his office. He said, "Whadda you want?" I told him, and he said, "Why should I help Howard, and why should I help you?" I answered, "Because I think that you're a decent human being, and you know that Howard doesn't belong where he is, that's why."

I almost shrieked for joy as he said, "Go write the letter, and I'll give it some thought." I snatched some of his stationery, ran to my car, and dictated the letter as I drove like a maniac back to my office. My secretary typed it up in about two seconds, and I drove like a maniac back to the Office of the Prosecutor.

I put the letter on his desk. It said that he knew the sentence, under all the facts, was harsh, and that he would have no objection to an early parole for Howard. HE SIGNED IT!

They're Singing Our Song

Two months later, Jeannie and I drove to the penitentiary to get Howard. Prisons are noisy places—steel doors slamming and banging, people shouting, buzzes, bells—but we heard the Mormon Tabernacle Choir singing, just for us.

That was many years ago. Howard has been calling me every two weeks for all those years. I just visited him, his wife, and child (my Godchild) in Oklahoma. It was a fine visit. I have tears in my eyes as I write this.

Anyone can be reached. Anyone.

More Tough Guys

It was my first big speech as a full-time professional

speaker and seminar leader, and I was facing 550 tough, independent electrical contractors. I'd done my homework, so I knew what their problem was— they weren't getting along with the union folks. It was risk time, and I said, "Would you like to spend less time at the bargaining table, have less hassle, and get back to work?" It got very quiet in that room, and their answer was an emphatic "Yes!"

"Well, I'm about to tell you how to do just that, but please let me finish before attacking. You see, you have a lot in common with those union folks." They started to hoot and boo. This was what Teddy Roosevelt must have meant when he said,

"FAR BETTER TO DARE MIGHTY THINGS TO WIN GLORIOUS TRIUMPHS . . ."

This was the time to get my message across about clear communication and success in the people business. Better relationships, lower divorce rate, fewer devastated adults and children.

"What you must know is that everyone wants to love and be loved, to feel that they're important, that they matter. You don't have to like what they're doing, and you can tell them so. But separate the behavior from the person, and see them as a fellow human being who wants to love and be loved, just like you. Then find a way to reach out and touch them where they live. Give them the wonderful gift of listening, catch them doing something right, ask them a question, let them know that you care. They don't care how much you know, until they know how much you care."

Anyone can be reached. We're fellow human beings. If we don't always see eye to eye, we can always see heart to heart.

Sincere words are not grand.
Grand words are not sincere.

—Lao Tze

THOMAS NARVAEZ, Ph.D.
Thomas Narvaez & Associates
6509 Southwind Drive
El Paso, TX 79912
(915) 584-6268

Thomas Narvaez, Ph.D.

A hypnotic, engaging communicator, Tom Narvaez is equally effective with executives and prison inmates. He is best known for his pioneering research in accelerated learning of human relations subjects. Quite comfortable before large audiences, Tom prefers to focus his talents on smaller groups, insuring that each attendee receives any special attention needed to internalize the material.

Dr. Narvaez trains groups in Neuro-Linguistic Programming (NLP), a model which uses the thought strategies and behaviors of outstanding communicators for teaching others how to become more effective. (This new discipline was described in Psychology Today *as "...the most powerful vehicle for personal and social change in existence.") As of 1985, over a quarter of a million people have been trained in NLP.*

Tom's career as a communicator started many years ago on the streets of New York as an instructor with the Police Athletic League. He has over 15 years in training and development, and now claims El Paso, Texas as his home.

Dr. Narvaez has taught at several institutes of higher learning as adjunct faculty. He is an active member of Texas A&M Home Economics Program Development Board, The American Society for Training and Development, The National Speakers Association, and The American MENSA Society.

6

How To Eliminate Negative Communication Programming
by Tom Narvaez, Ph.D.

"Put on the role of the humble enquirer."
—Benjamin Franklin

"Discretion of speech is more than eloquence."
—Francis Bacon

A Predictable Saga

Tears welled in his eyes as the five-year-old looked down at the ice cream from his cone melting on the sidewalk. His mother said, "I told you ten times, don't drop the ice cream! Now, see what you did?"

I had watched as this somewhat predictable saga unfolded. The mother was right; she did tell him at least ten times not to drop the ice cream. What she didn't realize was that she was a co-conspirator in the event and had actually led the child to imagine what the words meant, and to at least consider dropping the ice cream. The outcome she communicated was not the one she wanted.

As I left the scene, I thought back to one of my seminars where I commanded the audience, "Don't think of the number 12!" As the smiles and giggles came, I playfully noted that they were disobeying me. We had a good laugh and then talked about Negative Communication Programming.

When it comes to communicating with one another, people usually do the best they know how under the circumstances. It's sometimes difficult to understand, however, that the very words we use help determine the outcome of the communication. History is full of examples of people influencing the outcome of an event by communicating with specific objectives in mind. With a little pre-planning, anyone can use questions and statements to influence the outcome of a conversation.

Negative Communication Programming

We also use questions and statements to bring about

negative outcomes. Take for example the question, "What's wrong?" On the surface it is a simple request for information. But what it is really saying is, "Something is wrong. Now go and find out what it is."

This negative question is really quite powerful. On one occasion, demonstrating its effect, I asked a woman in the audience, "What's wrong with your 12-year-old child?" Her face turned red and she could hardly talk. She seemed quite embarrassed and flustered, and looked around nervously. Then she exclaimed, "Wait a minute! I don't even have a 12-year-old child!" The audience roared, but the question had already demonstrated the point. She had spent time and energy trying to make the question relate to her. Had she had a 12-year-old, she might have easily become a victim of negative programming.

Responses like this to negative questions are typical. Consider the effects of such questions as, "What's wrong with your job?" or "What's wrong with your marriage?" Even if nothing is wrong, the person will spend some time trying to find out. Negative assumptions are part of the question.

There are a number of equally devastating questions in use. Many communicators suggest replacing the word "problem" with another word, such as "challenge" or "opportunity." But what about "Who is to blame?" and "Whose fault is it?"

These not only suggest that someone is at fault, but possible that they should even be punished!

Constructive Criticism?

Have you ever seen a company where "constructive criticism" is no more than an ongoing review of everything that is wrong? Take for example this XYZ Corp. Harry is talking to Joe, a salesman.

Harry: "Okay, Joe. What went wrong?"

Joe: "Well, I think I have lost the Green Blivet account."

Harry: "Why did you lose it?"

Joe: "They got a new purchasing agent and I wasn't informed of when they were having their meeting for discussing bids. They bought from the competitor."

Harry: "Why didn't you stay in contact with them?"

Joe: "I took them for granted. They have been buying from us for the past five years. I just assumed they would call me."

Harry: "Joe, just why do you have problems like these?"

Joe: "I don't know. I guess it's because I'm not all that organized."

Harry: "And whose fault is that, Joe?"

Joe: "Mine. I should be more organized, but I'm not."

Harry: "How long has this been going on?"

Joe: "All my life. I'm just not an organized person. Maybe I should get out of sales!"

Uncommon? You know it's not. Joe feels terrible, and now he has labeled himself as unorganized, probably not suitable for a career he's had for a number of years.

Positive Communication Programming

Negative Communication Programming seems to have several characteristics. First of all, it concentrates on past mistakes. While it is often useful to analyze something that did not accomplish what it was supposed to, all too often much time and energy is wasted looking for a scapegoat, someone to blame. It would be even more useful to determine what was learned. Was this a failure? Or was it feedback, letting us know that something had to be changed?

Secondly, these expressions have implied negative assumptions. "Whose fault is it?" suggests that someone is at fault and that the person should be identified for one reason or another. "How did you fail?" even suggests the idea that you have no need to try again.

Positive Communication Programming, on the other hand, keeps the outcome in mind. It constantly asks the question, "What am I trying to accomplish?" It assumes that people have positive intent in what they do, but they need additional choices. These choices can be suggested by the proper design and use of questions.

To use Positive Communication Programming, start off with an objective. What is it that you want out of the communication? You may want to gain information, make a sale, be of assistance, get to know an interesting person, counsel an employee, or even just pass the time of day. You'll have a lot more control and you may even be helping others in their thinking process, if you communicate with an outcome in mind.

The Positive Alternative

What do you think Henry's objective is in this example?

Henry: "What's going on, Joe?"

Joe: "I think I have lost the Green Blivet account."

Henry: "What do you want to do about it?"

Joe: "I want to get it back."

Henry: "When do you want to get it back?"

Joe: "I want to do that right away, but I'll probably have to wait until they have another meeting to talk about bids. I missed the last one because they got a new purchasing agent and I didn't know about it. We could have given them a better price."

Henry: "What else can you do?"

Joe: "Organize my activities, that's what. I'll use this as a lesson to make sure it doesn't happen again."

Henry: "Who can help you with this?"

Joe: "I'll talk to Anne. She's a lot more organized and she can give me some pointers."

Henry: "How specifically can Anne help you?"

Joe: "She can show me how to keep track of clients more effectively."

Henry: "Well, what's your first step?"

Joe: "I'm going to see Anne right now. Next, I'll call that new purchasing agent at Green Blivet and make an appointment to let her know how we can be of service."

Henry: "Looks like you're on the right track. You've certainly gotten a lot of good feedback from this experience."

People Do Things For a Reason

In the previous example, Henry's outcome was to get Joe to come up with the solutions. The questions required Joe to use his own resources to come up with ways of dealing with the situation. Even though the answers may seem obvious to the reader, "real world" situations often demonstrate that many people are locked into a limited thought pattern. The questions were designed to direct the thought pattern into more productive directions.

Note that outcomes are not necessarily objectives. They are more personal and have to do with what we really achieve as compared to what we verbalize. Thus, an outcome is the specific end result that a person really wants to achieve. Flexibility and creativity may be needed in order to achieve it. There are many people who seem to accomplish little despite their goals and objectives. The actual outcomes are often influenced by factors outside of consciousness.

Use the presupposition that people do things for a reason—the best reason among a limited number of choices. You may not agree with what they do or why they do it, but this is not the issue.

Even though people do things for a reason, they may not have a specific outcome in mind. The reasons they give may be no more than rationalizations of some hidden agendas. If you can learn what people's outcomes are, you can improve communication tremendously. Not only that, you can lead them into thinking creatively.

Four Responses

I have encountered four different responses to the question, "What do you want?" In one, the person doesn't consciously know what he/she wants, in which case you can come up with a list of possible outcomes. In this example, Betty is watching Frank for any kind of nonverbal reaction which she will use to help explore new possibilties.

Betty: "What do you want out of good investment?"

Frank: "I really hadn't thought of anything more than making a few bucks. Why do you ask?"

Betty: "Well, some people are interested in retirement..." (No response from Frank.) "...or for a special trip around the world..." (Sees a slight response in Frank's face.) "...or perhaps an island in the Caribbean..."

Frank: "I have a fantasy of spending a year in Europe, just traveling around!"

In another, the response is more of what the person doesn't want. Here you can rephrase the question until you get a response that includes an outcome, or you can reply with, "So what you really want is..." Keep in mind that if you allow a person to dwell on what it is they don't want, you are allowing the conversation to move in a negative direction. Here, Henry is dealing with a problem employee.

Henry: "What is it that you want?"

Bill: "I just don't want a big hassle all the time!"

Henry: "If you don't want a hassle, are you saying you want to be left alone on the job?"

Bill: "Well, not really, but I do want that job

explained to me so I know what I'm doing."

Henry: "How can you get that?"

Bill: "I guess if I asked the supervisor in a nice way..."

A very common response is for people to want things for someone else and not themselves. These are not outcomes, but rather attempts to change people. In one interview I was told, "I want people to take responsibility for their actions." This was refined to some degree with, "I want Larry to get punished for lying about his reports." The actual outcome was, "I want to feel that I am being treated fairly."

The fourth and hoped-for response is that the person tells you the outcome. When you do get it, your next step is to probe even deeper. Knowing what is wanted still does not provide you with a person's motivation. Nor does it always make a positive effect on someone. It does give you some points of agreement which can be used as a basis for further communication.

Regardless of the response, we can generally assume that it will take several questions to learn the real outcome that the person wants to communicate. A good communicator will listen for patterns in the responses and watch carefully for nonverbal cues that may indicate incongruency. Most people hesitate to be offensive in communication, and the responses you get may be more of what they think you want to hear rather than of what they really want to say.

Following Up

You can get a lot more information by following "What do you want?" with "What will having that do for you?" The reply to this follow-up question will usually be much richer with information. It could even provide you with the basic motivation that a person might have for buying a home, making an investment or taking on a new career. Here you can rephrase the question again and again until you get as much information as you might need to close the sale, counsel the employee or ask for a date.

Anne: "John, what do you want out of a relationship?"

John: "I want to feel that I'm able to communicate with and help another person."

Anne: "And what will that do for you, John?"

John: "It will make me feel useful and needed."

Anne: "What will feeling useful and needed do for you?"

John: "I never thought of that before, but it will give me the opening to let someone else know that I have needs that I want met."

Also, you can use the question, "What's important about that?" It can get you even more of what you want.

Anne: "What's important about having these needs met, John?"

John: "Even more important than having them met is the opportunity to communicate them to someone."

After using this approach to communication, it becomes apparent that the questions are designed to make people think.

Questions of Power

In many of my seminars I have been asked to come up with a list of questions which could be used under different circumstances to help influence the outcome of the communication. The following is but a small example of such questions. In each case I have included the underlying meaning behind the question in parentheses. Feel free to modify and adapt them to your own circumstances. As you use them, keep notes on how your effectiveness as a communicator improves.

"How will you know when that happens?" (There are certain things you can detect which will give you information about the event when it occurs.)

"What does that tell you?" (There is additional information for you. All you have to do is listen.)

"How do you know that this is true?" (There

exists some kind of evidence that must be available to you.)

"How can we find out?" (There is a way to find out, but you may have to search for it.)

"What will it be like when...?" (You are able to imagine the end result as this task or operation is completed).

"What will have to happen before you...?" (There is a stimulus that you need to get you moving on this.)

"How does that lead to our objective?" (If that leads to our objective, you can explain how.)

"How would you go about doing it?" (You either have some ideas on how to do it or you should come up with one right now.)

"If that were resolved, what would you do next?" (There is an obstacle confronting you which should be temporarily ignored for the sake of discussing the outcome.)

"How would you make this decision?" (You already have a way of making this kind of decision. Not only that, you are capable of explaining it to me.)

"What will it take to convince you...?" (There is something which, if presented to you properly, would lead you to take this course of action.)

"What specifically do you mean by...?" or "Can you say that another way?" (You are using a term which requires further explanation for me to understand it. Give more detail and/or use other expressions which mean the same thing.)

"Does that make sense to you?" (You have ways of knowing if you understand something. Check and let me know if you understand it.)

"What additional information do you need?" (You need more information, you know what that information is, and you should let me know what it is, too.)

"If you were me, what would you do?" (Look at it from my point of view.)

"How will I know when you've completed the project?" (There is the suggestion that someone has the responsibility of keeping me informed and it is probably you.)

"What will having that do for you?" (Having "that" will do something for you in addition to what has already surfaced in this conversation.)

The Implied Question

It's no secret that some people don't like to respond to questions. They may feel challenged or defensive. You can communicate outcomes with Positive Communication Programming without using direct questions. There are a number of statements that you can use that seem to have the same power as questions.

"I wonder what time it is" is a statement about

what I am thinking. It is not necessarily addressed to anyone in particular, but used in a group of people, it will bring several responses giving me the correct time. Properly rephrased, I can ask someone about what it is they want. "I'm wondering what it is you really want" will usually bring about some kind of useful response.

"I don't know when you plan to make that decision" is another approach. By stating that I don't know something, the implication is that someone else present should respond. When my wife says, "I don't know where my eye glasses are" we usually have a number of people looking for them or commenting on where they might be.

The implied question is softer, less challenging, and usually as effective as a direct question.

Conclusion

You can learn to communicate your outcomes and eliminate Negative Communication Programming. Teach other people to do the same. You'll find they will begin to think in ways that are beneficial to themselves and to the people around them.

*Can there be a more horrible object in
existence than an eloquent person not
speaking the truth?*

—Thomas Carlyle

CHARLES M. PERKINS
PPS, Inc.
4900 Flower Valley Drive
Rockville, MD 20853
(301) 929-9245

Charles M. Perkins

Charles M. Perkins is the president of Perkins Protective Services, Inc. Prior to his founding the security consulting, training and investigative firm he was Chief of Training for Executive Security Consultants, Inc. of Philadelphia, PA.

From 1976 to 1981 Mr. Perkins was Chief of Counterterrorism, Threat Analysis, and Attache Security for the Defense Intelligence Agency. His responsibilities included the training and briefing of all attaches of the armed forces in the 88 countries of the world where the Defense Attache System was represented in U.S. embassies. He supervised and conducted on site security surveys of attache offices, homes and other facilities in 25 to 30 countries each year.

The series of over 50 studies in counterintelligence, area analysis and counterterrorism which he initiated and edited during 1978 through 1980 was unique and trend setting in the U.S. intelligence community.

During this period he served on a subcommittee of the National Security Council and was selected to be the U.S. representative to an international counter-intelligence conference at SHAPE headquarters (NATO) in Europe. Prior to his assignment to DIA Mr. Perkins was a Lt. Colonel serving as Vice Commandant of the Air Force Special Investigations School in Washington, D.C. where he trained investigators of the USAF, U.S. Coast Guard, and Defense Investigative Service.

7

Abraham Lincoln:
The Great Communicator
by Charles M. Perkins

"The Moving Finger writes; and, having writ, Moves on."
—Omar Khayyam

For a Score, and a Score, and a Score . . .

Small town, Pennsylvania, 1863

A young man about 23 years old is visiting his birth place, a small village he hasn't seen since he left at age 14. As he hustles across the dusty and rutted street, he stops suddenly to avoid a passing horse-drawn carriage. He waves at nobody in particular. Continuing on, his head down and holding the brim of his hat against the wind, he feels an unexpected relief that no one has recognized him this morning. He found out yesterday, his first day here, that it can be quite embarrassing to be recognized by someone you know and who has known you most of your life, only to find you can't recall that person's name anymore. Oh, he could remember faces all right—but names, names gave him problems.

His daydreaming was broken by a voice calling out to him—"Jonathan, Jon!" He stopped, and raising his head, shielded his eyes against the early morning sun. "Jonathan, is that really you?" The voice was that of an elderly man striding toward him. It was Caleb Hunnicutt, a longtime friend of his father. "Jon, it's been a while. How yuh be?" "Real fine, Mr. Hunnicutt, and how 'bout yourself?" "Oh, I've been some poorly, but then I'm gettin' on a mite. Say, Jon, how long since we seen yuh in these parts? How old yuh be now Jon, 'bout one score and three?"

Your Town, USA, Late 20th Century

One score and three? In the little scene set in 1863, did the actions and the words of the two characters seem to fit with what you thought might have been reality in 1863? A small town in Pennsylvania would likely have a dusty street and horse drawn carriages then, would it not? And conversation in the vulgate or common language of the period would probably include expressions like ". . . gettin on a mite," and ". . . seen yuh in these parts." But, would you expect Caleb to ask Jon if he was ". . . one score and three?" Would you expect Caleb to have responded to a question regarding his own age by saying, "Oh, I'm 'bout three score and ten—give or take."?

I think not. I think we would expect Caleb to say he was seventy. We would be surprised at any more formal language from Caleb or from most folks in that small Pennsylvania town because most people didn't talk that way in 1863. They didn't convert common everyday numbers to scores and remainders. To do so would have been unusual— odd—it would have attracted attention.

The Address and the Paradigm

Why then, why, did President Abraham Lincoln, near this same little dusty Pennsylvania town on 19 November 1863, begin his most famous address at the dedication of the Gettysburg National Cemetery with the words, "Four score and seven years ago . . ."?

Why did Lincoln not say for instance, "Some eighty-seven years back . . .," or "Eighty-seven years ago . . ." or some more common and more easily understood reference to time than that measured in scores of years?

The reason, in my view, is that he chose his introductory words for precisely the reason that they would not be immediately familiar or grasped. He wanted them to sound "different." It was a solemn occasion, some 50,000 men had been killed or wounded on this battlefield a few short weeks before. He knowingly and purposefully chose a formal, almost Biblical phraseology to begin his speech because he knew it would capture the listeners' attention! Now, of course, President Lincoln probably felt solemn, and he was intensely concerned with the content of his words, his message; but don't forget Mr. Lincoln has been called a great communicator. And with good reason, with thousands of examples of good reasons over his career. And very important among these, Abraham Lincoln understood effective form and organization for an informative speech. We don't know whether he learned it from teachers, for he had little formal education, from associates, or whether he simply reasoned it out on his own—but it's there! And you can see, as we will explore in this speech, in his speeches, lectures and addresses, repeated examples of his superb organizational form. It is the same supremely effective outline being taught in colleges, universities, seminars and communications courses today. The speech to inform, we are taught, begins with an attention step.

An attention step may be a quotation, a bit of humor or a joke, a reference to the speaker's experiences coming there (an "on the way to the forum" anecdote), or a flattering reference to the audience or some of the community or organizational leaders connected with the celebration, the place or the event.

No doubt Lincoln considered several of these options and rejected most of them because they would have been superficial, in poor taste, or not suitable for other clearly apparent or perhaps subtle reasons. But Mr. Lincoln knew, as we modern communicators know, that just because one person is on his feet and the rest of the people in the vicinity are sitting down does not mean that all sitters must give rapt attention to and listen to the stander. There is an arrogance on the part of some speakers that is demonstrated by their belief that when they stand up—by that act alone they have earned the right to be annointed with everyone's immediate attention and devoted listening. Not so— and Mr. Lincoln knew this. He deliberately chose his words because they were more formal, even scriptural in tone, than would be expected in the vernacular. And because the words were thus, they seized peoples' attention. They did not capture the audience in a burlesqued or unrelated way, as a modern day television comic might do with an outrageous act, costume or gyration. Such calculated and bizarre actions may capture an audience's attention, but it is quickly lost when the audience realizes it has been tricked into paying heed to the stander. No, Mr. Lincoln's attention step tricked nobody, offended nobody, amused nobody, yet encompassed everybody, caused all to pause in their myriad of random thoughts and brought them to reflect on his words. A moving and splendidly effective technique!

Attention
Step:
Four score and seven years ago our fathers brought forth on this continent, a new nation, conceived in liberty, and dedicated to the proposition that all men are created equal.

Every speaker faces an immediate problem after capturing the attention of the audience, whatever technique has been used. (Let's hope it was a method with character and charm.) That problem is—attention span. Authorities disagree on how long people can dwell on, or give attention to, a subject without mentally drifting away. There is agreement though that the span is short and thoughts have to be tugged back to the heart of a matter from time to time. People differ and attention spans vary but most have problems after a few minutes. This is not a problem for an entertainer. A humorist paces jokes and one liners so that they are spaced every few minutes and he or she keeps recapturing the audience's attention. It's also easy for the magician who conjures up some minor miracle every few moments. A rabbit changing to a lovely lady will get attention easily enough, as will sawing that rabbit or lady in half.

But for the speaker with a serious subject, the task of retaining the attention of the audience can be indeed trying. And to simply assert that one's subject is the most important thing anyone in the group has ever heard will not insure attention either. In fact, studies by educational psychologists have shown that when a message is conveyed in the most extreme terms possible (with regard to the damage done by tooth decay in the absence of brushing, for instance), it is less effective than if explained in moderate terms.

For Mr. Lincoln, he knew the war was not yet won in 1863. He knew more battles must be fought, more soldiers must die, more sacrifices must be endured. But he did not choose to continue to hold  his audience's attention with a reference to the extreme hardships ahead. Instead he motivated them to continue to listen by complimenting them for what they were doing—together. He said, ". . . we are engaged . . ." and "We are met . . . ." He endorsed and approved what they had chosen to do that day. It is likely that many in the crowd on hearing these words were reinforced in their own resolve that their decision to attend the dedication was a right and proper one. You can imagine even some of the people in the crowd quietly looking around at each other, and smiling or nodding in agreement at these words, and reassuring each other and the speaker with their subtle feedback. The President had motivated them to continue to give him their attention and hear his message.

Motivation
Step:

Now we are engaged in a great civil war, testing whether that nation, or any nation so conceived and so dedicated, can long endure. We are met on a great battlefield of that war.

What would a modern speaker expect next in a speech to inform? An overview, of course. And Mr. Lincoln does not disappoint. He has a simple but effective overview of his main point. Yes, point. In many speeches to inform, which may extend for 15 to 30 minutes, perhaps even 45 as in a college lecture, it is not uncommon to find three to five main points. Some experts argue three is best, and with supporting data, examples, quotations from authorities and so forth, will, with necessary transitional devices between one point and another, easily take the time allotted. Five to ten minutes being an average time to develop a point.

But the President did not intend to speak for 30 to 45 minutes. He knew his carefully structured speech would last about two to three minutes. He, therefore, limited himself to one main point, one theme for his address. The main point is dedication. He mentions it throughout the speech, six times in fact. Dedication of the field itself, to the proposition of equality, and to the great unfinished task before them of enduring—of saving the union of states intact, and surviving the war.

In one of his most effective moves in speech organization, Mr. Lincoln even begins to thread his dedication theme or main point into his attention and motivation steps—before the overview! Masterful content—Yes! Masterful form and organization—assuredly—Yes, Yes!

Does he tell folks what he's going to tell them in his overview? Clearly he does, and we will see that he also tells them in the body, and tells them what he told them in the summary as well.

Overview   *We have come to dedicate a portion of that field as a final resting-place for those who here gave their lives that that nation might live.*

Now we encounter an unusual step in the organization of a speech. Not often seen, it is exceptionally effective in settings of enormous impact such as that Gettysburg had on the history of a nation.

Mr. Lincoln here uses a *reinforcing* of motivation step. Perhaps he believed the subject of the speech to be so profound, so overwhelming, that he needed to remind the audience again that they were to be respected and recognized for what they were doing. Whatever his reasons, he chose to once again say to his listeners that what they were doing together, they the audience and he the President, and by implication the whole Union which he and they represented, was the right thing to do. One can almost see the long arms on this tall and stately

 figure swing out in a warm embracing fashion, gathering everyone there in a common activity, purpose and goal as he says, ". . . we should do this." Note, please, that Mr. Lincoln never says, "I as your Chief Executive," or "In my office as President and Commander in Chief," nor does he say, "This great country" or "The nation is engaged"—listen carefully. He says, ". . . we are engaged . . .," "We are met . . .," ". . . we should do this." Is there any question in our minds what a powerful motivating device this was? For the President to figuratively wrap his

arms around each soul in that audience and say we are in this together my brother, my sister, and it's proper that we should do this—this was powerful motivation indeed.

Reinforces   *It is altogether fitting and proper that we*
Motivation: *should do this.*

With such exceptional care to the steps which brought us this far, we now are conditioned to be fundamentally receptive to the main point in the body of the speech. Because our focus in this chapter, however, is on form and organization and how this can insure success for content, and not an analysis of content itself, we'll not explore content as a separate subject. Whole treatises have been devoted to the substance of this most remarkable of speeches. And by scholars more qualified than this writer to measure and evaluate the message the Gettysburg speech conveys.

For our purpose it is sufficient to observe that the theme of dedication is fleshed out in the body of the speech and the main point is firmly established. So much so that historians in later years would say that President Lincoln in this exquisitely short but magnificently gigantic speech, took the national calamity which was Gettysburg and drew from it a sense of national purpose and direction which then carried the Union victoriously through the rest of the war.

Body: *But in a larger sense, we cannot dedicate— we cannot consecrate—we cannot hallow this ground. The brave men, living and dead, who struggled here, have consecrated it far beyond our poor power to add or detract. The world will little note nor long remember what we say here, but it can never forget what they did here. It is for us, the living, rather, to be dedicated here to the unfinished work which they who fought here have thus far so nobly advanced.*

Some texts and some teachers of speech plan only a summary after the body of the speech has concluded. They believe in the efficacy of the three phase format of overview, body and summary which we considered earlier. The summary, being the place where you "Tell them what you told them," is an effort to reinforce and prop up that rapidly declining memory curve which promptly forgets 80% of everything it just heard before the listener reaches the door of the auditorium or the saddle stirrup on the horse, in the case of Gettysburg. Studies have shown that in stating and restating a main point with an overview, a body and a summary in a speech, a communicator can insure a much higher than 20% degree of retention in his audience.

Well, Mr. Lincoln surprises, yet again. He is not content simply to summarize; rather, he uses his summary in a most sophisticated way to also remotivate the audience once more. In referring to the need for dedication to the great remaining task, he again identifies himself, and by implication the nation, with the audience. He does not say "they" should be dedicated or the more abstract "nation" should be dedicated. Rather, he stands with them, figuratively in their very midst, as he says "us" (together), we together dedicated to the great task remaining before "us"!

Remotivation *It is rather for us to be here dedicated to*
Step *the great task remaining before us—that*
and Summary: *from these honored dead we take increased*
devotion to that cause for which they gave
the last full measure of devotion;

Finally, in his conclusion Mr. Lincoln has an

implicit call for action which flows from the resolve that he asks for from the citizenry. The resolve that "we" share with regard to what we owe to those who have already given full measure. What we owe to ourselves and to each other and to our God, and to all that this nation and its people and its freedoms mean on this earth.

Conclusion   *That we here highly resolve that these dead shall not have died in vain; that this nation, under God, shall have a new birth of freedom; and that government of the people, by the people, for the people, shall not perish from the earth.*

A powerful close to a speech which became itself a momentous historical event, its message, its thrust, its purpose, its effect still having impact on our lives even today. Over 120 years later. This, dear readers, is a speech! That was a great communicator!

Epilogue

Would that the moving finger which recorded this great man's life not have been obliged to close his chapter so abruptly and so early at Ford's Theater in Washington just 17 months later. He could have communicated so much more to us had he been permitted the opportunity. If only it might have been.

> *"Nor all thy Piety nor Wit shall lure it back*
> *to cancel half a Line, nor all thy Tears wash*
> *out a Word of it."*   —**Omar Khayyam**

M. KAY DuPONT
DuPont and Disend
2137 Mt. Vernon Road
Atlanta, GA 30338
(404) 395-7483

M. Kay duPont

Kay is Vice President of duPont and Disend, a consulting firm that designs and implements communication programs. Kay's clients represent such diverse industries as banking, real estate, ultilities, medical, universities, insurance, government, and retail services.

Kay specializes in four major areas of communication:

(1) BUSINESS WRITING: Kay is considered America's #1 correspondence trainer, and offers comprehensive writing programs for management and staff—communicating with readers. Her innovative grammar style book, DON'T LET YOUR PARTICIPLES DANGLE IN PUBLIC!, has been nationally acclaimed as America's most enjoyable and easy-to-read style book.

(2) PROFESSIONALISM: An invigorating, motivational program on professional image—communicating with customers on the phone and in the office, with co-workers and executives, and with the world around you.

(3) MOTIVATION: A highly inspiring program on self-talk—communicating with your own inner voice and power, believing in yourself, setting achievable goals, and being the best you can.

(4) PUBLIC SPEAKING: A hands-on program on presentation skills—communicating with an audience. As a winner in the World Championship of Public Speaking, and voted the best speaker in Georgia for two consecutive years, Kay certainly knows how to overcome stage fright and develop an audience-winning presentation.

8

Seven Ways to Put More Power in Your Business Writing
Write the Way You Speak!
by M. Kay duPont

"Good writers are not born; they are created by their own hands."
—M. Kay duPont

Ernest Hemingway rewrote the ending to his novel, *A Farewell to Arms,* 39 times before he was satisfied. When his agent asked him why, Hemingway said with a shrug, "I'm just trying to get the words right."

How many times have you struggled to "get the words right"? How many times have you sat staring into space, wondering how to get more power, more clarity, in your writing? How many times have your hands sat poised over your keyboard waiting for help from "above"?

When I became a professional speaker, I thought my need to speak better would relieve me from the need to write better, but I find that I still write more than I speak. I now own a company that specializes in helping organizations and individuals improve their written correspondence, and I am the product *represented* by my company. So it's critical that my correspondence be as sharp, clear, meaningful, and easy to understand as my workshops and speeches.

Your business correspondence needs to be as professional and up to date as your products or services too. Every company (and you *are* the company, no matter what your position or duties) has to communicate its products, services, complaints, visions, and dreams to other people. Much of this communication is done in writing. And, just as the products and services of most companies have changed in the last 10-20 years, so have the rules of written communication. The correct forms of spelling, punctuation, letter styles, sentence structure, word usage, and addressing have all changed. Not using currently accepted correspondence styles and rules is as bad as trying to sell products that have been outdated for a decade. It doesn't convey a quality, up-to-date image of *you,* and many people react negatively. They think, "If this is a reflection of their products or services, I don't want to deal with them." That can cost you money.

How's YOUR Written Image?

What about you? Is your correspondence up to date? Or is your image one of longwinded stuffiness, pompous words, run-on sentences, and six-page letters? If so, it's time to shape up and learn to write the way you speak! If you *speak* in longwinded, pompous, run-on sentences, it's time to take another look at that too.

Writing simply is hard for some of us because someone (can you remember who?) told us we have to follow a certain *style* when we write. We have to be formal and sound important. We have to "suffer." For that reason, we can't just put pen to paper and say what we mean. We have to outline what we want to say, then go to the thesaurus to figure out how to say it. Baloney! William Zinsser, author of *On Writing Well,* calls clarity the first test of writing:

"If you write clean, elegant sentences with as much simplicity as possible, style will eventually come."

Writing the way you speak will help take the pain out of writing for you, and make your correspondence sound more natural. Now I don't mean to put "you know" and "like, I mean" in your correspondence (or **any** communication, for that matter). What I mean is to pretend your reader is sitting across the desk from you. Visualize your reader and talk to him or her on paper as you would talk to them in person. Be friendly. Use contractions and personal pronouns. Use one-syllable words and short sentences. Don't try to be stuffy. If you use words and phrases that sound superior and snobbish to your readers, they won't be impressed—they'll only be confused, bored, or offended!

You can train yourself to write the way you speak! Clear writing is an art, like dancing or singing, and can be learned. Unfortunately, many people don't take the time to learn properly. You've probably been writing one way all your business life, so changing may be difficult. But it's time—unless you want to stay with the dinosaurs!

Good writers are not born; they are created by their own hands.

The following ideas will help you get out of your writing rut and put more power (and less pain) in your writing:

Tips for Better Writing

1. GO STRAIGHT TO THE POINT. Let's face it, the hardest part about writing a letter (or speech, or anything!) is getting started. We know what we want to say, but we feel like we have to be formal when we start. We don't! There is no need to drag out your first paragraph. Just use a short opening sentence, go to the point, and stick to the point. Readers don't have time to wade through pages of fluff to find out why you're writing. By "fluff," I mean those phrases that don't really add anything, those clauses that are set off by commas, those "nice" words that could really be left out. (**Having nothing else to do,** *I went fishing.*")

Most people won't read a two-page letter, they'll scan it. Most people won't read letters of more than 10 paragraphs, paragaphs of more than 10 sentences, or sentences of more than 20 words (no more than 15 if the words aren't broken by the proper punctuation). So why spend a lot of time constructing an eloquent, wordy, superfluous opening paragraph if no one is going to read it? Use a short opening sentence acknowledging the reader's letter, phone call, complaint, or praise, and then get to the point.

WEAK: I'm writing in reference to your letter dated May 8, 1985, in which you requested information about our Mousetraps of the Future. We are delighted to send you this information, which you will find enclosed.
STRONG: Thanks for your letter. We're delighted to enclose information about our Mousetraps of the Future.

Once you have gotten to the point, for Heaven's sake, stay there! Rambling will confuse your readers and cause *them* to lose the point—not a very smart move when you're trying to explain, request, or demand something.

2. PUT THE STRENGTH FIRST, THE FLUFF LAST. There is a sign on the ceiling of the Library of Congress that says, "Order is Heaven's first law." It's also the first law in effective writing (or speaking!). Remember that readers only scan letters. And when they scan, they usually read only the first half—the first half of paragraphs, the first half of sentences. If you want to make sure your reader gets the point and hears what you're saying, you need to put the strength right up front. This will also give you a more powerful sentence, and keep you from needing as much punctuation.

WEAK:

While on my father's shoulders, I could easily see the parade.

   (Fluff)   (Comma)   (Strength)

STRONG:

I could easily see the parade while on my father's shoulders.

(Strength)   (No comma)   (Fluff)

Another construction to avoid is the fluff that falls awkwardly in the middle of a sentence:

WEAK: She is, I believe, a fine communicator.

STRONG: I believe she is a fine communicator.

3. DON'T LET YOUR PARTICIPLES DANGLE IN PUBLIC.

Many people have asked me why I gave my book such a strange title. I chose it for several reasons: to catch the reader's eye, to prove that learning the English language can be fun, and to remind people that effective writing must still follow certain structure rules. A participle is not something to make you blush—it's simply a verb form that ends in "ing." It's often used as the first word of a modifying phrase. It's fluff!

A participle dangles when it's placed in the sentence incorrectly and appears to modify something it doesn't. For instance:

"Sitting on my mother's lap, the circus was more enjoyable."

Doesn't that sound like the *circus* was sitting on my

You may not realize when your participles are dangling in public . . . but others will!

mother's lap? *That's* a dangling participle.

Participles aren't the only modifiers that dangle. Adjectives and adverbs can dangle too. Modifiers can add a lot of beauty and color to our sentences, but they detract if they are not the right words or not in the right places.

It's not up to the reader to determine what's being modified—it's up to the writer to make it perfectly clear. A sentence that has to be dissected is not a good sentence, and readers won't stand for it often. So here's the rule: Make sure your modifiers are adjacent to, and preferably in front of, what they modify.

WEAK: Covered in chocolate, you can really enjoy ice cream.

STRONG: You can really enjoy chocolate-covered ice cream.

4. USE THE ACTIVE VOICE. An active sentence begins with the person (subject) doing the act (verb) to something (object). A passive sentence is backward. It has the object being acted on by the subject. For example:

PASSIVE/WEAK:

The conference was attended by many people.
    (Object)   (Verb)   (Subject)

ACTIVE/STRONG:

Many people attended the conference.
   (Subject)   (Verb)   (Object)

A passive sentence also may leave out all information about who is responsible for the action. For instance:

PASSIVE/WEAK:
Your request is being considered. (By whom?)
ACTIVE/STRONG:
We are considering your request.

Active construction is always preferable to passive. Let your subject do to your object, rather than having your object done to by your subject. Because passive verbs are impersonal and indirect, passive sentence structure is usually weak and awkward. Passive sentences also require a lot of unnecessary words and prepositional phrases that steal power from your sentence.

5. USE PROPER GRAMMAR. Whether you're an office supervisor, a plant manager, a secretary, a housekeeper, or a speaker, you're faced daily with grammar choices. Unfortunately, many people make the wrong choice. Sometimes that's because they never learned correctly in the first place, or because they've been doing it incorrectly for so long that it "feels" right, or because the rules have changed.

Yes, the rules have changed. They have changed in your lifetime; they have changed *this year*. People who write dictionaries are only historians, because all they can do is record how words have been used in the *past*. By the time a dictionary gets to the bookstores, some word has been added to, or deleted from, our language. Remember when there were no such words as **palimony, watergate, timewise**? when **judgment** had an "e" in it and **reevaluate** was hyphenated? Remember when it was unacceptable to begin a sentence with a conjunction or end it with a preposition?

The skill to weave words together and use them to their best advantage is vital to communication. The magic wand required for this ability is grammar. Words, as irreplaceable as they are, are only words; it takes a careful hand and knowledge of the rules to make words most effective. Even the right words will be ineffective if you use incorrect or outdated grammar.

Choose your words wisely.

The best way to improve your grammar skills is to buy a good style book. Just be sure it was published in the last five years so it will be up to date and not lead you astray. After you buy it, don't put it on a shelf with your copy of the 1953 phone directory—read it and find out what's changed! If you shudder at the thought of actually *reading* an

English style book, buy one that's entertaining as well as informative (like **mine!**)

6. USE SHORT WORDS, PHRASES, SENTENCES.

Professionalism is also judged by whether writers say what they intend to say, and say it in the best manner.

Effective writing is concise. Words are very much like extra pounds—the more you have, the worse the whole package looks. A sentence should contain no unnecessary words, and a paragraph no unnecessary sentences, for the same reasons that a drawing should have no extra lines, a machine no extra parts, and a body no extra flab.

Short words and sentences are more easily understood by the average reader. Good publications have always known that. *The Wall Street Journal,* one of America's most widely read newspapers, insists that the first paragraphs of its lead articles never exceed three sentences. More than half the *Wall Street Journal* paragraphs contain only a single sentence!

This doesn't mean that we must make *all* our sentences short, or that we must avoid all detail and always treat our subjects simply. It just means that we should write like we speak! We seldom use the same length sentences in our speech, and we seldom use long, unbroken dissertations. So vary the length of your sentences to insure best reader attention, and remember that overly long sentences tend to drag a reader into complacency, because the reader has to hold on to the statement in the first phrase until he or she wades through all the commas and deadwood and reaches the connecting point in the final phrase. *(See what I mean?)* Fifteen words per sentence is a good average.

If some lovely, dramatic, inspired phrase or sentence comes to you while you're writing, fine. Put it in. But then, with a cold, objective eye and mind, ask yourself: "Does it detract from clarity?" If it does, take it out. "Is it essential to get my message across?" If it isn't, take it out.

How About a Punch in the Nose?

Whatever you write, condensing almost always makes it tighter, crisper, and easier to understand. The reason a punch in the nose hurts so much is that the attacker has channeled all their strength into a small area—the fist. The same goes for words. As you pack more meaning into a smaller space, you gain power.

A short word containing the same information as a longer word or phrase is almost always more powerful. "Rape" is stronger than "physical abuse." "Propose" is stronger than "ask him/her to marry." "Poor" is stronger than "financially deprived." "Kiss" is stronger than "quadrilabial osculation."

Being concise also means avoiding redundancy.

You should never, ever, ever repeat yourself by using repetitive redundancies again in your whole life as long as you're living, and I mean that from my own personal heart inside me. *Do you see how silly some redundancies sound?* Still, we use them regularly without even being aware of them. Here are some common redundancies:

hot water heater	free gifts
tuna fish	mentally insane
future plans	advance warning
live audience	pizza pie
ugly eyesore	my own personal opinion

Stuffiness or pomposity is another form of wordiness that's especially noticeable in written communication. It isn't hard to write a message that is absolutely clear if someone takes the time to study it. But a message that has to be studied is not a good communication. We must choose our words so that our readers will understand them without wasting the readers' time or thought. Using everyday words will help. For instance:

If I said that my "cranial habiliment came asunder in a squall," would you know that my hat blew off in a gust of wind? If I told you that I had "ova for my matutinal refection," would you know that I had eggs for breakfast?

Using words like those can put our readers in the same bind as Albert Einstein's wife. She was once asked whether she understood everything Dr. Einstein said. "I understand *some* of the words," she said, "but *none* of the sentences!"

If you resolve never to use a longer, fancier word than you need to convey your message properly, you'll help stem the tide of misuse and lost meaning. More important, your readers will *like* you better. You won't sound superior, pompous, dull, or uninterested in them. You'll sound like you're writing to *communicate* rather than to impress. And, no, you won't sound too elementary. Do people accuse Abraham Lincoln, Mark Twain, or John Kennedy of being too simple? They were all great communicators who resisted the urge to show off.

Economizing with words is just a matter of packing the same, or more, meaning into a smaller unit to improve your chances of communicating what you have to say. It isn't always easy. Your idea is so clear to you that you may not realize how difficult or confusing your words may be to someone else.

Just be sure your idea *is* clear to you. Many people aren't sure what they want to say before they write. Their letters ramble because they just put their thoughts down as they think of them. If *you* don't have a clear objective in mind before you start writing, how can you expect the *reader* to follow your thoughts?

7. MAKE YOUR ENDING COURTEOUS AND BRIEF. If the hardest part of writing a letter is the opening paragraph, the next hardest part is the closing paragraph. This is true for the same reason: We've been taught that it's impolite to stop writing when we're finished. I find that very odd, because one of the tenets of other forms of communication is to stand up, speak up, and then shut up. As a public-speaking trainer, I always tell my groups that they will never offend an audience by keeping to the point and finishing *early* with a smile and a thank-you. As a business-writing trainer, I say the same thing. Don't waste your time or the reader's time by trying to think of something else to say when you've said what you wanted.

In *Alice's Adventure in Wonderland,* the King of Hearts told the White Rabbit, "Begin at the beginning and go on until you come to the end. Then stop." Good advice. Use a short closing sentence—perhaps repeating your opening sentence ("Thank you again for your interest") and close.

Summary

I believe our language is the most important part of our lives. It's what sets us apart from the animals—

and from each other. Our words are the way we communicate everything we feel, believe, and attain. They have an impact on every aspect of our lives.

It's through our language that our businesses, schools, governments, judicial systems, and every other aspect of our lives are run. Your writing should be as important to you as speaking, especially when you realize that your career could depend on it.

Write as though your career depends on it.

Writing should also be as easy for you as speaking. I know it will be if you'll just remember this one basic principle:

WRITE THE WAY YOU SPEAK!

MICHAEL A. AUN, II
Aun and Associates, Orators
U.S. One at Interstate Twenty
Lexington, SC 29072
(803) 356-0777 • Res. (803) 359-5220

Michael A. Aun, II

Michael A. Aun, II is a successful businessman. He presides over a real estate development firm, a construction company, a two-state insurance and estate planning company and his immediate family runs a nationally acclaimed restaurant. He is a syndicated columnist and his column, "BEHIND THE MIKE," appears in a number of southeastern newspapers and periodicals. He has authored and produced five cassette tape albums, dozens of custom-designed booklets, over 25 audio cassettes and has co-authored the 26 volume series "BUILD A BETTER YOU— STARTING NOW!" Vol 5. His section entitled "GET UP, YOU'RE KILLING THE GRASS!" has been widely acclaimed.

Michael Aun rose to speaking fame in 1978 when he won the "WORLD CHAMPIONSHIP OF PUBLIC SPEAKING" for Toastmasters International, an organization of over 125,000 speakers in over 50 countries throughout the world. He has since shared the lecturn with such speaking giants as Paul Harvey, Dr. Norman Vincent Peale, Art Linkletter and others. Today, he presides over two speaking firms, AUN AND ASSOCIATES—ORATORS and THE AUN HUMAN DYNAMICS GROUP. He speaks over 100 times annually to audiences all over the world.

In 1983 Michael Aun was presented the prestigious Certified Speaking Professional (C.S.P.) designation by the National Speakers Association and is one of fewer than 160 speakers world wide that hold that honor.

9

Twice As Long, Twice As Hard For Half As Much
by Michael A. Aun, II

"If you want to succeed in life, you must be willing to work twice as long, twice as hard for half as much!"
—Elias S. Mack, Sr., 1960

Most of the successful people I have met in my lifetime were people who had an important role model in their life, a mentor, if you will. My mentor was a man who was perhaps the most important person in my life, my grandfather. His name was Elias S. Mack, Sr. and he was indeed a remarkable man.

Born Elias Skaff in a little village outside of Beirut, Lebanon, my grandfather came to America unable to speak the English language, owning nothing but a primitive third grade education. When he arrived on the shores of Ellis Island near New York City, the immigration people immediately asked his name. Unable to understand their request, his puzzled look frustrated the immigration officer. "Look Mac, you've got to cooperate or we can't let you into America. Name please."

My grandfather said in broken English, "My name is Elias Skaff."

The immigration officer responded, "Too difficult to understand Mac. You gotta choose an American name."

"You keep calling me Mac," my grandfather said. "Is this a good name for me?"

"Yeah, let's name you Mack," he countered. "We'll put a 'k' on the end of it to give you a little class."

And with the stroke of a pen, the Mack family was born of the frustration of an immigration officer in the 95 degree New York City in the late 1800's. And a legend had come to life.

Long before he mastered the English language, Eli Mack had built a reputation as a hard working man who succeeded in business. His philosophy was simple. "To succeed in life, you must work twice as long, twice as hard, for half as much," I recall him saying it time and again.

By the time I was born in 1949, my granddaddy had become something of a local legend in the little town of Lexington, South Carolina where we lived. After a brief stay in New York, Elias Mack decided to try to make his fortune in the south. He had heard of the opportunities. He had heard of the slower life style. He had also heard of the prejudices of the south, but came to Columbia, South Carolina anyway.

We Lebanese people are all rug-dealers, we're merchants. The old joke about why we never win wars is so true. We always stop and pick up the lumber when the enemy blows up the bridge so we can resell it. Facetious as it sounds, it's true. We are an industrious people who appreciate free enterprise and profit. Left alone, I am convinced that the war-torn nation of my ancestors would be rebuilt in a matter of months or certainly a few short years. How? Through the industriousness of the Lebanese people.

The Lebanese word for grandfather is "jidy." My jidy used to call me his "hayati," which is an Arabic word roughly translated to mean "the breath of my life," which I have always felt is a lovely expression.

In the 13 short years that I knew my jidy

before his death in the early sixties, I came to respect him as a remarkable man of many resources. His greatest talent was his ability to "out-love" his neighbor. And in the deep south, where blacks, Jews and other foreigners were looked upon with equal disdain, that love was paramount in order to overcome the hatred you faced every day of your life.

My grandfather was Lebanese by blood line and Lutheran by faith. But in the deep south, you were one of three things. You were a white man, you were a black man or you were a Jew, the common category for all foreigners. No matter whether you were Greek or Lebanese, you got thrown into the Jewish category. Jews and Catholics were hated with the same vengeance. Naturally, my grandfather's daughter, Alice, my mother, had to marry a New Jersey Catholic boy, Michael A. Aun, Sr., my father, to make the circle of hatred complete.

So welcome to Lexington, South Carolina, a bedroom community of Columbia, the state's capitol. Welcome to Lexington, home of the Ku Klux Klan, home of black-haters of the thirties and forties and the anti-Jewish/Catholic sentiment of the fifties and sixties. Also the home of a man affectionately known as "Jew Mack," a man they thought so much of that they elected him to town council for two terms and Mayor for a third.

He out-loved them. That's how Jew-Mack got elected Mayor. He out-gave them. He fed them on credit from his little grocery store on Main Street. He made them lunch from his luncheonette. He sold them jewelry at his jewelry store. You couldn't hate Jew-Mack because he wouldn't let you. And the day he died, there's no telling how many thousands of dollars he was owed that was never re-paid by those who called this man of love Jew-Mack. Someone once told me, "If Jew-Mack had taken mortgages on the land of all the people that owed him money at the time of his death, he'd own three-quarters of Lexington County."

In the thirteen short years that I knew and loved my jidy he taught me the ways of a shrewd business man. He'd say to me, "Hayati, if you want to be successful, you must first of all walk in the shadows of successful people. You must study their ways . . . their lives . . . their shortcomings . . . their strengths. Then, you must avoid their errors and duplicate their successes."

Not bad information from a man who barely knew the English language even when I knew him after living in America for 50 years.

My jidy left me with many lessons over the years. In this short chapter, I'd like to share a few with you. There were many more, too numerous to list. Perhaps a full-length book would be appropriate one day. But for now, here are a few golden nuggets from the man who called me "the breath of his life."

Don't Trust Your Memory

"Hayati," jidy would say, "never trust your memory. Always write things down."

And so, at the age of 13, I began to write things down that my granddaddy and others would tell me. He encouraged me to begin keeping a journal. I remember the first one he bought me. It was a lovely, leather bound book with blank pages. At the age of 13, I began to take the notes of my life. I took notes after the Sunday afternoon cookouts at my jidy's house. I took notes in school. I took notes at ball practice. I took notes at sunday school. I even took notes in church. Today, those notes comprise many of the early scripts of speeches I have delivered all over the world.

I'm proud to say that I now have over 200 journals that I have kept over the years. They reflect the good times and the bad. They reflect the loves I enjoyed and the heartbreaks I endured. They reflect the pain I felt in losing my mother. They reflect the struggle our family faced when my father had his heart attack and how we had to all work together to help raise a family of 13. They reflect the fight to keep my brothers and sisters in school. They reflect the success and failures of business and rebuilding from scratch. They reflect the fight to support a family . . . to find a wife . . . to raise children. I've captured all these moments on paper because my jidy taught me at a very early age to write things down. The journals tell it all—how I lost the "World Championship of Public Speaking" for Toastmasters International in 1977 before coming back to win it in 1978. They tell of the heartbreak of losing a race for the House of Representatives. Those memories would have all been for naught were it not for my jidy.

Listen to Others

"You know something, hayati," my grandfather said one afternoon in the jewelry store, "the word listen contains the same letters as the word silent."

I never thought about it but it does. Jidy used to say to me, "Hayati, God gave you two ears and one talker. You ought to do twice as much listening as talking."

And so true it is. If we listen to others, we can better understand their problems, and we can certainly solve them a lot quicker. Jidy would add, "If you'll close your mouth, it might help to open your mind. Better listeners do better work. You see," he would chuckle, "it's virtually impossible to sound dumb if you don't speak!"

Most sales people lose sales because of this one

problem—they don't know when to shut up. They keep talking and they end up buying their product back.

"You've got to listen to the customer," he'd say to me. "People don't *have* to buy jewelry. They buy it because they *want* to buy it. Listen to the customer. Take a walk in his shoes. And for God's sake, when you're up to your nose in it, DON'T open your mouth."

Jidy gave me another important piece of advice on listening. "Listen to other's criticism, but DON'T support them," he once told me. "There is no such thing as constructive criticism. All criticism is destructive."

I can't begin to tell you how important that last statement is in my life. Life is full of self-appointed critics who have to get their two-cents worth in. In the process, they chip away at the self-esteem of the person they are criticising.

"If you'll listen to a customer long enough hayati," jidy counselled, "he'll tell you how to sell him what he wants. And if you'll help him to get what he wants in life, God will reward you with the things you want from life."

Fear

Of all the definitions of fear, I guess the best one came from jidy one Sunday afternoon just two days before he died. He was on his death bed and had been in this condition for several months. It was the dead heat of summer. I remember it well because I chose to spend that summer "baby-sitting" my sick grandfather. I would run back and forth from his bedroom to the kitchen. I would fetch things he wanted or needed. I was elected to be in charge of the television, which was a relatively new thing for us back then. Jidy hated commercials, so when a commercial would come on, I would turn off the television for 60 seconds and then I'd turn it back on. This went on most of the summer in the year he died.

During those last days, we became even closer to one another. I asked him if he was afraid to die. By now, I knew that he was very sick and that it wouldn't be long before God would call him. "Are you afraid jidy?" I'll never forget his response. "Never fear anything Hayati," he told me. "Fear is just an absence of knowledge . . . it's a lack of information. I know I'm going to die . . . I'm ready to meet my God."

Not a bad definition for the word fear— "absence of knowledge." Get the knowledge and you'll no longer fear the unknown.

Being Different

Jidy always encouraged us to be different. In a

family of 11 children, it's tough not to get some duplication of talent along the path. Each of us had strengths and weaknesses that overlapped. We fed off of each other's positive traits and we tried to avoid duplicating the other's errors. But being different in a family where so much positive attitude existed was tough.

In my first year of junior high, I went to jidy and explained that I had to come up with a science project for the next year and I wanted to get an idea from the projects on display this year. "Hayati," he smiled and said, "go study the competition this year. Find out all the things you can about what they're up to. Study the categories, study the style, study the actual ideas. Once you have all your information, toss it aside and try something different. Don't be like the rest of them; be different!"

The next year I won the State Science Fair Award with a simple project that the judges loved. I suspect the reason I won was that it was the only project of its kind in a category all to itself.

Wealth

Jidy used to take me to see the old Columbia Red Legs play at Capitol City Ball Park in Columbia. I cherished those evenings with him because I got a chance to see some great minor league baseball.

Many of those players went on to be very successful athletes in the major leagues. Great baseball was not the only reason I liked going with jidy. He always had some pearl of wisdom to share with me.

For instance, he asked me one night, "What do you want to be when you grow up hayati?" I didn't really know, but I did know one thing; I didn't want to be poor. "I'd like to be wealthy, jidy," I responded. "How do you plan to do that?" he asked. "I don't know" was about the only response I could muster. Then he said something very interesting to me. He said, "Find out what the poor people are up to, and don't do it. Find out what they read and don't read it. Find out what they eat, don't eat it. Study everything you can about them, and avoid their habits like the plague."

In other words, check up on how the rich got rich, how the wealthy got wealthy, and then try on some of their good habits. One of those good habits was and still is the accumulation of cash flow. "How much money have you saved?" jidy asked me when I was 11 years old. "Why, none," was my response. "Who sold you on that deal?" He went on to say. "Ninety per cent of all the money you make should be for today's needs—ten per cent should be for tomorrow's. If it's good enough for God, it's good enough for you. If you'll practice that formula, you'll be wealthy one day."

Knowledge

The beautiful thing about being in a large family is that you learn by the experiences of others. I learned very early that reading helped to unlock a lot of doors for many of my brothers and sisters. I was the third child in the group of 11 and I had the privilege of following a brother who hated reading and a sister who loved it. But it was my grandfather, the man who had but a third grade education, who turned me on to books very early in life.

"Hayati," he'd say, "You should be reading four books a week." FOUR BOOKS A WEEK! You gotta be crazy! I did well to read four a year. So jidy got me in the habit by taking me to the library. We'd look first at books he knew I'd like. Slowly, he built my habit until I felt lonely without a book in my hand. I'd take books to baseball practice. I'd take them to church, which was a 45 minute ride away, and read them on the way to and from. "Some of us are born in the A.D. with a B.C. mentality," jidy would say. "Build your knowledge and you will conquer the world."

I'll never forget the year I came home with a poor report card. I had just discovered girls, or at least, I had discovered that God made them for something beside making fun of and taking an occasional shot at. Upon making this startling discovery, my grades slipped with the same enthusiasm as my heartbeat. I failed my first course.

I went to jidy first. I had to know how he would handle this because daddy was of the old school: You play—you pay! That was his philosophy. School wasn't for horsing around. Jidy's response was unique as the man himself. "It's not your teacher who fails you in school," jidy said. "She just delivers the bad news!" In other words, I had no one to blame but myself and if I was going to get off the hook, I would have to get to work, not the teacher.

"Until the mind is moved, hayati," he added, "the carcass will stay parked!"

Truth

Like most of the people of the old south, we raised our own chickens, cattle, and horses. In fact, many a time a dozen eggs were traded for a gallon of gas. Jidy would have me cutting grass in the summer. He'd send a dozen eggs from his grocery store over to Red Powell's Esso station for a gallon of gas to cut neighborhood yards. One year, he swapped chickens with the hardware man so I could get a bicycle to deliver newspapers. In all his dealings with his neighbors and customers, jidy had a basic philosophy—"NEVER sell a man a crippled horse! Always give the customer a baker's dozen. Promise quality, but deliver quality plus a little extra!"

Jidy loved to quote the Bible. He was fascinated by the Lutheran faith, a faith he adopted as a matter of convenience. It could have just as easily been Baptist or Methodist. All were prominent in Lexington. One Friday night we were on our way to see those great football teams of Coach J.W. Whiney Ingram. It was a tradition in Lexington to see football on Friday night. Just as closing on Wednesdays and going to church on Sundays, football was the social event for Friday nights. By the thousands, people would pack the old Lexington Stadium behind Hite's Restaurant to see the Wildcats go at it with some hapless foe. In 33 years at Lexington, Ingram had only one losing season. I asked jidy one Friday evening how Lexington always managed to be so good. "They fight the *GOOD FIGHT OF FAITH!*" was his response, quoting Paul from the Bible. "They believe in themselves and so should you!"

Truth was vital to the success of the small businessman. If you beat somebody out of something, it was around town before the day was out. You just didn't take advantage of people in a small town. Quoting the New Testament one afternoon, jidy said, "Know the truth and the truth shall make you free!" He added, "Were it not for the freedom we enjoy here in America, we might still be living in poverty in a village outside of Beirut."

Goals and Planning

During the early years of my childhood, most of my work activities around jidy's business were confined to sweeping up, delivering groceries, putting up stock and can goods and general "go-for" type work. As I grew older, jidy would show me how he would mark up his jewelry. He would show me the system of letters, based in part of the Arabic alphabet, that he used to price a watch or a ring or a bracelet. At any time, I could go to the showcase, look at the letters, figure the cost of the item and determine how much I could discount it for the customer. The customer had to always win in the end.

Jidy would laugh, "I buy it for a dollar and I sell it for two. I take my one per cent profit and go!" Actually, his whole philosophy of business was to build on sound goals and proficient planning.

"You can't teach a duck to chase mice," he'd jest, "nor can you teach some people in business the importance of planning and goals. If you don't know how much an item cost, how can you know how much to sell it for? You're in business to make a profit. Why else should you stay in business? But a profit must be made by the customer as well. Each side must win. If one side loses, then both will lose sooner or later."

"Hayati," he'd say, "Plan without action is

futile. Action without plan is fatal." In other words, how can we know where we're going in our life unless we have a plan to get there? We wouldn't leave the east coast in a car heading for the west coast without a map. Why should we go through our lives without a map? And yet, most of us have not mapped a course in life. Thus, any road will get you there because we don't know where "there" is.

"You see, my hayati, you will grow up to be that which you tend to think and dream you will be," he once told me. I never will forget my response. "If that were the case jidy, I'll probably be an ice cream sundae or a good looking girl, because that's all I think about sometimes!"

Worry

If we had known about things like Type A and Type B personalities back then, you would have classified jidy as a card-carrying Type B. He simply never worried about anything. If a customer owed him money, he wouldn't worry about payment. He'd say to me, "Hayati, worry is the price we pay in advance for something that has but one chance in ten of happening. Most customers will gladly pay their bill when they can afford to. In any event, worrying won't get it paid any sooner."

And jidy was right, worry never changed a thing. Jidy would rather devote his time finding a way to make a profit on another sale than to worry about the fish that got away. "Worry," he would say, "kills more people than work. Why? Because more people worry than work!"

Motivation

There were many times my own inexperience behind the jewelry counter cost us sales. I would talk too much or I would not know when to write up the order. Jidy would listen patiently to my pitch and would discreetly bail me out if it looked like I was about to go under. He let me help customers on small ticket items. Sometimes I felt like he just wanted me to baby sit his jewelry, not sell it. But I still learned a lot during these early encounters with the public.

Jidy would say to me, "Hayati, people buy from emotions, but they justify their purchase with logic." What did he mean by that? Simply this: "Eighty per cent of the decision to buy something is made by the emotional mind, twenty per cent is based on the logical mind."

"Sometimes I can't get people to buy," I once said to jidy. "People can't be motivated to do anything they don't *want* to do, hayati," he said. "And yet all our customers are motivated. Some are more motivated *not* to buy than they are to buy, but they are motivated nonetheless." And then he added as almost an afterthought, "People will buy from you for their reasons, not for yours. Price counts, but reason counts more!"

"What about those who hedge?" I querried one evening over a hamburger steak at Rawl's restaurant just down the street. His response was a classic, *"Maybe* in Lebanese it means NO!"

"Emotions dictate many reasons why customers buy," he explained, "and emotions are caught, not taught. If you show enthusiasm, the chances are greater that your customer will act more favorably toward you."

On Failing

Perhaps the greatest pleasure I derived from my childhood was my participation on the Little League Baseball Team. Jidy's sons, my uncles (my mother's brothers) sponsored a baseball team that they affectionately named Mack's Meatheads. My uncles ran the grocery stores in the family and they were known far and wide for their excellent beef. So why not name the baseball team after them. Some of the other teams in the league included the Harmon's Pill Rollers (after Harmon's Drug Store) and the Dispatch Newsmakers (after the Lexington Dispatch News, our weekly newspaper). I later had the privilege of having my syndicated column "BEHIND THE MIKE" appear for some 17 years in that and other southeastern newspapers.

It was the bottom of the sixth and last inning. Mack's Meatheads were trailing the Pill Rollers by a run, but we had the tying run on third and the winning run on second. In fact, the bases were packed, but those were the two that counted. I was at the plate. Two men were out. Everything rested on my shoulders. Frankly, I was scared to death. I was hoping to get a walk, allowing the tying run to score and at least send us into extra innings. I knew that Grover Ray Revels was to bat behind me and he'd plumb knock green off grass if I could get him to the plate. But I had to get a hit or a walk.

Just before I walked up to the plate, jidy called me over to the fence. He told me something that didn't sink in right away. He said, "Hayati, 100% of the swings you don't take won't go for home runs."

I could have frankly cared less about a home run. I was praying for a blasted walk. Hit me with a pitch. Heck, I didn't care. I just didn't want to strike out.

Well, the crowd had gone hog-wild. Everybody was there. It was Wednesday afternoon. All the stores were closed. And I was at the bat. The first pitch was over for a strike. My thinking was I'll shoot for a walk. The second pitch was also right down the middle. Now I was getting nervous because I was one strike away from public humiliation. They would remember this for years. I could see the headlines in the Dispatch News the next week. "AUN GOES DOWN WITH BAT ON SHOULDER!" And then it occurred to me what jidy had said. Well, I fouled the next three pitches off before knocking the fourth over the left field wall for a grand slam home run. We had won and I was spared the public humiliation.

I wonder how many times in life I would have waited for a free walk rather than take a chance and swing for the fences were it not for the wisdom my jidy shared with me on an August afternoon in the late fifties.

Failing is a critical part of success in life. I know I would not have won the "WORLD CHAMPION-SHIP OF PUBLIC SPEAKING" for Toastmasters International in 1978 had I not gone through the agonizing pain of losing it in 1977. I went eight seconds over the allotted time frame and was disqualified. When you do something dumb like that, naturally, you have to have a "pity-party" for yourself. There I was in Toronto International Airport having this wonderful pity-party for myself . . . as my plane taxied off without me. It was then that I realized that I wasn't going to win the World Championship that year. But I was fortunate to get a second chance. I came back and won it a year later in Vancouver, British Columbia. But may I dare to suggest to you that you have to go through Toronto to get to Vancouver?

That wasn't the only time I failed at something

major. I remember getting my clock thoroughly cleaned when I ran for the House of Representatives. A friend of mine who refused to vote for me told me afterwards, "If I didn't have any more friends than that I'd carry a gun if I were you." I told him if I did I'd probably shoot him first. We laughed. I later asked why he didn't vote for me and he said that it'd be cheaper for me to buy a politician than to be one.

Still, I tried at something very big and failed. It wasn't fun but it was most rewarding, to say the least. I learned how to deal with the "agony of defeat" as the ABC Sports ad so graphically depicts.

Jidy once asked me if I was an eagle or a buzzard? I said, "What do you mean jidy? I'm a human being."

"No," he chided, "I mean are you more like the eagle or more like the buzzard? From a distance, both these birds look alike. They have similar shapes. Their wing span is about the same. They are the same color. In fact, if you didn't know one from the other, you'd probably think they were the same bird. The only difference between the two is their attitude. The eagle kills his own lunch, the buzzard sits around and waits for the remains. He's a scavenger. He's not responsible for anything, not even his own well being. The eagle takes charge of his life, the buzzard lets life take charge of him. The buzzard won't risk failure. The eagle will."

I remember my response to my jidy. "I don't want to fail in my life jidy. I want to fly with the eagles."

"If you want to be an eagle you must fly with the eagles," he said. "And that means taking the risk that the eagle takes. Remember this hayati, anything worth doing well in the end is worth doing badly at first!"

That was pretty good advice for a 13 year old boy who had had the privilege of knowing a great man for but a few short years. My jidy died in the early sixties when I was on the threshold of becoming a teenager. I miss his love and affection. I miss his home-spun humor and his remarkable way with people. He out-loved people and he out-gave them. I call this one-up-man-ship. He practiced it to a "T."

Jidy once told me, "The problem with most people in this world is that they fail to realize that life is but a huge banquet. Sadly, most of them are starving to death."

If I have any regrets in my life, it's that I didn't get to show jidy what I've done with the gifts he gave me. The first great gift he gave me was a great mother. Like the great man who was her father, my mother left a legacy that few will surpass. She gave birth to 11 talented children and she was simply "mama-Alice" to hundreds of others who were our friends over the years. She died on my 35th birthday and even though she never worked a day of her life outside of the home, a church packed with over 500 people came to pay her homage.

The only regret that I have is that I never had the chance to see my jidy off when he died. Our family felt that children should be seen but not heard and that funerals weren't the place for children. I cried my heart out on the front porch of our home, which was next door to my jidy's as the hearse came to claim his body for the funeral. I never got to say good bye.

When I speak of my grandfather to audiences in South Carolina, invariably some old-timer will come up and tell me some hilarious story about something that happened between the two. Some of his old poker playing buddies still get a great laugh out of the story about the time he served the town council a new chocolate candy at a council meeting. Council was bogged down in a sticky political issue and it looked like a compromise was out of the question. To ease the tension, Jew-Mack brought out the chocolate candy. The name of the new chocolate was Exlax. The council compromised shortly thereafter.

Perhaps his most embarrassing moment was after he was elected Mayor in 1948. He tried to get a visa back to Lebanon to visit his family in Beirut. After applying, he was told that he couldn't get a visa from this country because he was not an American citizen. He had served two terms on Town Council and had been elected Mayor unanimously and he wasn't even a citizen of the United States of America. Of course, every one got a big kick out of attending his naturalization ceremony.

Jidy would have been proud of me, I think. In 1985, I had the privilege and honor of being the keynote speaker at a naturalization ceremony in South Carolina. I don't know how many spoke English in the crowd of some 500, but those who understood were inspired by the story of how a young Lebanese boy came to America with no money and no education and went on to become one of the great men of our time. Indeed, he was truly one of our "GREAT COMMUNICATORS."

BILL BARNETT
DAWN, Inc.
Two Dallas Communications Complex
6309 N. O'Connor, Suite 119
Lock Box 147
Irving, TX 75039-3510
(214) 869-4416

Bill Barnett

Bill Barnett is the creator and executive producer of the DAWN television series. DAWN (Dynamic Achievers World Network) is an internationally syndicated success show, not to mention a success story itself.

Barnett, now 30, conceived the show after leaving a four year stint in the transportation industry; a period in his life that Barnett describes as "a time my brain just went numb, I wasn't using my potential." Barnett and his DAWN company can't be accused of that now. With 102 television episodes completed and more on the way, DAWN seems to have struck a real need in the television world, good wholesome, positive programing.

DAWN's current expansion has included the beginning of it's first feature film, a light hearted adult comedy called "T-Bird and the Fudge Man."

Bill Barnett was born in 1955 in Birmingham, Alabama. After a childhood filled with love he began attending the University of Alabama as a marketing major. During his freshman year Bill was a "walk on" for coach "Bear" Bryant's Crimson Tide. One of Barnett's most valuable lessons in life came after he quit the team out of frustration. The lesson, never, never give up, has been a major factor in his accomplishments.

10

The Birth of a New DAWNing
in American Television
Communicate Love for a
New DAWN in Your Life
by Bill Barnett

"Why do we wait until a person's gone
Before we tell his worth
Why do we wait?
Why not tell him now he is the finest guy
on earth?"

—Jess Kenner

I'd like to share with you my personal experience. Communicating totally changed my life, the lives of my family and at the time of this printing, has positively affected the lives of over 1,000,000 people across America. The spread of this message will soon go worldwide. I share this with you in the hope that you will be moved to put this invaluable lesson to practice in your life. If you do, I can confidently promise you a positive effect that will make you wonder why you haven't been communicating love like this for years.

The Surprising Start of Something Wonderful

Here's the scene: I am twenty four years old working in a not so promising job, but enjoying my life, knowing that I will find my destiny soon and be on my way. I'm spending my days in our family-owned shoe store. That's right—selling shoes. Not exactly a job for the future. It's late one afternoon when I get a phone call from Dr. Travis Tindal, the Registrar for the College of Medicine at the University of Alabama at Birmingham.

For me to receive a call from Travis was nothing unusual. He had counseled and guided me for over 10 years. Travis was just checking on me to see if I was doing all right. In the middle of this routine conversation, Travis stopped and said, "Billy, I have never told you this..." (Then there was a long pause, my mind was racing to negative thoughts like, "Oh no, he's got cancer and has only a few months to live" or "he and Rosalyn are getting a divorce." Now, those two statements may seem out of place being used together, but trust me, either would have been just as much of a shock.) Instead, what he told me was, "I love you."

I was totally numb. I didn't know how to react. No man has ever told me that he loved me. My DAD's never even done that and here I was twenty four years old. After what seemed like three days had squeezed into ten seconds, I was able to come up with a response that was just as revealing and just as warm and compassionate, "Thank You." Wow, what a let down. This grown man that I had known for over 10 years, dares to open his heart to me and all I can come up with is, "Thank You." After a few more confused seconds, I mumbled, "I have to get back to work."

I don't believe that any one statement has had such a disturbing effect on me. For the next three weeks his statement consumed me. Why would he say that? Doesn't he know that men don't say that to other men? I didn't speak to Dr. Travis again during this whole three week period.

The Second Shockwave

Then I receive a call from another close friend, one I happen to respect very deeply, Wayne Rhoads. Wayne is a successful businessman with a beautiful, loving family. Wayne's claim to fame was that while he was becoming an all Southeastern Conference defensive end for Coach "Bear" Bryant's Alabama Crimson Tide, he became the only man to ever tackle Ole Miss quarterback, Archie Manning, for a loss of yardage. Wayne and Judi (Wayne's lovely wife of twelve years) had called to invite me over for supper (dinner if you don't happen to be from the South). Well, I wasn't about to miss some of Judi's fine cooking, so I was on my way. After an excellent meal and lots of laughter, it was time to leave. Judi said good night at the door and Wayne decided to walk out to the car with me. I was just really getting over the trauma of Dr. Tindal's statement, when out of nowhere, (yeah, you're way ahead of me) Wayne says, "Hey, I want you to know how much your friendship means to me, and that I love you."

I thought, "Now this is ridiculous, I've gone twenty four years without ever having a man tell me he loves me and now within a three week period, it has happened to me twice. I've either got to make some major adjustments or put an end to this." At this point I was not sure which to do.

But this time I was much more prepared. Yep, I was able to say, "Thank You" without the long pause. Driving home I wondered if the whole world had gone bananas on me. Over the next couple of weeks I thought about these two events constantly.

Why would these men open their hearts to me? What prompted this sudden voice of love and concern? Why in the world did I have to get both barrels so close together? You will be proud of me because within two weeks I had called them both and said, "Thanks again for letting me know how you feel," (I know you thought I'd say I love you) but listen, just because they went a little bonkers, was no reason for me to get caught up in this thing.

But it just wouldn't go away. After another month I had become much more comfortable with the idea. Not to the point that I might do the same thing, but recalling these two events did make me feel good. Then I got a really wild idea. I would work up enough courage to tell my Dad that I loved him (then I thought it might be a good idea to take out additional life insurance on him before I did it.) Of course before I made this incredible revelation to him, I was going to have to practice. Who better to practice on (hey you guys are way ahead of me again!) than Wayne and Travis. After all it was their fault that this whole thing got going anyhow. So within a week of each other, I told them each face to face that I loved them. Boy, it was tough, but it was nothing compared to what was about to happen. I hadn't seen anything yet!

The Next Step

After I told them about my love for them, and about my plan to tell my DAD, I had a tremendous feeling of energy and well-being. I asked them both to be thinking of me. I would need all the support I could get to muster up the courage to tell my DAD. I decided that there was no need to wait any longer. I was to go to Mom and Dad's on Sunday afternoon. "I will just do it then," I thought. Gosh, wouldn't you? Hey, I was on a roll. Already two in one week. I'm throwing it out there in faster time than it came to me.

Oh, how quickly it became Sunday afternoon. The fear became too much to handle. I just couldn't see Dad and not tell him, so I chickened out all together. Later in the afternoon I was feeling guilty about backing out of my decision. A compromise was in order. I called Dad (it was going to be now or never).

After all the small talk I could manage, he sensed that I wanted to discuss something, so he just said, "Whatever's on your mind, just say it." (Ha, easy for him to say, he didn't know what I was up to.) After pulling all of my nerves together and fighting a cracking voice and tears in my eyes, I struggled through the hardest sentence I have ever said, "Dad, I just wanted you to know how much I love you and appreciate all the things you've done for me." Probably only my father's many years and the experiences of his life, allowed him to respond with such a unique answer. After a long pause, he said, "Thank you son." With tears of happiness trickling down my face, I hung up the phone.

Wow, I had done it. My DAD knew what he really meant to me. Then I began to roar with laughter, remembering his reply, "Thank you, son." Now there is an original response if I have ever heard one. The most important fact was that I now realized that it is okay to share emotions. I was now free to express my feelings completely. I had broken the barrier. I made a promise to myself not to talk to either one of my parents ever again without telling them that I love them.

Love Is Reflected in Love

As with anything, the more I told them that I loved them, the easier it was. My Dad made this slow transition from saying, "Thank you" to responding with a phrase like, "me too" or "and you know I do you." Of course my mother was ecstatic about all of this. It was during this that my job (I had left the family business and entered the world of transportation) required that I move to Montgomery, Alabama. It was only 90 miles south of Birmingham, but for me it was a big move, hey I didn't go that far away to go to college. The move and my new responsibilities prevented me from being home on my birthday, October 20th.

As that birthday and my work day came to an end, I drove across town to get a good night's sleep. It was around 8.00 p.m. Most days required I work for 14 hours, I was a tired pup. When I got home and started going through the mail, I could easily see that several pieces were birthday cards. Then I noticed that one of them was in my Dad's writing. Boy, what a surprise. You see, in all the years past, any cards had come from my Mom, carrying both her and my Dad's signature. I was impressed, my Dad had actually taken the time to send me a card from him, just him. Mother's writing or name appeared nowhere on the card. I was extremely happy about this card. As I opened it and read through, I came upon his signature. Dad had signed the card, "I LOVE YOU, DAD." Wow, I had to sit down. This message has become one of the single most significant events of my life.

There I sat, twenty five years old with tears streaming down my face. The happiness of that moment has only been surpassed by the joy our entire family has come to know. Since then my Dad is able to tell all of us, without hesitation, that he loves us. It has totally revolutionized our family as a whole. The next natural step was for my brothers, who are nine and eleven years OLDER than me, to start telling our feelings for each other.

No matter how close you are to someone, you will always become closer by taking the time to share those three most rare and valuable commodities of the English language, "I LOVE YOU." At the beginning of this chapter I said that this event has totally changed my life, the lives of my family and at the time of this printing, has positively effected the lives of over 1,000,000 people across America with the spread of this message soon to go worldwide.

The Light of DAWN

How does a moment of sheer terror become a positive influence to over 1,000,000 Americans? Easy, make a TV show! No, it's not the "Dad, I love you" show, it's "DAWN." (Now, aren't you impressed?) No, seriously, the communication breakthrough I experienced with my Dad led to many changes in my life. One of these changes was the ability to take an idea and put some love into it, without being afraid someone might know.

After spending almost four years in the transportation field, I became bored. Boredom has to be one of the worst human states possible. I'd wake up in the morning, and could hardly wait . . . to turn over. Does that aptly describe the overwhelming excitement in my life at that point? If there is anything that will eat away at your personality, it's boredom. I decided that I had to do something that I enjoyed, something I loved to do. When mulling over the tremendous range of possibilities, there were only a few things I ruled out: Brain surgeon was first on the list; I'm not so great around blood. Astronaut sounded good, but I'm not into training that much. After that, it looked like a wide open topic. I had to admit, as much fun as it looked like it might be, my atheletic days were pretty well over. Oh, I run to the fridge in record time, but Haagen-Daz has not sponsored an Olympic Ice Cream Team yet. It just doesn't sound right to say, "The Run for the Rum Raisin."

The thing that kept coming to mind that really appealed to me, was that those guys (pro athletes) get paid for having fun. After two solid weeks of prayer and meditation for thirty minutes daily, it came to me, TELEVISION. I've always thought it would be great to be an actor or maybe even a producer. Yeah, I could get into TV. Hot dog, we've got it now! Television, it's a natural.

Now you might find this hard to believe, seeing how I've just turned 30, but I have quite an extensive television background. I've spent almost twenty-five years in TV. No kidding! Wow, that's a long time. Yeah, I've been watching television for as long as I can remember. (Had you going there for just a second, didn't I?) Ok, since my resumé was void of anything that might be construed as broadcasting, how does one get started? Easy, just create a show. That way, if it doesn't look right, no one will know but you, 'cause you created it.

Communicate the Power of Love

Thank goodness nobody ever said what you're doing needs to be logical. Now the ideas were starting to flood into my mind. What type of show should it be? Easy, one that would communicate the power of love and commitment in a realistic way, a show that's positive. Lord knows there's enough garbage on already. Great, this will give me a chance to involve the two great interests in my life; the self-help industry of books, tapes and public speakers with my fascination of television. Super, I've got a good idea. Where do I go from here? (I guess you noticed the questions are getting harder as we go.) Besides talking up my idea to everyone, I needed to learn as much about the industry as I could. As I entered the library for the first time in years, I thought I heard the roof crack. Nah, just an overactive imagination. For the next four months, I spent every spare moment reading about television. No, I didn't learn it all in four months, but my eyes were beginning to look like they were ready to make a blood bank deposit. What all this reading did do was give me insight on how things flowed in the business, and also helped me to pick up a lot of the vernacular. Now when I spoke about the project, the people in the industry thought I knew what I was doing! I cannot overstate how important those trips to the library were.

My new-found ability to express my deepest feelings was now playing a very important role in moving my dream from concept to reality. As you take an idea and begin to expand on it, you simply write everything down that comes to mind and sort through it later. If your mind is as "creative" as mine is, you'll have a lot of sorting to do. None of it may be useful, but you'll at least think you're doing something right.

Selling Is Loving

Moving from the concept stage requires the ability to SELL (I know, I promised Mom that I wouldn't use any four letter words, it just slipped out) your idea to others. Let's face it, the bigger your idea, the more people you're going to have to have to love and support you. The selling of the concept is a transference of feeling. One of the most influential people in my life, Zig Ziglar, puts it this way: "If I can make you feel about my product the way that I feel about my product, you're going to buy my product." So, the key is simply being able to communicate to others the belief, faith and love that you have in your idea. If other people can detect that you have a deep desire about the project, they will support you. Don't get me wrong, it's not that you're not going to get rejection; you are! And lots of it. For awhile I thought I had gotten into a self-hatred group; I mean, why would anyone want to bring this abuse upon himself? However, if there is a passion for what you're doing, it is going to support you through all the tough times.

The first step for me in selling the concept was to get to someone who could help by lending his name to me. (No, I didn't sign his name to my restaurant tab!) I've already told you how important Zig Ziglar has been in my life, so he seemed the best person to begin with. My first meeting with Zig about DAWN was a very short one. He said my idea was good, and that he would help if he could. I asked for his support, to increase my personal credibility with people that didn't know me. Zig's response to this was all I could have hoped for. Zig said I could have anyone call him to "check me out." (So, the next day, I had American Express . . . no, no, I'm just kidding . . . .) This first step was a big one, because most of the people that I wanted as TV guests for the first season were members of the speaking profession. With Zig's tremendous stature in that field, his support would at least buy me enough time with everyone to sell my idea. You may also be surprised to find that there are very successful people who will help you because they like you, and perhaps because they see a little of themselves in you. It will also mean a lot to your determination knowing there's someone (other than your mother) out there who believes in you. For me, selling the concept was easy. You'll never find it hard to talk convincingly about something that is so exciting to you that you can hardly sleep for thinking about it. The circles under your eyes might scare off a few people, but talking about it won't be a problem.

Finding a Top Team

After securing the support of Zig, I was ready to start seeking the technical help I needed. I had a good clear picture of what I wanted DAWN to look like, and what it's content would be, but you might catch me looking into the wrong end of a camera. That wouldn't prove too dangerous. (If my decision had been to shoe horses, there could have been some real problems!) It was time to seek professional help. (A lot of people tell me I need to seek "professional help.") Getting professional help is terribly easy. Our nation has become one of specialists. Anytime you find yourself lacking in an area, seek your advice from the most successful people in that field. Please understand that you don't necessarily have to pay these people. Many of them will at least go to lunch with you if they think what you are doing is good. Others will help if they see the possibility of doing some cash business with you later.

The television production companies I interviewed were not getting me where I needed to be; I didn't feel like I could talk or communicate with them. It is vitally important to be able to sit down with someone that you're going to be heavily involved with, and talk through the difficulties and misunderstandings that are going to come up.

I was beginning to feel really frustrated when a friend suggested I call a fellow he knew who is half partner in a production company that is located in the Dallas area. Charles Yates' production company had won several national awards. Bingo! From the very beginning, he and I hit it off. The ability for us to communicate openly with each other led to deeper discussions which included his partner, Jim Rupe. Through the course of our working so closely together, I've grown to genuinely love these two guys. It's wonderful to be able to look them squarely in the eyes and tell them so.

Now Things Began to Roll

I had a great idea, and now the folks who can actually put the technical end together. Then,

Charles asked a question that slowed everything considerably. "Who's going to pay for all this?" It was at this point that I realized that maybe there was a basic flaw in my plans. If not there, then in my checkbook. See, if there's one thing about Charles, it's details, details, details. Being able to communicate your idea in detail will determine whether or not it becomes a reality. The best advice I could give you about communication is to know exactly what it is that you want to accomplish. Have an extremely clear idea of what you want to say, then, say it sincerely. This focus will allow you to get to the heart of the matter, and stay on target. Especially important when you are talking with potential investors. You will have to communicate very specific goals and objectives. Your words ARE critical. The use of words or phrases like, "MAYBE we can do this," or "I THINK we could" are dead giveaways that you are not clear on what you are going to do.

Consequently, potential investors will be very clear on what they're going to do; that's right, they'll keep sitting on their money. Frankly, I've discovered it is much easier to get "there" with money! Investors are a special breed. Rich? No, that's not what I mean! Most private investors are people who have built their own fortunes. Because they have, they are much more likely to see the value of what you're doing. They've already been through many of the same problems you'll face. The communication process here has to be fine-tuned.

An investor has to be able to clearly understand the goal and objectives of the company, while understanding the risk involved. Being able to clearly and succinctly tell someone your plan may turn up the capital that you need. By being able to share openly that you have the capacity for genuine love, you'll become a more readable person, which is very important. Openness makes it easier for people to see that you are trustworthy. For me, this was the hardest part of the plan. The reason it was so hard was that everyone knows there is a lot of money to be made in television, but they seem surprised that there would be heavy risk involved. While almost everyone, at one time or another, has wanted to be in "show biz," and while everyone was willing to talk and get excited, I didn't see anybody writing any checks! I realized this was more than a minor problem.

Do It Now

In October, 1983, I was returning from a trip to Denver (made on borrowed money), to meet with potential investors, that, frankly had been a waste, when "Fate" stepped in. Gosh, that really makes it sound dramatic, but it wasn't. (Most "fateful" things happen in the course of just everyday living.) My plane had just landed when I thought about calling the girl I was dating at the time. Normally, I would have waited until I got home, but something said that I should call now. Strangely enough, she told me that a couple of her friends whom I had never met were on their way over to take us to a Cowboy's game. If you live in Dallas, you don't miss a chance to see the Cowboys live, and, better yet, for free! (I mean, what are you, a communist?!) So, I rushed over to my girlfriend's house in time to meet this couple.

The guy was Barry Friedman. During the game, Barry asked what I did for a living. Now, there's a loaded question! My response was filled with hope and encouragement. I must have said the "right" thing, because Barry decided right then and there to fund my pilot. (I thought this was a nice gesture, but listen, "pilots" are already making good money . . . I'm the one who needs "funding" . . . . It's ok in life for us to not take ourselves too seriously, and as you've seen, I don't!) So with Barry's financial help, the expertise of Charles and Jim, and my direction, we had moved to a point of reality.

Zig Ziglar on Camera

On January 3, 1984, after much work and planning,

we shot the pilot. And who better to be our guest than Mr. Zig Ziglar? As I told you, he has been quite an influence on my life. The day that we had the privilege of working with Zig on that pilot was one of the most memorable days in my long and storied life. (OK, so it's not that long, but it IS storied!) Without any major problems, the pilot was finished and ready. Ready for what? Oh yeah, I knew I was forgetting something important . . . ready to be sold. The pilot of which I was so proud, had to be used to convince stations across the country that the series would be good enough to air on a daily basis. For that job, I hired a New York firm (after all, we had hit the "big time.")

It was now mid May of 1984. With sales efforts through the summer, we started running the show five days a week in 14 markets, five of which were Top 10. The first day of broadcast was September 10, 1984. (A date that will live in infamy, or no, was that Pearl Harbor? Although it was debated whether or not we would bomb . . .). By mid-November, DAWN was covering 29 cities, and almost that same percentage of American television households. The growth of DAWN continues. We now have 100 shows airing. (If we are not on in your local T.V. market, please, call your favorite station, tell them about us.

You don't know enough about DAWN to tell the station anything? OK, DAWN is a success show! An "I did it, you can do it too, here's how" show. It's motivational, and frankly, I think it's a fun show. Our host, Ty Boyd, (one of the world's greatest human beings and one of the finest speaker/trainers in the country,) each day introduces one of America's most dynamic personalities. People like Victor Kiam, the guy you see on TV saying, "My wife bought me this electric shaver. I liked it so much, I bought the company," the President of Remington Products; people like Norman Brinker, former Vice President at Pillsbury, and founder of the "Steak and Ale" restaurant chain; Wally "Famous" Amos, founder and President of "Famous Amos" Chocolate Chip Cookies; Ken Blanchard, author of *The One Minute Manager*; 1975 Miss America, Dr. Shirly Cothran Barrett, and Mr. Ed Foreman, the only man in this century to hold U.S. Congressional seats from two different states; Cavett Robert, Chairman Emeritus of the National Speakers Association and Dottie Walters, publisher of this book. These people, Zig, and the list goes on and on. Wow! Just imagine spending 30 minutes a day with these great people, having them share with you their personal secrets of success in a lively presentation. That is the DAWN show.

Communicate Love

The page numbers are telling me maybe it's time to

wrap up this chapter with the story of the change in my life, and how DAWN resulted from that change.

There are three thoughts I want to leave with you on "Communication:"

1) **Don't hesitate to let important people in your life know that you love them.** It will do more for your ability to communicate with everyone in your world than you can imagine.

2) **Know what you want to represent, be focused.** Keep an open and loving heart.

3) **A challenge—one that will make you and others realize their true value.** Select the 10 most influential people in your life, the ones who've had the most influence on you. THEY MUST BE LIVING. Write them a letter telling them just how special they are to you. It'll be an eye opener and heart opener for you.

Please know that we're all in this life together. Let's love each other. I hope that by sharing my experiences with you, that you will be touched and that love's message will communicate as much impact in your life as it does in mine. Thanks for taking time out of YOUR life to share a little bit of my life, straight from the heart. Don't forget to turn your dial to DAWN!

Thanks for taking time out of your life to share a little bit of my life, straight from the heart.

DAN MORTENSEN
FAA Accident Prevention Counselor
B105-227, 32221 Camino Capistrano
San Juan-Capistrano, CA 92675
(714) 493-1866

Dan Mortensen

A noted speaker in aviation "circles" (he gets lost a lot); an instructor; race pilot; test pilot; aircraft builder; holder of several world speed records; Dan Mortensen, affectionately known as "Crash" by his friends, is a real "survivor." Following a two year tour of duty as an infantry officer and eight years with the Federal Aviation Administration (FAA), he became an aviation pioneer in synthetic lubrication while air racing, and now serves as an Amsoil company spokesman at airshows and conventions nationwide. In addition, he teaches three day cram courses for Airline Ground Schools specializing in the Airline Transport Pilot and Flight Engineer written examinations. Featured on national television, radio, and numerous publications including six magazine covers, his other credits include a B.A. in the Russian language (Arizona State University); a California Community College Teaching Credential; past president of the United States Air Racing Association; A Rotarian, and a Paul Harris Fellow.

Dan's proudest achievement, which you won't find listed in his resume, however, is his son, Tye. "The most challenging job I've ever had is living up to the full measure; the expectations of a three year old. It certainly is the most rewarding experience I've ever had!" Dan enjoys working with young people of "all" ages on the topics of "Success," "Setting Records in Our Lives" and "Safety." Whenever time permits, he can be found indulging in his all-consuming dream—flying.

11

Crash at 200 MPH
by Dan Mortensen
FAA Accident Prevention Counselor

"One has never lived 'til he has almost died; life has a flavor the protected will never know."

—Unknown

Monday, June 13, 1983, 4:05 p.m. over central Wisconsin at 6,000 feet enroute home to Superior indicating 190 MPH. A routine flight home suddenly becomes an in-flight emergency. A tremendous vibration shakes the race plane as 17 inches of propeller snaps off causing an imbalance.

It lasts only four or five seconds and then...
complete silence. Serious damage has occurred and
the situation is doubtful. As oil obscures my
canopy, I can see that my one and only engine is
hanging at an unusual angle. It's broken from the
engine mount and appears to be precariously
balanced; about to fall away. I smell avgas and
immediately close the fuel valve. A fire in the air; a
pilot's worst fear, and I'm not wearing my 'chute.

Fly the airplane; the first rule. I push over and
dive for the ground. Any piece of it will suit me
just fine right now and the sooner the better.
Somebody is looking after me because just ahead
amongst the deep woods of Wisconsin is a 9000
foot runway—Volk Air National Guard Base. I
"Mayday" my position on the emergency frequency
only to discover my radio is dead. All the instruments in the cockpit are also shattered. That
doesn't deter me in the slightest. My mind is made
up! I have no more desire to fly today. The runway
is unoccupied. The deadstick landing was unevent-
ful and anti-climatic.

Inspection of the aircraft moments later dis-
closed a vertical crack in the fuselage just forward
of the tail of 180 degrees. Another second or two
of continued vibration would have broken her back
in mid-air. In the engine compartment, the starter
had broken from its pad and punched the battery,
spewing acid. The exhaust stacks had separated

from the aircraft along with other assorted pieces. Later scientific examination of the prop by the FAA determined that the blade failed due to a harmonics problem at that particular engine RPM setting. This resulted in metal fatigue and subsequent failure; and it was a brand new $800 propeller.

My next problem, I thought, will be the Guard. I was an uninvited guest and they usually impound civilian aircraft. What I needed was a hangar and several weeks to effect repairs. Summoning all my skills as a public speaker, I eloquently threw myself upon the mercy of the base commander, LTC Nichols. I quickly attained my goal only to find out that he knew my employer, Al Amatuzio. They flew together in the Guard. So much for my apologies for intruding and disclaimer of pilot error.

The airplane, the AMSOIL Rutan Racer, had started as a DREAM some 25 years earlier. It slowly took form as I nurtured it closer and closer to reality. What kid doesn't dream of flying a beautiful one-of-a-kind airplane to heights nobody has been before? I knew that the CHALLENGE would incorporate some RISK. I was prepared to pay the price for SUCCESS and FAILURE. Two WORLD RECORDS and two national speed records were the rewards of my efforts. The lesson learned from this accident was that I had become complacent. Having achieved a degree of success, I began to take a lackadaisical attitude. I neglected to take precautions to insure that success. I forgot about safety. I should have been wearing that parachute!

How does that apply to you? Don't become complacent with your life or your job. Take steps to insure your continued success. Don't assume or take for granted your social and financial position. The status quo is constantly changing. Continue to learn—to educate yourself. There are people below you climbing the ladder of success and if you don't keep moving up, you'll be pushed aside. I took the world speed records from some very successful people: Barry Schiff, a TWA Captain and noted aviation writer; and Hal Fishman, a news anchor-man on KTLA Channel 5 television in Los Angeles. Obviously records are meant to be broken and someday some upstart will take mine. I had a dream and did something about it. There are records just waiting for YOU. Your name is already inscribed on them. All you have to do is stand up and look around you. Here's how I did it.

A Dream

We all have dreams or goals in life. Sometimes we misplace them; forget them; or place a low priority on them. The only difference between you and me is that I stopped talking about my dream and did something about it. I wrote it down on paper and posted it where all the world could see it. I put it on the refrigerator at home and I put it on my desk at work. You do the same no matter what your dream might be. It's your dream and seeing it everyday will help keep it alive. Besides, making it public will have several benefits, if you're serious. First, people will ask about it. You'll talk about it and communication will net you several allies who share similar dreams—positive reinforcement. Sure, you will also encounter the doubters, but their negativism will also reinforce your determination to prove you really can do it! Run it up the flagpole and see if anyone salutes it! *Right now! Write down some of those dreams or goals that immediately come to mind in the following space.* Keep this in mind: some people only have one dream; some have several; but those who dream the most—do the most!

D R E A M S — G O A L S

1.
2.
3.
4.
5.
6.
7.
8.
9.
10.

Living your dream is something you can do, if you want it badly enough. For several years, I was known as "Last place Dan" on the air racing circuit because I had the slowest airplane when I first started. There is nothing wrong with starting at the bottom. When you're in last place, you are no threat to anyone. Everybody likes you. Popularity is fine but it doesn't win races. I talked about my dream—a faster, single seat, high performance composite job that would walk away from the competition; an airplane light years ahead in technology. Oh, I'd get the usual lip service and heads nodding in acknowledgement, but nobody really believed "Last place Dan" would ever do anything about it. The more I talked about it, the more I convinced myself I was really going to do something. There was also anger because my family didn't share my confidence that I could do anything in this world that I wanted to do. They were indifferent! Have you ever noticed how family members are the hardest people to convince (or sell anything to)?

It takes sacrifice to live your dream. It means giving something up: it could be financial; it could be personal; or it could be both. One day I stopped "talking" and started "doing." I wrote my dreams and goals down just like you did a moment ago and buried "Last place Dan" along with the TV set beside "Walter Mitty." With the television gone, I now had time to follow a more successful and rewarding life—being a winner! Don't stagnate in a quiet life of desperation. You deserve better. Listen to that little voice talking to you right now. Do something!

I challenge you to do something with your dream; your life! Sure, it involves risk and you certainly will encounter adversity along the way. Fly above it. Your dream is your magic carpet. Think positive. Don't let your dreams evaporate or turn into problems. Don't let your problems turn into nightmares. Problems are simply opportunities. You have to overcome life's setbacks—the crashes of life—for your dream, when achieved, to have any value. Everyday of your life is filled with little disappointments. We generally shrug them off and continue on without a second thought. First, there is the freeway traffic jam in the morning; then you discover your associate called in sick and the boss assigns his workload to you in addition to your normal duties; next you face the freeway traffic on the way home; your son was fighting at school today; and the wife burned the water while trying to make dinner. We won't mention what the dog did. Hey, nobody said anything about a "challenge" being easy. A positive mental attitude will take each of these insurmountable obstacles and cut tunnels right through them. There is an old saying, "You don't get to the top of an oak tree by planting an acorn and sitting on it." I might add, "It doesn't do any good to climb an oak tree unless you look around when you reach the top and then yell a lot!" Do Something! A wrong move is better than no move at all. Am I communicating loudly enough to be heard over that TV set; that temple of mediocrity? You are responsible for your success or failure in life. Pick up that challenge. Take a little step each time which has a good chance of succeeding. A lot of little steps in the right direction add up to a big success story! Minimize the risk in that fashion. Success breeds success.

If you don't accept the challenge, you reduce your chances of truly being happy. You know what happens when you're not successful—you lose your job to someone who is. In our achievement oriented, upwardly mobile society, you had better be aware of the risks of complacency. The janitor sweeping the floors at the office tonight (and going to school during the day) is looking at your desk and dreaming about the day he'll be sitting at it...and he will if you don't do something. I challenge you to continue your education; improve yourself; continue to grow as a human being; be more successful.

There are lots of success stories. You might as well be one of them. Your little voice says you are, so reinforce that winning attitude. It's there within you; bored to death. Don't let your life be polluted with complacency and boredom. If I could just motivate you a little, as others have done for me. Remember the Greek shipping tycoon, Aristotle Onassis? He was one of the richest men in the world—pure 100% success. When he arrived in the New World in the early part of this century as an immigrant, he had only $68.00 to his name. Why, I bet you've got at least twice that much in the bank and you're already here. Do something!

Take an analytical approach to risk just like a businessman or a racer. Neither are unduly reckless. Onassis bet his life that he could successfully cross the stormy Atlantic some 70 years ago in primitive shipping (the living conditions were deplorable and many died). Later in life he also lost millions on several business ventures but he never gave up. He weighed the risks against the opportunities and took calculated risks. He gambled, took chances, and succeeded.

Another example is Bobby Unser, three time Indy 500 winner and considered by many to be the premiere auto driver in this country. He raced at Indianapolis some 18 times, crashing in his first two years. The fact that he did not finish in first place in all but 3 years does not detract from his victories in the least—Bobby Unser is a winner! He had a dream; it involved hard work; it was a challenge which was met with perfection. Having worked with Bobby on several occasions at conventions speaking on behalf of AMSOIL synthetic lubricants, I've had the opportunity to observe him close up. His personal life away from the track also demands that same perfection; his secret for his success. Reckless people simply don't survive in or out of a cockpit.

What I'm suggesting is that racing is no different really than our day to day existence and if you are just existing, isn't it time you got back on the highway of life and started living? Take a calculated risk. Getting in the family car and going to the supermarket is a calculated risk. You do it everyday and you minimize the risk or increase your chances of success—returning safely, by taking advantage of optimum conditions. You usually go during the day when traffic is light; you put on your seatbelt; you check the gas gauge, and so on.

We did the same thing with the race plane. We analyzed the risks and took precautions to insure survivability in the event of a malfunction or mistake in the race. We weighed all the possibilities. The cockpit was designed for a 22g impact. A five point safety belt system was installed. A military crash helmet and Nomex suit for fire protection was worn. Minimum fuel was always checked. The checklist goes on. There is no limit to safety—no such thing as being too safe. I accept the challenge of competition and the calculated risks.

214 / The Great Communicators

Success and Failure

Following the prop loss and subsequent damage, it took a superhuman effort by the crew (Mike Arnold, Duke Dodge, and Kit Sodergren) to repair the racer in time for the National Championship Air Races in Reno just six weeks later. The aircraft was almost totally rebuilt, including a new engine. We arrived just in time to qualify only to discover we were not going as fast as the previous year. We worked feverishly all week trying to improve the performance with little gained. Pat Hines, the current champion in "Sundancer" even offered some help. It looked as if this was not going to be our year.

The race course is laid out just like an auto racetrack with two straight-aways of a mile each. The two turns are marked by three telephone poles each with 55 gallon drums painted red and white and mounted atop, so the pilots can see them. As many as eight biplanes race together as low as pylon height. We actually take off together on a race horse start just ten feet apart. Engines at full throttle; brakes on with several crew members holding the tails down; we roll when the green flag is dropped. It can get real exciting!

It's Saturday, September 17, 11:20 AM and down comes the green flag for the heat race. I'm off first and approaching the first pylon for a left turn. Another aircraft accelerates past on the outside already banking into the turn and slightly below me. I'm looking down and to my left toward the pylon and planning to start my turn when I reach the pylon. Out of the corner of my eye I see movement. Looking forward I see the wingtip of the "Sorceress" in my windshield. I am angry; my first thought is mid-air collision! I look again to the left quickly for the pylon as I immediately roll into a left 90 degree bank and hope I've miss both the other aircraft and the pylon. I must have already passed the pylon now for I do not see it again.

Having just started the race, all the aircraft are in close proximity to each other. I suspect I have traffic just above and behind me and also behind and outside. The only place to go in a squeeze play is into the turn with the traffic. Suddenly I hear that little voice telling me I don't want to be here anymore. Something else is wrong! It takes only a fraction of a second to realize what is going to happen but that is a fraction too late to get out of the unintentional trap that is set. The classic race start with everyone bunched up to the tune of musical chairs, and then the music stops. My engine is roaring with full power but the silence is deafening!

The aircraft making the pass is ahead now but I can't see him. I'm inside the turn with my belly to him. I realize he is going to climb through my altitude when he rolls out and I have to do something. I pitch up slightly. I want to do it more quickly but am concerned I might hit somebody above me out of my field of vision. It's too late, though. I encounter wake turbulence; mini-tornadoes from the wingtips of the "Sorceress." The vortices try to spill me over on my back and down. There is absolutely no control over my aircraft. Total time elapsed is two seconds. I strike the ground at 200 MPH and scatter airplane for a thousand feet through the desert. The video tapes are awesome!

It's amazing what happens in a life-threatening situation. Things happen in slow motion. The body is trying to give you time to react to stress. I wanted to live but knew I was going to die. I've faced it before. Each time my thoughts progressed to a higher level of consciousness picking up where the previous event ceased to be life-threatening. With the prop loss six weeks earlier, I saw my life flash before my eyes, and felt remorse at the thought of never seeing my wife and child again. This time, simple resignation. "It will be instantaneous—no pain—the lights will simply go out." I hit...and waited...and waited. There was so much dirt that I couldn't see a thing. It felt like driving down a "washboard" dirt road. The aircraft stopped and I pushed the quick release on the safety belts and scrambled out the broken canopy. I was in a hurry for the old fear of fire was a distinct possibility. I tripped and fell over something and sprained my ankle. Now who would expect an engine to be laying out there in the middle of the desert? How embarrassing and with all those spectators watching! I got my Nomex suit dirty.

Failure? No way! CBS said, "Dan didn't complete one lap this year and still came home a winner!" Folks have commented that I had some bad luck in '83 to which I always reply, "Hell no, it was the best year of my life!" You've got to think positive! I survived. Survival of course sometimes involves a lot of luck. NASA and the FAA have identified several factors, though, that contributed to my success. The angle of impact was shallow with the left wings taking the brunt of the initial impact. It was a slow decelleration over a long distance versus an abrupt stop. The aircraft was built of composite materials; fiberglass, graphite and foam—frangible materials.

What did I learn from this? They say the first person to arrive at the scene of an accident is usually the pilot. At first, I thought it was just one of those fluke accidents over in coffin corner. The FAA didn't cite anyone for a violation. I didn't hold my friend, Don Beck, in the "Sorceress" responsible. He was simply flying his usual aggressive race. Al Kramer in "Cobra" just above and behind mentioned to me later that it wasn't my fault. That made me feel good but it distracted me from the truth for several months. With the passage of time, I was able to detach my emotions and look more analytically at cause and effect. I realized that I should never have been in the airplane that morning! I had been too tired to fly competently. Fatigue from working all night reduced my reaction time. I reacted too slowly to an adverse situation. It may or may not have made a difference on the outcome, but I compromised not only my life but the lives of the other pilots.

The crash, like any other, was the subject of considerable discussion. My friend, Weldon Britton, of the FAA in Washington, DC asked if I would tell my story to the pilots across the country through the Accident Prevention Program. It was difficult the first time to stand amongst my peers and admit a mistake. I've been surprised by the response. Others have had similar experiences and had not realized what fatigue can do or have been reluctant to admit the fact. It has been rewarding. I like to think that I've saved a few lives.

You don't have to be a pilot to understand that message. Fatigue is an incipient little monster sitting in the other seat while you drive to work in the morning. You've experienced it before. For some reason you were up too late. Your reaction time is not what it should be and the freeway is more dangerous than a race course. Accidents are 99% human error. Now you drive home in the afternoon after a rough day in the office and the little monster has grown so big that he now takes up the whole back seat. Is it time to begin exercising some caution in your life? This is risk with reckless abandon. It's stupid! You're the driver. Take charge of your life. Perhaps this should be one of your goals. A life is a terrible thing to waste!

1983 was just one of those years. "Last place Dan" was back. I was asked by reporters if I would return to Reno in 1984? I answered, "Of course! If you break a leg while taking a bath, that doesn't mean you should never take a bath again." My fantastic wife, Cheryl, upon reading that the next day in the newspaper, commented, "Yes, Mort, but you broke your bathtub." To which I can only say that behind every successful man is a woman telling him what he did wrong! It doesn't matter if you fall down as long as you pick up something from the floor when you get up. Learn from your mistakes. Fortunately, you probably don't need to make life and death decisions while pursuing your dreams. Don't let a little pothole in the road of life slow you down. Keep on driving! I came back in 1984 with another biplane and broke the qualifying record. I didn't win but I will continue trying. I will not accept failure. I'll win it this year! I wrote it down!

World Records

What is a record? Something to remember; celebrate; in sports or business—the best performance. It doesn't take an airplane to break world records or raise yourself to a new plateau of excellence; of success. Within each of us is the catalyst for action. You can set a record tonight at home with just a little effort. Surprise the wife with some flowers; cook dinner for her; or just do the dishes. You'll be an instant success and have just set a world record as far as she is concerned. Now try it on the kids. Spend a few minutes with them tonight. Watch their eyes light up when you ask if you can join them! You'll be a hero and again, an instant success.

Now take that success into the office with you tomorrow and continue your winning ways. Work on improving your performance over that of yesterday. Set some goals; just little ones for starters, and records will begin to fall. It's really that easy! When you reach those initial modest goals, then set some larger goals. Work a little harder and someone will notice YOUR contribution. There is an energy crisis of people not living their lives to their full potential. There is no limit to your potential, your horizon. Columbus proved there is no limit to the horizon over 500 years ago. He had a dream...

Hard work and dedication will accomplish everything. You don't have to finish in first place to be a winner but you do need a positive attitude. Every successful businessman has it. Every successful marriage has it. You have it! You took the time to read this book and by doing so, have already taken the first step toward achieving your dream.

Do you realize that in the same amount of time many people will achieve success while others fail? Make every minute; every opportunity productive. If a door closes on you, use the window. Go for it. The most successful way to achieve failure is never take a chance. Why not take a chance on yourself? Set some personal records. One of my little goals is to start the day by smiling. It increases your face value. They say it takes more energy and involves more facial muscles to frown than it takes to smile. Think about that. Life will give you whatever you are willing to accept. Don't accept anything less than SUCCESS!

MARCIA FINE
L'Image / Casablancas
6900 E. Camelback Road
Scottsdale, AZ 85251
(602) 941-4838

Marcia Fine

Marcia Fine, President of L'Image/Casablancas Modeling, Personal Development and Career Center and L'Image Model and Talent Agency, has a varied background encompassing the fields of image, education and public speaking.

A member of the National Speakers Association since 1980, the year she founded her company, she has made presentations on visual image communication to many groups and corporations including Valley National Bank, League of Women Voters, Arizona Heart Institute, American Graduate School, Arizona League of Cities and more. Frequently interviewed on radio and television, she speaks on image as well as women and their success.

She is the Vice President of the National Association for Women Business Owners (Arizona Chapter) while serving on the Advisory Committee of Apparel Design to Phoenix College, the Advisory Board of the Phoenix Film Commission, and the National Board of the American Society of Fashion and Image Consultants. She was also named one of the "Outstanding Women of the '80's" by Arizona Living *magazine.*

Included in Who's Who Among American Women, *she has written numerous articles including "Beauty Plus," a weekly column for* The Arizona Republic.

A former English instructor at the high school and college levels, Marcia is an avowed people watcher who resides in Tempe, Arizona with her family.

12

The Impact of
Visual Communication
by Marcia Fine

*"Personal beauty is a greater
recommendation than any letter of
introduction."*
—Aristotle

We have all had those times when a decision at a crossroads leaves one's life radically altered. Sometimes these crossroads occur when we are in the position to take full advantage of the opportunities presented. I have always been the type of person to accept a challenge, learn from an experience and look for a new and better way to approach a problem. Little did I know in 1980, the year I founded my company, that I would push that philosophy to its limits.

For five years I was involved in a very successful and rewarding career as a high school English teacher and curriculum designer. I often marvel at how much I learned from the students. I will never forget the excitement of turning them on to ideas and to reading. "Antigone" and *Of Mice and Men* may not have much in common; however, the values they teach are vital to young minds. I loved every day of it and remember being embarrassed a few times because my name was called over the loudspeaker. I was the only teacher who had forgotten to pick up her paycheck. I couldn't believe I was being paid to do something I enjoyed so much. To this day I still correspond with some of my former students.

When my family and I moved to Arizona in 1976, I chose at that crossroads to go back to school for a Masters in English Education and Women's Studies. For many years I had become increasingly aware of inequality, particularly in the job market. I learned what women had accomplished over the years.

By the time I finished my degree my children

had entered elementary school and I was at the next crossroads. Option number one was to enter the Doctoral program at Arizona State. I enjoyed learning and the academic life always held a fascination for me. More degrees, however, do not necessarily make one more employable and I wanted a career with a capital "C." I had not had many options when I entered college. Most young women with my background became teachers. Although teaching had been rewarding, I now had other choices I wanted to explore. Fortunately, I had wonderful parents who always built up my self esteem so I felt confident pursuing new directions.

Option number two was to become involved in a women's center or teach a course on Women in Literature. That would certainly have been in keeping with what I had learned. However, a career based on a particular movement might not have longevity.

A third alternative was to test myself in the world the way men had been taught and to keep score by the same standards: money and power. Could all I had learned over the years about managing and communication with people be put to use out there to play the "success" game? These are some of the ideas I was pondering in 1979 when a trip took me through Philadelphia where I had worked 10 years earlier as an instructor for a well known modeling school.

I visited with my former boss and he encouraged me to start a similar business in Phoenix. I immediately vetoed the idea. I had not been involved with modeling for quite some time. Besides, it wasn't exactly an intellectual pursuit! On the other hand, I had been doing makeovers on friends for years. Modeling skills had taught me the importance of self presentation and confidence. Marcia, the educator, was also intrigued by the idea of actually running a school. What better way to take on the success quest than to go into a business I already knew?

I have always been fashion-conscious and a people watcher. My background as a model and instructor made me keenly aware of what style and quality add to one's credibilty. With a burning desire to be of service, I set about developing a curriculum that would allow women to project the best possible image in any situation. Consultants were employed in necessary areas and an educational philosophy evolved. I also did my own market research to find out if there was a need for what I wanted to share.

After exploring the subject of image thoroughly, I found we communicate an almost unbelievable amount of information about ourselves before we even open our mouths. The more sophisticated the observer, the more obvious we are. We wear our socio-economic circumstances, or politics, our likes and dislikes and our background all over ourselves. These are expressed by our clothing, grooming, posture, and manner of speech. L'Image started by putting this message out to the world in a straight-forward way, and people listened. More and more people have heard our message and even large corporations paid attention. As a result we've been able to guide many successful men and women in developing a style that makes them feel good about themselves.

The Right Place and Time

The idea worked and the enthusiasm was definitely high level. I was fortunate enough to have the support I needed from my family and employees. Positive, enthusiastic attitudes created an exciting work atmosphere. We were growing every day and I felt as though my business was a new colt on shaky legs. My first year I wrote all the curriculum, bought the supplies, sold the classes, and lectured in the public school by day, women's groups by night and anyone who would listen in between. I had a receptionist and four instructors to assist me in my mania. Today, a short five years later, I have over forty employees and thousands of graduates.

So much had to be learned: dealing with employees, the technique of selling an intangible, making people believe in my idea and creating a pleasant and professional image for the business. I soon realized I could not do it alone. It was necessary to find salespeople who were professionals and others to whom I could delegate carefully defined tasks. Hiring turned out to be easier than firing. It wan't easy telling two early employees they had to leave when I caught them lying. I'll never forget how it felt as I sat there answering the phone that day. Yet I wasn't sorry I let them go. The truth always works.

As it turned out there was a tremendous market for quality model training in our area that I had not even anticipated. Advertisers contacted us almost from the beginning to inquire about the availability of good models. Our graduates were in demand, so we opened an agency to represent them. The number of people we chose to represent was limited, so it was clear to students that enrolling in the school in no way guaranteed signing with our agency. This up-front candor with everyone coming through the door gave us a unique credibility in the industry.

The agency thrived and I ran out of time in the day. Robert Black, who had been with me from the beginning as a model, men's instructor and booking agent, bought an interest in the agency. As its director and vice president, he has done a superb job. He has also become something of a power in the model/talent industry in the Southwest and I'm quite proud of his growth. Today our models and talent can be seen in national commercials, magazine ads and major motion pictures, a testimonial to our success.

In 1983 L'Image Ltd. purchased a franchise from John Casablancas, a powerhouse in the international modeling industry, to give higher visibility in our new, expanded quarters at a prestigious mall. The association with the Casablancas organization gave access to even more comprehensive curricula and world wide placement of models. The name L'Image was retained because of its already considerable recognition value. The L'Image Agency became one of only two in North America permitted to use "in affiliation with John Casablancas Elite Model Management." Our graduates are now models and talent who work in glamorous places all over the world. Karin Manson, who began as my babysitter that first hectic year, has been to Paris twice for modeling assignments. It was exciting to watch her evolution from gawky teenager to magnificent model. And I just might mention in case you're of the mind that all models are dumb, Karin received two full academic scholarships.

How Image Communicates

Obviously only a small percentage of the people enrolling in our school are professional model material. What about the rest? What do they get out of it? When I watch a previously awkward teenage girl smile when she looks in the mirror because, for the first time, she likes what she sees or when a shy young man begins to make eye contact with his handshake I know we are being of service. My greatest reward is to see a talented secretary move up to a management position because of the new image we have assisted her in creating. Sometimes there's even a bonus in her social life, too.

What exactly is an "image"? It's the total picture that we put out there in the world. The *initial* three minutes are crucial. The visual information is immediately available and the mind takes it in as an indelible photo. Our eyes catch the lightest item a person is wearing and then travel to the face and feet. All of that visual data is processed instantly according to our generalizations based on culture and experience. Involuntary and instinctive, the judgement may not be acknowledged, but it overwhelmingly influences the remainder of the encounter. In fact, if the visual impression is enough of a "turn-off," the relationship may go no farther. Conversely, a favorable visual image enhances the meeting and allows the rest of the feeling-out process with a positive attitude. This is especially important in the business and professional worlds where we do not always get to choose with whom we interact.

Recently John Molloy made a tremendous impact on the business world with his books for men and women about dressing for success. Throughout corporate America, with the appropriate variations according to sex, business people rushed out to acquire the prescribed navy or dark suits, white or light blue shirts, silk ties or scarves and, for women, pumps. Within a short time Molloy's words became a required text for success.

Now that the ground rules for business dress are established, people have gotten bored with being navy blue clones. Minor rebellion is at hand. Everyone wants to succeed and the question is how one can express individuality, style and taste without running afoul of the formula that will produce the best results?

In terms of the way we are perceived, nothing has changed. If you are making a presentation, all research says that the darker the main garment, the more authoritative the wearer. White is the most powerful color so it helps to have it close to your face. The question is whether this has to be a daily uniform to consistently establish power. The answer is no. Success is not so narrowly defined that it can only be expressed in one way.

Probably the most frequent question I am asked by both men and women is, "Do I have to wear a dark suit?" The answer varies according to the situation. It is "yes" if what you are doing that day is of the utmost importance. If you need to convey your most powerful image in making a presentation or asking for a raise, wear a suit. The answer is "no" if you are comfortable in establishing a prosperous image without it.

An aura of power can be maintained with a grey suit, a well tailored blazer, pastel shirts or blouses and unique accessories. Any layered look adds to authority. A pink suit for a woman or a very light one for a man say "ineffective" in a business situation. What we choose to wear when we wake up in the morning may influence us all day long. If it happens to be a favorite article of clothing that makes us feel good, our day will usually have positive results. Everyone needs to know how to use image to their advantage.

There are many colors available that add style, taste and variety to a wardrobe. Hunter green, taupe and teal work well and there are others depending on the individual's preference. Gone are the days of only light blue and white shirts. Subtle stripes, pastels, and a range of beiges give men and women more alternatives. There is also nothing wrong with using a strong color as an accent. If we are interested in making these choices, the impact of picking a successful image will be especially rewarding. Remember, if you *look* successful you *are* successful.

Accessories still speak the loudest for us in our visual signal system. Quality never goes out of style and it is most frequently observed. Choose ties, belts, scarves, briefcases, jewelry with the utmost care. People notice. A plain suit with no attention to detail is boring. Suntan hose, polyester ties or open toed shoes diminish our power. One study says that men gauge other men's success initially on their ties. Polyester does not make the same statement as silk.

Use your accessories to express yourself. Let them give hints about who you really are and what interests you. They can assist you in having fun with your wardrobe. A funky pink, crazy socks, or a favorite hat may add the dash you need for play clothes. In business the details of a tie bar, pocket scarf or colored hose can all add a dash of flair. What they say is, "I'm paying attention and keeping up with what is going on. I'm interested in my work, myself and in you." If we are outdated, it says, "I'm not keeping up." Accessories need the most attention in terms of quality and choice.

There is an art to dressing well and it does not have to cost a lot. We are giving out a visual signal when we put together our clothing. Our clothes drop hints about our economics, our politics and even our sexuality. Classic good taste is *always* in style. When you get dressed look in a full length mirror and ask yourself if your image communicates the two "C's" and two "R's":

**Confidence and Competence
Reliability and Responsibility.**

The Specifics

We now know a matched suit is no longer always necessary. Men and women can be well dressed in coordinated separates as long as attention is paid to quality. If the budget is tight spend more on the finishing touches—ties, belts, scarves, bags, etc.— than on the main garment. A memory accessory, one which will make you remembered, always helps. It can be an unusual belt buckle, a unique piece of jewelry or a special tie or scarf. Even a hat! Emphasis near the face is most effective and a light colored shirt or blouse will keep the audience's eyes riveted on you.

It is no secret that dressing well makes us more secure. The confidence of security makes us more comfortable with ourselves and our words flow more easily. We become our own best advertisement.

Try your own experiment. Go shopping "dressed down" and see what kind of service you get Wait a week and enter the same store well dressed. The difference will be obvious.

Fact: People who are well dressed get preferential treatment.

Fact: In this competitive world the "look of success" is not a phrase; it is a truth.

Fact: Image can affect how much money we command as we advance in our careers.

So here you are, ready to start building a visual image. How do you go about it? First of all, go to your closet and get rid of everything you haven't worn in the past year. If you are like most Americans that will be 50-60 percent of what's in there. All of that new space will immediately give you incentive and motivation. Next classify what is left into dress-up, business and casual. Ask yourself these questions about each piece:

1. Is it in style?
2. Is it a quality item?
3. Is it in good repair?
4. Does it reflect the image I want to project?

If the item does not meet the criteria, then it should be replaced. What's left in your closet will form the basis for your new wardrobe. Remember: You may play many roles and you are allowed to choose the image to fit them. If this is a game of dress up, let's make it fun.

Classics never go out of style. The secret of a wardrobe that works for a man or woman is to have few (or more depending on economic circumstances) pieces that are essentially immune to fads. For men conservative suits and blazers with well tailored trousers form the core which can be constantly enhanced with the latest shirts and accessories. For women it may be a wonderful silk blouse that is worn for business during the week and then matched to jeans on the weekend.

By building a lineup of clothing in this manner one avoids the frustrating experience of what I call the "Great Closet Stare." That's when you peer into your closet full of clothing you don't wear and cannot make decisions. Your day may get off to a bad start because you don't really feel good about the way you look. Why not set it up to begin with strokes?

Quality cannot be stressed enough. Buy the best you can afford even if it means buying less. Quality also includes clothes made from natural fibers such as wool, linen, cotton or silk alone or combined with synthetics. The less expensive suit, well tailored of course, can be made to look like quality with leather shoes, a silk tie or scarf, leather belt and real jewelry. However, an expensive suit worn with vinyl briefcase, polyester shirt and canvas shoes will not portray the image that success oriented people are anxious to communicate. It may seem harsh to think we judge others this way; however, it is a truth. We cannot possibly get to know every person we meet and what is really inside. Visual image communication simply assists us in making our decisions.

Finally, when you are deciding what to say with your clothing language, think of IMAGE and you'll look terrific!

I =Imagination. Be creative. Give a hint of your individuality.

M =Make a statement. Decide what you want to say visually and do it well.

A =Accessorize. Go for the silk tie or the leather belt. Quality counts.

G =Gauge your audience. Who are you meeting? Who do you want to attract?

E =Expensive talks. Buy the best you can afford. People who look successful *are* successful.

Remember to make your image work for you. People are not born with style. It has to be learned. The positive attitude that you create with your visual impact makes a tremendous difference in the way the world treats you and therefore in the quality of your life.

If you are still not sure of what to do, here are some guidelines:

1. Be colorized. It's not to learn your season. It will show you which colors are flattering and those that are not.

2. See an image consultant. Qualified, professional advice from a neutral source is always a good start.

3. Prepare to change. Don't be afraid of it. If you haven't altered your hairstyle, makeup or glasses in five years, it is time to do so.
4. Look at the details. Your nails, the polish on your shoes and the fit of your clothes are all crucial.
5. Wear solids instead of prints. Prints always make a statement. A jungle motif or little flowers bring on an instant reaction.

Make your image work for you and have fun with it. It will influence your career, your earning power and even who you bring into your life! It gives you the opportunity to express who you are and sometimes whether you have a sense of humor. I know that I'm enjoying what I have created with IMAGE.

EUGENE A. SCHRANG, M.D.
240 First Street
Neenah, WI 54956
(414) 725-6661 • Res. (414) 729-9611

Dr. Eugene A. Schrang

Dr. Eugene A. Schrang was born and raised in Milwaukee, Wisconsin. He received his Baccalaureate in Science from the University of Notre Dame in 1953. He earned his Doctorate in Medicine at Loyola Medical School, Chicago, Illinois, and graduated in 1957. For his internship he attended the Los Angeles County Hospital, Los Angeles, California, followed by four years of general surgery residency at both the Albany Medical Center, Albany, New York, and St. Mary's Hospital in San Francisco, California, six months of which was spent as Clinical Instructor of General Surgery at the Sacramento County Hospital, Sacramento, California. He then served the next three years in plastic surgery residency training at the University of Texas Medical Branch, Galveston, Texas, where he was associated with the Shrine Burn Center.

His eight years of post-graduate specialty training preceded the private practice of plastic surgery in which Dr. Schrang has been engaged for twenty years in Neenah, Wisconsin. He is presently on the staff of Theda Clark Regional Medical Center.

Dr. Schrang has applied his skills in helping hundreds of people add more years to their lives and more life to their years by not only correcting their physical abnormalities, but by helping them cope with their personal deformities, thus, improving their attitudes about themselves and their relationships with others.

Dr. Schrang enjoys sharing the insights he has discovered which can more effectively deal with the headaches and heartaches of life—a life which can, in virtually all instances, be made richer for everyone.

13

Beautiful People Are the Greatest Communicators
by Eugene A. Schrang, M.D.

*"Through the beauty of His creation,
God communicates His essence to
man...and through the beauty of his art,
man conveys his feeling about himself."*
—Unknown

Ancient Man Had High Esteem...

Several thousand years ago mankind reached a level of civilization far above those of his ancestors whose main interest was sustenance and the preservation of life. His culture reached lofty heights with the advent of the Greek and Roman empires. We can easily understand how those people thought because their literature was profound and their art work reflected how they felt about themselves. Their great writers taught us that we as humans have value and showed that, indeed, we can be on a level with the gods themselves. I marvel at their great statuary and have often wondered if the people of those days really possessed the physiques of Hercules, Venus de Milo or their olympic athletes. The ancients must have possessed *great self-esteem.* It is the nature of man to feel good about himself and through the centuries we see evidence, time and again, in music, literature, architecture, and in renaissance painting that mankind has a burning desire to express the good within himself. Man has always sensed his inner beauty and has never waivered in his search for excellence.

What Is Different Today...

Nothing has changed in modern times except, perhaps, that so often we have lost sight of the fact that we are important as individuals; that we are persons worthy of self-respect and have the obligation to treat others with that same self-respect and dignity. But if we do not have high regard for ourselves, we cannot communicate well with others which brings up the question: What is lacking in modern man that prevents him from developing himself fully and helping others do the same? What is there in our makeup that is blocking this ability to communicate our feelings freely and clearly? I firmly believe that man's lack of self-image is the answer. Those who possess pride and a sense of identity are the great communicators and are easy to recognize. We feel them, we sense them, we like them. They stand above all others. They relate well with their fellow men no matter what their socio-economic level may be. A great communicator can relate comfortably with a child, an adult, a rich man, a vagrant, nobility and you and I.

What Are the Essentials of Communication...

Somehow we find it difficult to define just what it is about these unusual people that makes them so "communicative." But the reason is really quite simple. They possess four important ingredients necessary for effective expression. Apart from the fact that they know how to listen, they have:

1. Self-confidence
2. Courage
3. Enthusiasm
4. Friendliness

Self-confidence Is Knowledge...

The great communicator has self-confidence because he knows his subject matter well. He did his
homework. He has researched his topic and more
than likely has been involved with it for a long
time. The surgeon who works deftly with his hands
is composed and sure because he is familiar with
human anatomy, how it can be manipulated, and
what he can do with it in various situations. He has
profound experience and with this knowledge goes
the ability to produce artistic craftsmanship which
cannot be done by the unskilled. The pianist who
confidently walks on stage to give a brilliant
performance is nothing more than a man who has
studied the basic fundamentals of music, applied
them to his instrument and then practiced the
technique and artistry of musicianship for many
years.

By no means is this quality of "confidence"
possessed only by those who perform for an
audience. Great architects, who work quietly in
their studios, create the images of buildings which
reflect not only their knowledge of materials and
how they can be applied to the shape of their
structures but their artistic ability, and above all,
how they feel about themselves. Examples such as
this could be given for all the activities of everyday
life. We can readily pick out and distinguish those

who know their work well as opposed to those who do not. They radiate self-assurance—and those who do not, reflect their lack of knowledge in the shoddy way they perform their daily tasks.

Self-confidence Needs an Element of Courage...

Hand in hand with self-confidence is that quality called courage. The greatest communicators are courageous men and women who believe in themselves and are not afraid to communicate the principles of righteousness to others. Self-confidence needs courage because so often we are called upon to express ourselves in difficult situations; and these situations are rarely planned; a crisis must be dealt with and the opportunity to deal with it effectively does not last long. The faint-of-heart can in no way express themselves to any degree necessary to persuade or convince others.

Like Yourself and Your Work and You Will be Enthusiastic...

Enthusiasm is also found in the man who likes himself , has great self-esteem, enjoys his material and wants to share it with others. This applies to all forms of communication. That surgeon and musician I mentioned enjoy doing their work because they like to show others how thoroughly knowledgeable they are. The salesman who confidently walks into a prospective customer's office does a good job because he knows his product, knows what it can do, has great faith in it and enjoys the art of selling. He could not do that if he did not like himself and others. How often have we seen people work with lack of enthusiam—they simply have no "zest for life," and this is nothing more than an example of lack of self-esteem. Those people who do not like themselves, have difficulty liking others and will not let others like them. They are people we would just as soon avoid.

Criminals notoriously do not feel very good about themselves. Someone once said that a criminal is a criminal because he looks like a criminal. We did some very interesting work at the University of Texas which has been repeated by other researchers. For many years the plastic surgery residents in training did cosmetic surgery on the inmates of the Texas prison system. We removed scars, set back protruding ears, reduced oversized noses and, in general, did what we could to take away that "criminal" look from those individuals. We found that the return rate to prison, or number of "repeaters," was statistically decreased in those inmates that had plastic surgery as opposed to the general prison population who did not. Obviously the plastic surgery we did, gave those men enough self-confidence and enthusiasm that they, in many cases, could go out and function normally in society without again getting into trouble. Does this say something for the way we look? It certainly does!

The Man or Woman Who Looks Good, Feels Beautiful and Communicates Well..

Not long ago I was contacted by the family of a teenage boy who had the residual scars of a cleft lip. As he grew up, he became shy and introverted, would rarely communicate with others and, as a matter of fact, became overtly hostile. He was first seen by a social worker who made the not surprising discovery that this boy was essentially normal. He liked girls, however, girls did not like him because of the way he looked. He wanted to ask them for dates but was always afraid that they would turn him down. The situation became worse until he was finally seen by me for evaluation. The boy did have a very noticeable and unattractive scar of his upper lip. In addition, there were deformities of his nose and teeth, all of which collectively made him a very unattractive individual. Fortunately, his problems were easily corrected by plastic surgery. This took several months to accomplish but once the work was finished, an amazing change came over him: His hostility disappeared, he became communicative, enthusiastic and friendly. His grades improved in school and he gradually socialized normally with others in his peer group.

Examples such as this are common in the busy plastic surgeon's practice. I will never forget the girl whose large misshapen nose caused her great anxiety and prevented normal intercommunication with others. The day that her dressing was removed, she stood before the mirror in my office and cried. Her life was changed forever from that moment on.

Disfigurement from serious accidents can be extensive and their psychological effects profound. A number of years ago a young woman was driving to town for the purpose of buying her wedding dress. Her automobile was struck from behind by another which caused a rupture of her gas tank resulting in a burn injury which involved her face and the entire left side of her body. Many months of care were necessary to heal this girl's severe burn wounds during which time she experienced a deep sense of depression. Because of the way she looked her fiance left her. Many more months of reconstructive surgery were necessary to bring this girl's physical features back to as near normal as humanly possible. Fortunately, the results were quite good and with the passage of time, this girl realized that she was not offensive to look at and, as a consequence, became calm and serene. The story ended happily because she found another man whom she married and with whom she raised a family in an atmosphere of peace and contentment. It was *how she felt about herself* that really counted.

But Physical Attractiveness ALONE Is Not What Is Important...

Any physical deformity can affect us deeply and can block our ability to communicate effectively, for the simple reason that we can be so self-conscious of the way we look, that free communication with others is interfered with. But there *may not even be any physical deformity* as evidenced by the fact that teenagers, as a whole, spend excessive time in front of the mirror trying to correct deformities which do not exist. What they are really trying to do is *feel beautiful.*

Keep in mind that physical beauty by whatever standards and measurements we use is NOT IM-PORTANT; what *is* important is *how we feel* and if we *feel* good about ourselves, have high self-esteem and self-respect, we can consider ourselves beautiful no matter what negative physical attributes we may have. The opposite is also true: If we *are* physically beautiful by the standards of Hollywood or some beauty pageant, but have low self-esteem, we can certainly consider ourselves unattractive.

If We Do Have a Real, Bonafide Physical Abnormality..

It was always said that we cannot help the way we

look but we can certainly do something about the way we appear. Well, this is no longer entirely true. Fortunately, in this day and time it is easy to get some of nature's imperfections corrected. We found that when a person's face is changed, almost invariably their future is also changed. Improve a person's physical appearance, and nearly always you change the person—their personality—their behavior and sometimes even basic talents and abilities. Maxwell Maltz, in his book *Psychocybernetics,* says that each of us has a "non-physical face of personality" which seems to be the real key to personality change. If a person feels ugly, scarred or physically inferior, that person will most often act out this role in his or her behavior. This could be changed in one of two ways:

1. Surgically remove the scars, defects, deformities, etc. and usually the basic personality changes, or,
2. Remove the emotional scars which allows the person himself to change without the necessity of plastic surgery.

Great Thinkers Have Always Understood the Problem...

Henry David Thoreau, the great American writer, once said, "Be careful what you set your heart on for you will most surely have it." For example, if

252 / The Great Communicators

you think like a millionaire, and I am not talking about the daydreams people have about being one, but actually think just like one, you will eventually become one. This is an automatic process that you can do nothing to stop. Mike Todd said, "Being broke is a temporary phenomenon, but poverty is a state of mind." This "state of mind" works for the way that we feel about ourselves. If we *think* that we are *not* ugly, distorted or peculiar in any way—as far as our minds are concerned—we will not be—no matter what physical deformity we may have. Let me emphasize that our minds profoundly govern our lives—*WE WILL BECOME WHAT WE THINK.* If we think well of ourselves, our attitudes about life's problems will be healthy and we will be able to deal with them effectively. Shakespeare said, "The problem, dear Brutus, lies not in the stars but in ourselves."

All that is necessary is to change our attitudes and the way we think and the problems of life will take care of themselves. Physical attractiveness does not in itself make us beautiful; beauty is *HOW WE THINK.* If we *think* we are beautiful, we will be. It has been said that the face we have at fifty years is the one we deserve. Look around you, consider the people you know and you will find that there is a definite correlation between facial expression and a person's attitude.

And as far as your physical appearance is

concerned, never be ashamed nor deterred from trying to do something positive to look better. Whether this means having plastic surgery to correct a deformity or simply making the effort to keep yourself neat and well groomed. "Nothing that is human is alien to art—it is the divine right of man to look human."

Friendliness Is a Sharing of Ourselves with Others..

Friendliness is a quality possessed in varying degrees in different people. Your measure of friendliness depends, I suppose, on the mood you are in at any one particular time of the day. But it goes without saying, that the more friendly we are, the more acceptable we are to other people and the more readily they will accept our efforts to communicate with them. One should be willing to help other people become more than they ever thought they were capable of becoming; this is an unselfish attitude and, in so doing, we improve ourselves immeasurably. Did you ever see anyone communicate better than a friendly dog? He wags his tail, he jumps up and down, he looks happy because he is happy and immediately we like him. He is readily communicating his feelings to us and we readily accept. On the other hand, do you think that a charging dog, foaming at the mouth, ready to leap upon anything that gets in his way is communicating? You bet he is! You may argue the fact that he may not like himself but that is beside the point. He is telling us that he is self-confident, courageous and enthusiastic about what he is doing. But this is a communication which we do not readily accept and we will usually do anything to avoid this overt hostility.

So the communication about which we are talking assumes that it is friendly communication, which in most instances evokes friendly responses from others. The cliche adage that bees are attracted by honey certainly holds true in any situation. What we should seek is friendly response and this requires friendly communication on our part.

Why Not Reach for Even More...

There is one more characteristic of the truly expressive person that is worthy of mention. That is charisma. This often used, difficult to define term is a quality that has been possessed by attractive, forceful and intellectual people of all ages and times. By definition they must be *different*. They must stand out from all others because of what they say and do, and because they are different they attract our attention. They must be *forceful* in a positive or negative way. We may not necessarily like them; Rasputin, Charles Manson, Adolph

Hitler, and those of like ilk would not likely attract any of us, but they certainly commanded attention and, admittedly, they possesed a magnetism which influenced the thoughts and actions of many. They must be *intellectual* (a dullard cannot be charismatic).

And remember that intelligence does not presuppose lengthy education—many imminent men have degrees from respected institutions who cannot be considered charismatic. On the other hand, many who have had no education, have had a great deal of charisma. And then they must possess a *charm and fascination* that can be defined by only God Himself. But do not be misled into thinking that just the great and famous can be charismatic. You and I can also possess that quality. I am sure that a father and mother are charismatic to a child; that lovers are charismatic to each other; and we can all name people that we like in particular because they have magic qualities apart from all others. Therefore, charisma is something which can be developed to varying degrees and in its development we automatically communicate our inner selves. Also, love and charisma are similar. That so called "alluring attraction" can be found in people in love—they consider each other charismatic and thus, they communicate well—but when charisma ends, love ends and so too, communication ends.

Remember, YOU WILL BECOME WHAT-EVER YOU THINK YOURSELF TO BE...

Be self-confident—know your subject matter well. The quest for knowledge is interesting, thought provoking and enriching beyond measure. The educated person communicates well with anyone, even animals.

Be courageous—a brave man cannot live forever—a coward never. A coward communicates nothing more than his inability to relate well with himself and others.

Be enthusiastic—enjoy yourself, your work and other people. Your zest for life will be contageous. Your bright eyes and laughter will be picked up by others and you will find bountiful rewards beyond all expectations.

Be friendly—there is no reason not to be. Never be too busy to say "Hello" to someone, even when that person does not return the salutation. You know in your heart that you feel good about yourself and the world and you will pass through the day with a sense of enjoyment and well being.

Be as charismatic as possible—work at its development, be different, energetic and knowledgeable. *You will become what you think;* you will indeed have whatever you desire. Think well of yourself—you are human, and therefore of special value.

Lastly, always look for **every opportunity to improve yourself** in any way you can. Self actualization or self development is the natural goal of man on earth. The rewards are great and are automatically communicated to all with whom you will ever come in contact.

God said, "Build a better world," and I said, "How?"
"The world is such a cold, dark place and so
    complicated now;
And I so young and useless, there is nothing I can do."
But God in all His wisdom said,
    "JUST BUILD A BETTER YOU."

                                        —Unknown

Beautiful people are those who think well of themselves, are confident, courageous, enthusiastic and friendly—they are the great communicators.

ROGER I. BURGRAFF
P.O. Box 909
Redlands, CA 92373

Roger I. Burgraff, Ph.D.

Roger I. Burgraff is a professional public speaker who has distinguished himself in four major areas of communication: (1) Public Speaking; (2) Speech Pathology; (3) Teaching; and (4) Acting. He combines this broad range of training and experience with his personal enthusiasm and sense of humor to present dynamic and informative programs focusing on various aspects of the communication process.

In addition to an earned doctorate in Speech Pathology from Denver University, Roger holds an M.A. (with distinction) and a B.A. from DePaul University. He has taught at several universities and currently lectures at the graduate school of Loma Linda University in California. He is a member of the National Speakers' Association and the American Speech, Language and Hearing Association.

In recent years, Dr. Burgraff has presented such programs as "The Power of Positive Speech," "Good Listening Is Good Communication" and "Actions Do Speak Louder Than Words." He has also presented training seminars to improve interpersonal communication to various health care groups and business organizations. His lecture material, demonstrations and exercises have all been designed with practical application in mind. Roger believes that communication is the key that unlocks human potential.

14

The Two-Way Power of Speech
by Roger I. Burgraff, Ph.D.

"Guard your inner spirit more than any treasure, for it is the source of life."
—An Ancient Sage

The Power of What We Say to Ourselves

Twelve weeks had passed since his laryngectomy, and Mr. W. was recovering beautifully. He was now healthy and living at home. In his late 50's, Mr. W. had many full years ahead of him, and he seemed motivated to make the most of them.

My job was to teach him esophageal speech. He managed to communicate with the aid of an artificial larynx, but he didn't like the sound of the instrument. He wanted the freedom of esophageal speech, yet he seemed unable to master the technique.

I was frustrated. I asked him how he felt about our progress. His reply, in an easy Colorado drawl, offered the key to his eventual success at esophageal speech, and it opened a whole new career avenue for me. "I can't do it," was his answer. "I just can't do it. I have thought about it, and I just keep telling myself I can't do it."

Bingo! Mr. W. had talked himself into failure.

After my talk with Mr. W., I began to pay particular attention to my other clients, to my colleagues, friends and family. How many of them were talking themselves into failure? What experiences in their lives had led them to negative self-talk?

When I was in the eighth grade in Chicago, I was 6'1" tall. I couldn't help that, but I was constantly reminded how I was different. Always placed in the back row or at the end of the line, I lived with the "How is the air up there" joke every day. Furthermore, since I was big, I also acquired the companion adjective, "clumsy." In time, of course, many of my classmates grew as tall as I, but it took me far too many years to stop telling myself that I was "clumsy."

Once I became aware of this negative inner story-telling, I found countless examples among the people around me. One colleague told me that she had been sickly as a child, and frail looking. Her loving mother often spoke of her as "poor little Grace." Unfortunately, "Poor little Grace" achieved an adult stature of only five feet. Though she liked to dream of being a willowy 5'10", her inner tape droned on, "Poor little..., poor little..., poor little."

The Inner Tape

Talking to oneself can be called inner language, thinking, or intra-personal communication. Whatever it is called, I believe it is one of the greatest powers available to human beings. Self-talk, to a large extent, makes us who we are. It engenders self-esteem, confidence, willingness to take risks, the power to overcome fears. Self-talk feeds our subconscious, which believes whatever it is told, particularly when the internal message is delivered repeatedly and with great emotional conviction.

Internal chit-chat can be positive, or it can be negative. We need to listen to our own internal monologues, and recognize when we are poking ourselves in the eye or patting ourselves on the back. If we recognize that we have a penchant for negative self-talk, then, surely, it is time to consider a change!

Negative Self-Talk

Do you talk to yourself in a negative way? Do you have a self-programmed inner tape recording that repeats, "I can't, I just can't," "Big and clumsy," or "Poor little..."?

I recently heard someone refer to self-talk as "head movies" and that struck me as a particularly apt and vivid word picture. In our heads we can play out whole scenes of negative (or positive) "what-ifs." We can direct these negative scenarios at a specific instance in life, as in the case of Mr. W., who used a negative inner monologue against learning esophageal speech. Or we can create broad, general signals of self-negation in which the inner message is, "It's no use," "You can't beat City Hall," "When the going gets tough—quit." That may be a clever play on the old version (in which the tough get going), but it can be devastating to self-esteem and self-actualization.

Dr. Albert Ellis, founder of a school of psychology known as Rational Emotive Therapy, points out that self-criticism based on negative self-talk leads to a majority of the emotional problems his patients have, such as depression, anxiety and guilt.

I came to realize that in my work as a speech pathologist, I must help my clients ferret out their destructive internal conversations. I encouraged Mr.

W. to change his negative orientation to a positive one. He eventually did succeed in speaking esophageally when he changed his inner message from, "I can't do it," to "I can do it, I want to do it, I will do it." I was especially gratified to hear Mr. W. pass on what he had learned when he began visiting new laryngectomees and admonishing them, "Now, don't you tell yourself you can't do it. Tell yourself you can, and you will."

The Power of Positive Self-Talk

I watched one of my sons intuitively use positive self-talk on himself. He was standing in the line for the great roller coaster, "Colossus." It was clear that he wanted desperately to conquer the monster. But it was equally clear that he was terrified. I edged closer to him in case he needed some support, only to hear him intoning under his breath, "It'll be OK. It'll be fun. I can do it." I suspected then that he would succeed, and was not surprised to see him go eagerly to the back of the line to ride again. He rode the "Colossus" seven times that day, and learned a little lesson in positive self-talk that enabled him to overcome his fear of the moment. Would he have been able to ride "Colossus" if he had been telling himself that he couldn't do it?

Most of us grew up on the story of "The Little

Engine That Could." It is an inspirational fable teaching the message of positive self-talk, and it is a lesson that is widely used by long distance runners and cyclists to keep themselves going. Mary Lou Retton, the Olympic gymnast, has developed her own very specific self-talk technique for use just before her run at the vault. As she powers up for her run, you can almost hear her feet repeating, "I know I can, I know I can."

There are people in desperate situations who have utilized the power of positive self-talk to enable themselves to survive. Time and again I have heard this from my rehabilitation patients, Vietnam veterans, and one-time prisoners of war. Their internal message, repeated endlessly for so long as needed, went something like this: "Just one more day," "Just one more mile," "I can do it." Like negative self-talk, positive self-talk *can* be a self-fulfilling prophecy.

Four Steps to Positive Self-Talk

We all have this choice: We can focus on past failures, personal weaknesses, fantasies of disaster, or we can take the power of our potential into our hands and shape a positive future for ourselves.

Learning to use positive self-talk requires effort in four separate areas:

1. **AWARENESS.** To become aware of the *good* in

ourselves and our actions is the first step toward change. Once we recognize it, we can begin talking about it, thinking it over, and projecting our conclusions into our future endeavors: "The next meeting will go better. Next week I will take extra time and improve on the graphics. I see that my approach is right—it just needs more practice." We can recognize the moments when we create positive responses in others, and we must learn to take credit for our power to touch others by our words. By "taking credit," I mean that we accept the fact that we have done well, and we embrace the feeling of warmth and satisfaction that goes with it.

2. **DENIAL OF NEGATIVISM.** Negative thoughts, doubts and recriminations will creep back into our inner monologues, but they must not be tolerated. Learn the technique of *thought-stopping*. When the negative rumble begins, say to yourself: "So what if he didn't buy my sales pitch," "So what if my deal fell through," "So what if the lady said no," "So what if my friend disappointed me." So it happened, that's what. Recognize the failure, look at it, profit from it, and then put it away.

Carl Sandburg, the beloved American poet, said, "The past is a bucket of ashes." Learn to see these doubts, recriminations and negative thoughts as a bucket of ashes. Then let go.

3. **REFOCUSING.** Most situations are complex, made up of many factors. When you reevaluate a situation, stress the positive areas. *Do* analyze the negative facets of the event to see what could have been done to make them better. Vow to incorporate these changes into your next opportunity. *Then* let go of the negative parts of the situation. Go on to give yourself credit for what was right and good in the situation, and decide how you can make it even better the next time. Consider a different slant, a little re-tooling, risk a bit of humor.

4. **REPETITION.** One of the oldest cliches I know is "Practice makes perfect." A saying becomes a cliche because it is repeated so often, and it is repeated frequently because it is recognized to be true. Practice does make perfect, or as near to it as we can get. Practice is nothing more than studied repetition, doing it until we get it right. Og Mandino, an inspirational writer, has a ten-point program guide to success. Each element is a scroll and must be focused on for 30 days, three times a day. This sort of spaced repetition is an effective tool for helping learning to seep into our consciousness.

You and I can never eliminate all of those influences around us that initiate our internal negative self-talk. What we *can* do is overwhelm the negative ruminations with positive self-talk. Those good things we say to ourselves repeatedly and with conviction become our beliefs. Our beliefs form the basis of our behavior and our ability to cope successfully with life.

The Power of What We Say to Others

"Man's supreme achievement in the world is communication from personality to personality."

—German Philosopher Karl Jaspers

After you begin to practice the four steps of positive self-talk, you will develop internal conversation, and you will then be ready to give serious thought to the impact of your words on other people. We *do* affect other people by what we say to them. Our words provide the feedback by which others come to know themselves.

Rarely is human communication a simple exchange of data. Speech is more often the vehicle by which we establish and maintain relationships. Most of what we do is in the context of a relationship, and, I submit, what we say to one another is the *key* to those relationships.

Talking to Children

A good example of the way positive speech influences another person is the actual process by which a baby learns to talk. As a normal child approaches one year of age, he is engaging in oral-sound play, just because it is fun. Parents hear strange combinations of coos, gurgles and burbles, and sometimes they imitate those sounds. Because large portions of the infant's brain are devoted to communication functions, the stage is set for real speech to begin. By chance or in imitation (and because it is a very simple sound combination), the child says "ma-ma." What do the parents do? They hug, kiss, smile and imitate the child's new word. When this happens a few times, the child realizes that vocalizing "ma-ma" is a rewarding thing to do. According to learning theory, behavior that is positively reinforced will continue and grow. The child may use other sound combinations, and he gets rewarded for "da-da" and "bye-bye" and "nigh-nigh."

Eventually this system of positive emotional reinforcement shifts to positive verbal reinforcement. As we grow up, we hear: "Nice report card," "Well done, son, we're proud of you," "Good game, you played well."

As I watched a videotape of one of my therapy sessions, I tried to detach myself in order to better analyze the therapeutic process. I knew that I was employing standard techniques in my therapy; I was using intermittent positive reinforcement to shape the child's responses; I had colorful pictures and games to make the situation fun for the child. But I realized that, most important, I was talking to the child in a positive way. I could see his eyes light up, even through the faulty medium of the videotape, when he did well and I told him so in positive words and tones.

The more therapy sessions I conducted, and the more adept I became at my chosen field, the more fascinated I was by the importance of the twin facets of communication—self-talk and talking to others. I came to see how very influential are the messages children receive, and how vital it is for professional people to communicate positive messages to their colleagues, clients, and in their personal relationships.

In therapy sessions, I have been able to put these principles into practice on a one-on-one basis. But, in my lecture career, I am able to reach larger audiences with the message that each of us has a responsibility to consider carefully what we say to those in our charge and to those we love.

Speaking Negatively to Others

Almost everyone was taught the positive message of "The Little Engine That Could:" "I think I can, I know I can, I knew I could." Why is it, then, that some people fail?

Unfortunately, the inspirational fables of our youth are not the only messages we receive from outside. As in my own case, messages of a general nature come to us from the reactions of people around us. People note that we are tall, short, fat, thin, and they let us know how they feel about it. The minute we speak, the people around us react to our high, squeaky voice, our lisp, or lack of fluency. One lady I know told me that when she was small, grown-ups mimicked her unchildlike low, powerful voice, with the result that she is now soft-spoken to the point of whispering.

Many negative signals come to us from people who should be wholeheartedly supportive. Usually their negative messages are unconscious and certainly not intended. Surely, "poor little Grace's" mother did not mean to cripple her with a sense of defenseless impotence.

How many children have been stifled in academic performance because someone called them stupid? How many people haven't even tried to express themselves artistically, even just for fun, because they have been told that they "can't draw a straight line" or they "can't carry a note."

How vulnerable we are to those negative comments people make! After a training seminar, I still have to remind myself not to give more weight to one negative reaction than to ninety-nine positive feed-back statements.

It is easy to label people in a negative way if we don't want to work out our problems with them.

"How can anyone work with a !@#$&%*(like that?" In marital problems, the spouse is usually called a slob, a pig, a sicko, or something worse. The problem with that approach to a relationship is that many people are in a vulnerable position and cannot defend themselves adequately. Children, the elderly, subordinates, the new kid on the block, the new employee, or even people in a current personal crisis usually are not equipped verbally, physically or emotionally to handle negative verbal attacks. They are likely to overreact to negative labels and perform in accordance with the labels which they have been given. This is why it was a problem to me to be 6'1" in the eighth grade, and why my colleague reacted so disastrously to her mother's well meant label of "poor little girl."

Because what we say to others can have a direct impact on them, we must guard against negative statements infiltrating our speech. As we become more fully aware of the destructive qualities of negative speech, our need to change becomes evident. Parents, teachers, supervisors, speakers and others in positions of authority have a grave responsibility to be cautious about what they say.

Speaking Positively to Others

How do you feel when someone says something nice to you? Compliments your work? Your appearance? You feel good! You probably think, "Here is a really perceptive person." You look forward to future encounters with this attractive individual, and you even create opportunities to meet again.

There are many good reasons to develop the habit of speaking positively to others. It enhances our authority rather than diminishes it. A person who is open, "together," and capable of speaking in positive ways to others is a person to be respected. Morale goes up, people are happier and more productive when such a person is working among them. It is necessary for employees to have frequent positive verbal reinforcement for their efforts. In this way, desired work habits continue and grow stronger. One supervisor nurse to whom I spoke said, "Well, Carol knows how I feel about her good performance." I wonder if she does?

Although people will go to great lengths to receive positive verbal reinforcement, there seems to be a reluctance to give positive verbal affirmations to others. People seem prone to criticize and find fault by letting the good things people do go unremarked. I do it, I know. If my sons take down the trash or tidy their rooms, that's fine—it's what is expected of them. But let them forget, and they are sure to hear about it.

It should not be embarrassing to affirm others. On the contrary, it adds to morale at work and to closeness in our other relationships. In social situations, it helps people to feel at ease with one another. Ignoring the good or pleasant things people do is almost as serious as punishing them, because unreinforced behavior tends to diminish. Why should we knock ourselves out beyond the job requirement if nobody takes notice? When others feel you expressing positive things, they see you as sympathetic, understanding and attractive. Your relationship with them is strengthened and, as a result, they are far more likely to open up to you.

Psychologist William James said, "The deepest principle in human nature is the craving to be appreciated." We demonstrate this appreciation most admirably through those positive things we say to other people.

Five Steps to Positive Communication

There are a number of excellent books that teach methods we can use to achieve more positive speech. Among my favorite techniques are these:

1. **Be specific in your positive statements.** There is more impact and reinforcement in identifying a specific feature for comment: "I appreciate the effort you put into those graphics" is much more effective than the general comment, "Good job."

2. **Use the person's name.** There are few things we like to hear more than our own name linked to

something positive. "Stephen, thanks for coming in early and getting things organized" is much more powerful than, "Thanks for coming in early."

3. **Compare a person's behavior to a higher standard.** "Jack, your poster really looks professional," or "Connie, you're among the most conscientious members of this organization."

4. **Make receiving affirmations work for you.** As you are complimented, it is a very good opportunity for you to express your positive feelings for another. "Thank you, David. It's nice of you to notice and mention it," or "That's really good to hear, Lilly, you've made my day."

5. **Ask people's advice or opinions.** It always makes me feel appreciated when I am asked for an opinion. "Chris, how do you feel about this?" or "Dottie, what do you think of this section of the proposal?"

Conclusions

> *"If I have all the eloquence of men or of angels, but speak without love, I am simply a gong booming or a cymbal clashing."*

—I Corinthians: 13

We can use speech, either within our own heads or outwardly to the world, to build up our own self-esteem and confidence and to help others achieve the same result; or we can use language, consciously or unwittingly, to destroy the self-image of those around us.

Knowing this to be true, it is urgent that each one of us gives heed to the thoughts we allow into our heads. It is crucial that we learn techniques for turning those thoughts toward positive self-realization.

Once we have our inner "head movies" under control, every effort should be made to govern our conversational approach so that we offer encouragement and positive reinforcement to those with whom we come in contact each day.

> *"When communication is guarded, hostile or ineffective, the relationship falters. Where communication skills are lacking, there is so much lost love between spouses, lovers, friends, parents and children. For satisfying relationships, it is essential to discover methods that will help us to at least partially bridge the interpersonal gaps that separate us from others."*

— **Robert Bolton**

Yours in the Spirit of Mutual Understanding,

ROGER I. BURGRAFF

To speak much is one thing,
to speak well is another.

—Sophocles

LYNNE G. HALEVI, Ph.D.
Halevi & Associates
1717 Ala Wai Blvd., #2305
Honolulu, HI 96815
(808) 944-4079

Lynne Grossman Halevi, Ph.D.

Lynne Grossman Halevi, Ph.D. is an author, lecturer, actress, and world traveler. Her eighteen years of professional experience has included teaching from preschool to university levels; gaining experience from city to isolated rural areas; moving interchangeably from research to administration, from writing to public speaking and consulting to guiding thousands toward success.

Dr. Halevi has coauthored Peabody Early Experiences Kit *(PEEK) published by American Guidance Service; authored and coauthored major grant proposals and fund raising requests as well as numerous in-house newsletters and publications dealing with improvement of communication, goal setting, motivational and problem solving techniques.*

She is listed in Personalities of the West and Midwest 1969-1970; *named Master Clinician in California; elected to Phi Delta Kappa; has the Certificate of Clinical Competence in Speech Pathology and holds teaching credentials in Arizona, California and Hawaii.*

Dr. Halevi is currently Chairperson (Hawaii) of the International Listening Association and a board member of National Speakers Association (Hawaii). She has presented listening workshops for IBM; Sheraton Resort Hotels; International Listening Association and numerous school districts in addition to business and professional organizations. Dr. Halevi is a dynamic trainer, speaker and listener. The central focus of her career has been to help others to learn to communicate effectively for personal and professional growth and success.

15

L.I.S.T.E.N.I.N.G.
An Acronym for
Successful Communication
by Lynne Grossman Halevi, Ph.D.

"Nature has given to each of us two ears and one tongue, because we ought to do less talking and more listening."
—Plutarch

The Listening Mode

How to turn your business, professional and personal encounters into major profitable experiences and endeavors instead of disasters! Imagine this: you are in the office, the phones are ringing, the typewriters are clicking, the copy machine is humming and the staff is asking you for directions. How are you reacting to this noise pollution? Imagine another scenario: You are in your car, horns are honking, sirens are screaming and the radio is blasting. What effect is this kind of auditory input having on your central nervous system? Has all this continuous bombardment of sight and sound taught you to tune out? Do you hear, but you do not listen? What are the consequences of this learned non-listening behavior in our personal and professional lives?

In the business world the result of half listened-to directions and misunderstood messages can equal financial losses measured in the millions. In our interpersonal relationships the consequences are hurt feelings, loss of self-esteem, family crises, arguments, stress and illnesses which can be devastating. Therefore, in order to eliminate these devastating financial and health disasters, we must learn to listen.

How Are You Received?

Plutarch, more than 2,000 years ago, understood that being an effective listener was twice as important as being a verbose speaker. Despite the fact that listening was discussed thousands of years ago, we still do not give enough attention to the listening process. The true test of communication is not whether a message is sent, but if and how it is received. Listening is the most difficult and overlooked aspect of the communication process. That is why such companies as IBM, Sheraton Resort Hotels, specialty organizations, and school districts have hired me to train their personnel in this very important skill.

In these workshops I demonstrate that what people have heard is often very different from what has been said. Listening, although the most used communication process, is the least understood and is, unfortunately, rarely taught in schools. Although the definitive definition of listening is still in process, each scholarly approach has moved us closer to understanding the complexity of the habits, behaviors, experiences, and environments which influence how we interpret what is heard. Dr. Ralph Nichols, an early, modern day pioneer in the study of listening behaviors, has developed the conceptual model upon which many communication trainers, such as myself, base our inquiry, discussion and training. "Listening is the missing 'L' in learning," Nichols declared, when he mapped out his listening theory.

I personally have helped thousands of students improve their listening skills using various techniques. I train people to overcome the eighteen barriers to effective listening and to understand that there are more than seven types of listening. By becoming active, creative listeners these students have improved their productivity, had career advancements and improved their life situations. Dr. Drakeford has written:

> "If I were to announce that there was one simple skill, which, if mastered would make the possessor a well informed, knowledgeable individual, a wiser person, a more desirable companion, a better communicator, a counselor par excellence, a more skillful administrator, I would be besieged by requests to reveal it, and listening is that skill."

The secret of successful communication lies in respecting the speaker by being an active, not a passive listener. We have come to believe, erroneously, that listening is a passive behavior. I cannot stress enough that effective listening takes much energy, concentration and work. Visualize, if you will, how you react to these two statements: Have you hugged your child today? Have you *listened* to your child today? Does the former make you feel warm, relaxed and comfortable? Does the latter give you an uneasy, sweaty palms reflex? Hugging does not take the same amount of time or energy that energetic listening demands.

Listening tells the speaker that you care

enough to spend time to allow him to share his feelings. It is a way of relating with love, without making value judgments. It allows for self-evaluation, to explore options, to talk out frustrations, problems, dreams, and goals in an atmosphere of trust and love. To increase your listening ability takes systematic training and practice. With such training I have enabled people to increase their listening efficiency and personal effectiveness. Kim Rosen has said:

> *"All human beings have within them a longing to communicate, to surrender fully to the song that sings in their heart and to bring it forth to the world."*

Despite this need to communicate we are not listening to the "song." Children complain that their parents and teachers don't listen to them. Most employers complain that employees don't listen, and employees say that employers are not listening. Our high divorce rate may be a result of spouses not listening to each other. In short, although we are bombarded daily with sounds of all descriptions, we, as a society, have become non-listeners. The act of merely hearing sounds is not the act of listening.

Listening Is an Art

The development of listening, as with the speech act, is a learned behavior which is influenced by our experiences, biases, and self-esteem. Effective listening must be considered an art as well as a very complex process. I conceptualize listening as occurring in five stages:

1) We take information in through our senses (hearing, smelling, tasting, feeling and seeing).
2) We interpret that information (evaluate, sort and categorize).
3) We store that information in our memory banks.
4) We retrieve it as needed.
5) We disperse that information in some way (respond, react and report).

In summary, we sense it, interpret it (identify), evaluate it, then predict, store, and finally respond to it in some way. We decide to either act upon the message or to ignore it.

Messages are too often misinterpreted and misunderstood. Our interpretation is based on our personal frame of reference. Tell a doctor that there is a consumption epidemic in the U.S. today, and he will infer something very different than the economist who thinks of it in terms of consumption of goods and products. Messages passed down through the organizational chain of command may be as easily misinterpreted. Messages go through our complex filtering system. Misconstrued messages in an organization may be monetarily costly. In personal relationships misconstrued messages are costly in damaged egos, loss of self-esteem and unneccessary stress and strife. In the world community it is presently felt that a misconstrued message may even cause a nuclear holocaust. "But I thought you said..." is the beginning of many a conflict among peers, families, and colleagues.

Winners Listen

Listening is central to our success as communicators, personally, professionally, and financially. Listening, and not how well we articulate the vowels and consonants, is the critical factor influencing our interpersonal relationships. A thought to ponder: A winner listens; a loser just waits his turn to speak.

Because I give entire courses, day long seminars, half day workshops, and many speaking engagements about listening, as well as individual consultations, for the purposes of this anthology, I have developed a concise methodology to get the information across. I shall use the word "L.I.S.T.E.N.I.N.G." as an acronym. Each letter will be used to describe the various components to be learned if you are to become an effective listener.

L - LOOK: Remember the old adage "Look before you leap!" Let's change it to, "Look before you speak." I repeat, listening is not the same as hearing, therefore, we must listen with our eyes and our heart as well as our ears. We must observe the speaker's body language very closely. Much can be learned by the look on the face, the tap of a foot, the movement of the hand and the turn of the head. The stance and the gestures help us to understand what is *not* uttered. Very often in life we are too busy to listen to all the hearts that are beating around us. At times the real message may be understood only through understanding the body language. Look at your own body language as the speaker is giving you the message; is the environment safe enough to allow for open communications in the home or office or are you listening with one hand on the phone and an eye on the clock?

Theodore Ricke wrote, *Listening With the Third Ear,* Halevi says, "Listen With Five Ears." That means two ears plus two eyes and one heart. The first four letters in the word heart spells hear.

Effective listening involves the visual as well as the aural message. When you look at the speaker he feels supported, loved, and respected. This allows for expansion of ideas on both sides of the listening-speaking equation.

I - INTEGRITY: Integrity is the essence of all things successful. The listener must determine if the message is 'full of sound and fury signifying nothing.' You must ask yourself if the message is meant to inform, amuse, teach, persuade, preach, or vent emotions. Perhaps the speaker's intention is to be sarcastic or ironic. On another level the message may be meant as the first step in the development of intimacy. Small talk or chit-chat is the necessary first step to the process of bonding so that deeper communication may evolve.

I instruct sales people not to overlook this step when dealing with clients. The successful professional identifies with his client. He is able to integrate the client's needs and purposes with his own so that what is offered adds value that is mutually beneficial. Many a transaction is culminated with a handshake because the two have built a bridge of mutual understanding and trust.

Managers, supervisors, executives, and family members must find some common ground between themselves and the speaker. When trust is established, what follows are successful interpersonal relationships and professional growth. We gain knowledge about ourselves, our clients, and our families when we listen and respond with integrity and honesty.

S - SYNERGY: The dictionary defines synergy as, *"Comparative action of discrete agencies such that the total effect is greater than the sum of the two effects taken independently."* Therefore, I teach how the combined effects of sight and sound work together to produce a sum greater than the individual parts. When the listener and the speaker work cooperatively to understand each other, problems can often be averted or solved with greater insights. The result of processing of information becomes greater through the collaboration of effort than when approached without synergy.

Research indicates that the speed of the mind is, at least, three to four times the speed of speech. Consequently, it is incumbent upon the listener to use this time differential productively. In my workshops we practice how not to become distracted, day dream, click-out, jump to conclusions, interrupt, or attempt to second guess what the speaker is going to say. Resist inattentive listening if you are to become an effective synergetic communicator. A good communicator is willing to listen to the speaker until the conclusion. You can synergize by using thought time to be alert to your emotions, prejudices, biases and preconceived notions. You must make cooperative understanding your major objective. It is the listener's responsibility to understand how what is heard is influenced by how emotions and self-concept interfere with the message. I advise my clients to evaluate sincerity, empathy and patience—theirs, as well as the speaker's.

A good listener stays attentive regardless of the prejudicial distractions; he uses sight and sound to produce and to create a receptive, open communication greater than its parts. Such behavior will give a quality of communication with clients, peers, subordinates, and family unknown before. With synergy, creative solutions evolve because this kind of working together creates a total effect that is otherwise impossible.

T - TUNEABILITY: Good listeners must learn to tune in to the central idea by being sensitive to the speaker's feelings. My clients learn how to decide if the message is a turn on, a tick off, or a tune out. Through tuneability and neuro-linguistic programming participants learn to tune in on the same wave length. Once the listener is able to define the speaker's underlying theme and to understand what is not stated, he is able to make judgments as to how much and the type of note-taking that may be necessary in order to follow through correctly.

In my workshops participants do exercises to

learn how to review what is being said and to understand how it is being said. They learn how the message affects their understanding and why tuneability is a major key to effective life long relationships. They understand if the message is a serious one to be acted upon immediately. They are taught the techniques for remembering and passing along precise data. To insure that your communication stays alive and well, think and practice C.P.R.R.—clarify, paraphrase, reflect and respond. Tune in to the whole message, the spoken as well as the unspoken.

E - EMPATHIZE: There was once a movie entitled *Tea and Sympathy,* but a therapeutic listener must be ready to offer "Tea and Empathy." Empathy is that characteristic which allows the listener to have the capacity for participation in another person's feelings or ideas without offering advice or passing judgment. There is no need to agree or disagree when called upon to be an empathetic listener.

In the business world the manager/supervisor is often called upon to be a sounding board for employees' complaints, petty grievances, personal problems and work related situations. Those administrators and CEO's who are able to allow employees to talk through their problems, grievances, and annoyances find that problems are quickly solved. Talking things out helps to clarify thinking and to release pent-up emotions. The guidelines for empathetic listening, whether dealing with peers, colleagues, children, spouse, or friends are the same. In my training sessions, I teach techniques for staying with the speaker and allowing the speaker to complete his message.

Do not enter into this kind of session, however, when you are rushed for time. Empathetic listening takes a great amount of time and energy. An empathetic listener needs to be alert to creating a positive, relaxed atmosphere through body language, eye contact and attentiveness. As a sounding board you do not offer advice, solutions, or judgments, but show warmth, understanding, and sincere concern. The listener is merely the mirror by which the speaker is able to see himself in order to solve his own problems through self disclosure. It is sufficient to nod or make a non-commital "uh-huh." Empathetic listening is important because among many persons today there is a deep sense of loneliness, a lack of true friendships, and a lack of those with whom we can simply *talk*. Persons need to be able to express pent-up feelings. No amount of saying, "You mustn't feel that way," will change feelings. As a parent, spouse, manager, school teacher, business executive, lawyer, or doctor, it is critical that you be able to listen without passing judgment.

The reward for this kind of listening comes in improved office relationships and greater productivity, as well as greater interpersonal communication in all spheres. When you are able to put yourself in another person's situation you will experience a positive impact on your personal and professional life. There will be noticeable personal and professional growth and improved cooperation with all the people with whom you interact.

N - **NEGOTIATE:** We generally equate speaking with power; however, listening can be equally as powerful, when conferring with others, so as to arrive at a mutually satisfactory compact. A successful listener knows when to respond. If a listener has a blank face and is totally silent, the speaker feels that he is speaking in a vacuum. It is incumbent upon the listener to give feedback in a positive, gentle, honest, and compassionate manner, both verbally and non-verbally.

The role of today's management teams differs from the past, when the old pyramidal structure of authority was the way of organizations. Today management must break the frame and be true facilitators by learning to listen and negotiate. This means that win/win negotiations are especially important because employees must be actively involved in those decisions that affect them. I train clients to use negotiation to resolve conflict so that no one feels that he is a loser. Don't operate from an, "I can top this," or from an opponent/victor position. I train clients on how to give appropriate feedback so that when negotiating for their time to speak the outcome will be mutually satisfactory. Always negotiate from this win/win position; do not explode, demean, or be rude. Without win/win negotiations, communication breakdown, hurt feelings, and loss of self-esteem is the result and nobody wins.

I - **INTERPRET:** A good listener must be alert to those preoccupations which cause the internal and external barriers that result in message breakdown and faulty interpretations. It is the listener who must assume responsibility for identifying his intra-interpersonal relationships and how these affect how he listens, interprets and responds to what is being said. The listener must understand how he reacts to authority figures, fast talkers, slow speakers, indecisive persons, and to those who are slovenly, poor, rich, older, younger, optimists, pessimists, physically handicapped, or speech impaired. In other words the listener must understand *why* and *how* his reactions prevent him from interpreting the message correctly.

How the message goes through the internal filtering mechanism is heavily weighted by our perception about the speaker and ourselves. Once the listener is able to overlook mannerisms, appearance and social position, the message is less likely to become distorted. In my workshops I train the listener to be able to read between the lines with an unbiased eye. How well we are able to modify our stimulus-response attitudes determines our degree of success as effective communicators. The real meaning may not come through because of external and internal static. Our personal awareness of the internal as well as external noise pollution will greatly increase our success in all interpersonal pursuits. Effective, open communication skills are the basic foundation upon which are built effective management and personal relationships.

To illustrate how bias influences our attitudes, I sometimes begin my workshops by speaking very rapidly and using gushy expressions and frivolous gestures. Then I switch to sound assured; I hold my head high, speak very distinctly, appear confident and important. The response of my audience switches as well and not very subtly. The audience's reaction to the self-assured, important sounding delivery is attentive, interested, and respectful. The authority of the presenter grabs the attention.

Another test I give my workshop participants to show bias is with this story:

A father and his son are involved in an automobile accident. The father is killed and the boy is rushed to the hospital. The surgeon that treats the boy says, "I can't operate on him, he is my son."

How can this be? The question invariably confuses the participants because they have listened through their filtering systems. The answer is simple! The surgeon is a woman.

N - NON-VERBAL BEHAVIOR: Our mannerisms, from the gleam in our eye, to the position of our feet, are all non-verbal messages that produce positive or negative responses. The non-verbal message is usually stronger than the verbal message. For instance, if the speaker says, "Everything is wonderful," but the eyes do not make eye contact, and the body appears listless, do you accept the speaker's statement as true?

The non-verbal component in the listener-speaker equation influences what is being said and how the message is being received. In my workshops we demonstrate how the message is impacted upon by our stance, body language, and eye contact. How well we communicate is influenced by our ability to read the non-verbal as well the verbal messages. Non-verbal behaviors may cloud or clarify the message. We tend to trust our eyes more than our ears. That is why the saying, "Seeing is believing," is used so frequently in our society. Once we understand how non-verbal and visual cues affect us, we begin to develop deeper insights into ourselves and others. When we learn how to eliminate from our thinking such stereotypical cliches as: "All blonds are stupid"; "All red heads have tempers"; "All bearded men must be old"; we are exercising cognitive and reflective learning.

G - GIVE AND GATHER: The final letter in this acronym, 'G', stands for giving and gathering information. It is the sum total of the synergetic essence of the communication process. We listen to gain information, to be alert to warning signals, such as fire alarms, ambulances, alarm buzzers, and crying babies. We also listen to relax, to socialize, to gain and give opinions based on reliable data, and to become knowledgeable about the world and our profession. We listen and exchange information to be friendly, to gain respect and to be polite.

As we listen we use the time to sort out main ideas, to clarify what is being said, to evaluate the importance of this information and to give the necessary feedback so that both the listener and the speaker are able to determine if they are on the same wave length. Participants in my workshops learn to identify the many and varied listening situations. They learn when to ask for clarification, when to paraphrase, and how to be aware of those words that elicit emotional responses that tend to excite or arouse. They learn when and how to recall C.P.R.R.—clarify, paraphrase, reflect, and respond for effective communication.

Summary

John Denver has written, "It's hard to tell the truth when no one wants to listen, when no one really cares what's really going on." Effective listening involves caring. Before reacting and responding to what is being said, try tuning in to what is really being sent, in that way you clarify what you think you hear. In our daily lives as well as in our professional lives, we forget that there is jargon related to our activities. If we keep C.P.R.R. in mind, our communication process will remain alive and well. When we listen with compassion and integrity we will interpret correctly and synergize with the speaker. With listening training you will be able to recognize difficult listening situations and to react with a clear and open mind. You will tune in to the message even when it may seem too long, too complicated, or too boring. Listening training will teach you when to ask questions and how to give honest, compassionate feedback and how to avoid information overload, thereby becoming a dynamic, action oriented, effective human being. By learning how to overcome the effect of auditory and visual over-stimulation you will reduce the cause of irritability, nervousness, high blood pressure and other stress related illnesses.

Listening training pays big dividends in every phase of our lives. Listening, when used effectively, can be the key to the clarification of goals, dreams, conflicts, and to the dynamic development of a more productive milieu for spiritual, mental, financial, personal, and professional growth and happiness. Good listening training seminars pay big dividends.

I will leave you to think about the message in the following poem.

ARE YOU LISTENING?

You may listen to the friendly chirpings
Of the cricket in the grass,
But do you listen to the silent plea
Of the hungry lad or lass.

You may listen to the music
A hundred times or more
But did you stop to really listen
To the lonely heart next door?

Perhaps it would be worthwhile
As we play our many parts
If we stopped sometimes to listen
With an open loving heart.

—Anonymous

Tact:
The ability to see others as they see
themselves.
                          —**Abraham Lincoln**

DAN AMMERMAN
Ammerman Enterprises, Inc.
4800 Sugar Grove Blvd., Suite 400
Stafford, TX 77477
(713) 240-2026 • Res. (713) 491-0553

Dan **Ammerman**

"From now through the year 2000 and beyond, those who rise to the top in any profession will be those who have mastered the art of communication."
Thus says Dan Ammerman, president of Ammerman Enterprises, Inc., the communications consulting firm which he founded in Houston in 1976. Ammerman has applied his experience with both the CBS and ABC radio networks and as news anchorman for the ABC-TV affiliate in Houston to become one of the world's most respected trainers in public speaking and electronic media communication as well as crisis training and witness preparation. The famous "Ammerman Experience" takes place in modern facilities including a state-of-the-art television studio to provide the most realistic teaching atmosphere possible.

Ammerman lectures widely on such topics as the art of communication, effective media relations, image making, motivation, and goal setting.

Ammerman has also enjoyed success in his hobby: acting. His television roles include several episodes of "Dallas" and "Guilty or Innocent." Recent movie credits include "Local Hero," "The Jesse Owens Story," and "The Sky's No Limit."

Ammerman is a member of the National Speakers Association, is included in Who's Who in Finance and Industry, serves on the Board of Directors of MBank Southwest in Houston, and is a national board member of the Volunteers of America.

16

Ammerman on Communicating:
"You've Got to Make Me Believe That You Believe Before I Can Believe What You Believe"
by Dan Ammerman

"To be believable you must be credible.
To be credible you must be truthful."
—Edward R. Murrow

D id you understand the title I picked for this essay? Did you have to read it more than once to get the drift? If you think it plays tricks on the eye, you should hear its effect on the ear.

When I begin my speeches with that same remark, I can see glazed looks come over the faces of some of the members of the audience.

Most people don't fully grasp the meaning of the statement the first time they encounter it, but it represents the essence of successful human communication.

In fact, if you're a communicator, it's your job description.

What do I mean by a communicator? In professional terms, a communicator is someone who is good at understanding those not good at explaining and explaining it all to those not good at understanding.

In everyday language, a communicator is anyone who must go before an audience, no matter what size and in no matter what capacity: as guest speaker, as trainer, as lecturer, as witness, as debater, etc. It's anyone with an idea to get across. It's the President of the United States facing a Joint Session of Congress and it's a mother teaching her child good manners.

Whether your public consists of a hall teeming with reporters, an office filled with employees or a station wagon crammed with teenagers, your task is the same: you've got to make me believe that you believe before I can believe what you believe.

As a communicator of any sort you must convince me that you believe what you are saying before I can entertain the thought that I might want to believe what you believe.

If I don't think you believe, we can't go on.

But if you can convince me that you believe what you want me to believe, the dividends will be immediate and obvious.

If you are a trainer, supervisor, safety meeting leader, general manager, vice president, or CEO, you will be able to measure the effects of what you believe.

Productivity increases because workers believe you believe.

Quality is maintained because workers believe you believe in quality.

Safety improves because workers believe it is a good idea because YOU believe it is a good idea.

Absenteeism decreases because nothing will prevent a worker from returning to a place where positive thought reigns and people believe in one another and in what they are doing.

Illustrations Abound

Remember when Tug McGraw was the premier relief pitcher in major league baseball? Philadelphia hadn't won a pennant in many years. The town was notorious for its negative attitude toward baseball, and the boo-birds reigned supreme. The team was ten games out of first and the All Star break had been long forgotten. Most baseball fans will quickly say that once you pass the All Star break, nothing really can be done to change the standings.

Tug McGraw would be called in to pitch when things had taken a nasty turn. He would retire the side and save the game, but he did something special after each stupendous performance. McGraw would come off the mound slapping his glove against his leg, then he would shoot his arm into the air supporting a clenched fist and shout, "YOU GOTTA BELIEVE!"

When he first began his challenge, no one in the stadium believed as Tug believed. But as the season wore on, he continued his extraordinary relief pitching and always ended his performance with his shout, "YOU GOTTA BELIEVE!"

After a while, another member of the team started to say, "As Tug says, 'You gotta believe, and I do." Sure enough, the teammate's performance improved. Others on the team began to believe because Tug McGraw believed. Before long the team had made up the ten games. And those same Philadelphia Phillies went on to win their division title, the National League playoffs, and the World Series.

Tug McGraw believed. He convinced others that he believed. Then they, in turn, believed because he believed so strongly.

A believer is a leader. Leaders motivate others—they don't wait for others to motivate them.

You can have the same effect on people. That same element that transformed a losing team into a World Championship team can help turn you into an effective communicator.

Of course, Tug had talent to begin with. And many teachers will tell a speaker that it all begins with having a wonderful speech with a carefully-crafted message prepared before getting up to face an audience. That's true. You gotta believe, and you also gotta have a good speech.

But a good speech delivered by a bad speaker might as well be a bad speech. The anticipated impact of that carefully-crafted message can be thwarted by a bad speaker.

On those happy occasions when a good speaker gets up to deliver a good speech, he still faces one great challenge that many would-be communicators forget: when that speaker steps up in front of that group of people, he must make them believe that he believes before they can believe what he believes.

To be believable, you must be credible. There is nothing more precious to a communicator than his credibility. It's the cement that creates the bond between speaker and audience.

I'm going to offer some insights on how to

create that bond, and how to avoid breaking it.

How to Establish Credibility

The first element is obvious. To be credible you must be truthful. Rhetoric is the art of persuasion, not the art of lying. "Don't tell me anything that isn't true" is still the best advice for a speaker.

But just because you say it, does not make it so. To convince me of your belief, you must possess a number of qualities that contribute to belief.

First, you must have an understanding of your role. When you address an audience, your job is to communicate. You are there to accomplish a mission—to lift these people up, to do something for them, to raise their spirits, inspire them, motivate them. You have a message to convey, yes, but you also have an attitude to communicate. And that attitude must be positive.

You must have conviction. Your belief can't be weak. It can't be mumbled. It must be stated with enthusiasm. Enthusiasm is probably the most catch-able disease known. When someone's enthusiasm is genuine and he displays it, others can't resist catching it. Part of being believed is your enthusiasm for what you are saying. People can see not only that you believe it but that believing it is good for you.

We have to be excited about what we believe. Our eyes will twinkle when we tell someone of our exciting belief. The fire will spread and other people will get excited. When that happens the work environment improves and everyone looks forward to new challenges.

When I speak, I like to give the audience all the energy I brought with me. In my briefcase I pack a tape recorder, spare tapes, extra batteries, my speech, a spare introduction, a few extra pictures and a few extra brochures—and all the energy I can cram into it.

And I want to go home with an empty briefcase.

I try to give that audience everything I've got. I want to sit down after I'm finished and feel that I've given something of myself to the audience, that I've expended myself. If a speaker doesn't finish with the feeling that he has expended himself, how can he expect to be believed?

The difference between a $2000 speaker and a $200 speaker could well be that the $200 speaker has failed to make the audience believe that he or she believes so they can believe what he or she believes. He or she has failed to transfer that energy to them.

CREDIBILITY. All that has been said is tied up with one word. We must be credible to be believed. We can't represent the opposite of what we are trying to get other people to be. Aristotle, the first great authority on rhetoric, talked about the *ethos* of the speaker. It means his ethical character—and his ability to communicate to the audience a clear impression of what kind of person he is.

The goal of communicating is to tell the truth and be believed. The one will do little good without the other.

There is an art to making the truth seem true. In law there's a saying, "It is not enough that justice be done. It must be *perceived* to be done." In making a speech, it is not enough that the truth be told. It must *seem* to be true.

Fiction writers have a good word: verisimilitude. It means simply "true-seeming." Naturally fictional stories are just that—fictional. They didn't really happen. They aren't really true. But they must *seem* true. Marianne Moore said the writer should create "imaginary gardens with real toads in them."

Similarly, in pursuing my hobby of acting in movies and in a television series like *Dallas*, I must be concerned with verisimilitude. The character I am portraying is not real. He is a product of some writer's imagination. But I must believe in him. If I don't, I certainly won't be able to make the audience believe. If I have my character say or do something out-of-character, the illusion of verisimilitude will be broken.

Once the spell is broken it's gone forever. If you have written a novel, and the reader ever says,

"Wait a minute—this didn't really happen, it's only a story," that reader will never finish reading your book. The spell is broken.

All communicators must strive to achieve verisimilitude. They must not only tell the truth, they must appear to be telling the truth. A businessman appearing on a television interview program will do his company little good no matter how candid he is if he sits in his chair with posture that suggests he has something to hide.

Your appearance is an important part of your credibility. That's why you don't see many successful salesmen wearing bow ties and brown suits.

Remember that your audience wants a reason to believe you. They also want to understand you. They can't believe what they can't understand. Talk at the level of the audience, but never condescend. You can't establish credibility if you can't first achieve intelligibility.

It is the responsibility of the speaker to be understood, not the responsibility of the audience to figure him out.

When Abraham Lincoln began a speech by saying, "Forescore and seven years ago," he was lucky indeed that the calculator had not yet been invented. People would surely have been pulling them out. (Years later, when people figured out what Lincoln had actually said at Gettysburg, the speech became famous—too late to do the speaker any good.)

Eye contact establishes believability. I cannot believe a person who won't look me in the eye. Whenever you look up from your text or your notes, look right into someone's eyes. Consider what you'll look like if you DON'T follow this advice! The audience will see you as a person whose eyes blink constantly, flittering up and down, always moving without seeing anything. You'll come across as someone who won't look at people.

I have conducted surveys after my speeches, asking those who felt that during the speech I looked directly into their eyes to raise their hands. Eight-five percent of one audience in Los Angeles raised their hands. I had actually only spoken to ten people. The people sitting around each of the ten I had looked directly at didn't know I was focusing on one person; they thought I was speaking to them individually. Electricity was there. That bond had been built, so that they were afraid to take their eyes from me.

How to Cancel Your Credibility

Your credibility is like your American Express card—it'll be cancelled if you don't meet your obligations.

The first obligation, of course, is to be truthful. But being truthful isn't quite enough!

I've got to believe that you believe that you

know what you're talking about before you can make me believe it.

I can't believe it if you cancel your credibility at the very outset by saying, "Of course, I'm no expert, but—"

Do you have enough confidence in what you are going to tell me to be relaxed yet energetic? I won't think so—if you grip the sides of the lectern so hard I can see the whites of your knuckles.

Noise

In communicating there is something we call noise. Noise is anything that compromises your message. Let me give you an example.

A mother is scolding her son for pulling up her prize violet. She tells him, "If you ever do that again, I'm gonna break your tongue." But as she says it, she smiles and winks. That's called noise in communication. That wink is the antithesis of the threat. Consequently, the child says, "She's not gonna break my tongue. I don't believe her."

That mother might as well be holding up a sign that says, "I don't mean what I say."

A doctor says, "You've got to quit smoking"— and at the same time, he reaches in his desk, pulls out a pack of cigarettes, gets one out, puts it in his mouth, and lights it. That's noise in communication.

Many speakers will get up and compromise

their believability with their non-verbal gestures as well as their verbal actions.

They will say to the audience, without ever realizing it, "Don't believe what I am saying because I don't believe it myself. I'm going to tell you what my research found, but I don't believe it."

If ever in the audience I get the feeling that there is noise coming from the podium, if I get the feeling you're saying something you haven't tried, something you yourself do not believe, what happens? I tune you out.

If I'm a woman, I dump my purse out on the table and start sorting out two years of accumulated junk. If I'm a man, I start going through my briefcase. I put it in my lap and start pulling out old business cards and messages.

You have broken the bond of communication.

Conversely, if I step up in front of that group of people and I'm dynamic, I'm excited, I'm enthusiastic, I build credibility in minutes. I entertain, I have their attention. Then I start to make pronouncements that I believe, and the audience feels that I believe. What is their tendency?

Their tendency is to start writing. The minute I see heads go down and hands go to the tablet, I know I have established credibility. I'm giving them my information, and they are writing it down, which is the highest compliment a lecturer can be paid. In effect, people are saying, "That is so important, I don't want to forget it." They know that only a part of what one hears is retained, and they don't want to forget the message.

It's one thing for the audience to start writing. But it's quite another for the speaker to start reading. When a speaker reads to an audience, he breaks the bond of believability. Reading to people has a demonstrable effect: it puts them to sleep. That's why parents read to their children at bedtime.

Most people in the audience would prefer to have you just mail them a copy of your talk than to have you read it to them. It is especially dangerous to read to an audience if one isn't a particularly good reader. In fact, as a rule only the most articulate and quick-witted people (President Reagan is a good example) can get away with reading a prepared text without losing the audience.

How much better it is to give your audience the feeling that you are talking directly to them, using fresh words.

That's even more true if you can make effective use of humor. (It is extremely difficult to make humor work for you when you are reading from a prepared text.) Humor can play an important role in creating the bond of credibility that ought to exist between speaker and audience. It relaxes people and prepares them to respond to the seriousness that comes after the humor.

Humor Is an Art in Itself

There's far more to humor than merely getting up and repeating the latest joke you've heard. For one thing, jokes can fall flat. And you'd be absolutely amazed at how often a speaker gets up and tells a joke only to find that last week's speaker beat him to the punch-line. News travels fast, but jokes travel faster—and wear out even quicker.

Instead of a joke, try telling something from your own life and experience that might be amusing. It takes a lot of work and a capacity for self-analysis to find just the right story from your own experience. But it's usually worth the effort. You will discover that in many cases the result is much funnier than the Las Vegas humor you planned to use. It helps you win the respect and affection and attention and belief of the audience— and on those rare occasions when everything works perfectly, it may help you win one of the highest compliments an audience can give you: laughter that grows quickly into applause.

When that happens, it signals that more than humor has been communicated; you've also gotten your meaning across with a delightful ironic twist, and the audience will show its appreciation for your skill.

If you decide to use humor from another source, be sure to follow the traditional rule of attribution that all honorable speakers employ. Credit your source! It'll give the audience one more sign of your integrity if you say something like this: "There's a story that So-and-So tells that illustrates my point perfectly..." Then tell the story or anecdote. But be sure it *does* illustrate your point.

Knowing when to quit is very important. Nervous repetition oversells the audience and undoes the good you've done. You begin to sound as if it's yourself you're trying to convince. Better to sit down too soon than to go on too long and have your audience think you've lost your place and started repeating yourself. Getting yourself into this kind of loop can be disastrous.

Conclusion

When a speaker conveys excitement, it's magic. (I don't mean hysteria, which merely annoys people; jumping from wall to wall and yelling at audiences is hardly the point.) It is as though a speaker says, "This spot in time and space is the center of your universe for the time we are together. I'm going to create that feeling by my enthusiasm, by my excitement. I am going to be so energetic, so dynamic up here, that you'll carry my energy level home with you."

If you aren't meeting these criteria, do something about it right now. Take action. Specifically, the next time you make any kind of presentation, tape it. Videotape is ideal if it can be done unobtrusively but sound alone will do. After the performance, analyze it. Give it the same objectivity you'd give your balance sheet. Go over it with a cold eye and an unbiased ear. Do YOU believe it? Why not? Do you find it hard to follow? Does your mind wander when you try to listen to it? Do you find yourself wanting to improve the way things are put?

If you're really serious, get some training. This can range from a few speech lessons to intensive seminars at a place like Ammerman Enterprises, where thousands of top executives have learned how to communicate in a variety of situations. For some, getting serious about communicating will include locating a good speechwriter.

The level of expertise you require will, of course, depend on the level at which you are competing. If you were a tennis player, would you go to Wimbledon without taking a full-time coach along? John McEnroe wouldn't and neither would Martina Navratilova.

Above all, drive out those negative thoughts and attitudes that wind up as negative gestures and messages to your audience.   Put yourself into a positive frame of mind and *stay there*. It's where everything worthwhile gets done in this world, including effective communication.

JOE CALHOON
New America, Inc.
Drawer 1210
Clovis, NM 88102-1210
(505) 763-4671

Joe Calhoon

Joe Calhoon speaks on prosperity and success from the principles set forth in the Divine oracles and the inherent strengths of a free enterprise system.

As an active member of the National Speakers Association and the New Mexico Speakers Association, he has assisted in promoting new chapter expansion.

He speaks to and consults with both business and civic organizations including the Clovis Chamber of Commerce, Clovis Downtown, Inc., the Clovis Board of Realtors, Gardenway Manufacturing, Realty USA, King Energy Systems and Nautilus Fitness Centers.

Joe Calhoon is founder and president of New America, Inc., a corporation which:

1. Engages custom marketing opportunities—turning ideas into profit

2. Introduces and promotes new business opportunities

3. Designs and implements sales and marketing programs

4. Contributes to ministries, charities, and other community and national projects.

5. Teaches pro-American and pro-Christian values; and

6. Is dedicated to serving God's most beautiful creation—you!

As a national management coordinator for an energy conservation company, he was responsible for opening fifteen new businesses as well as professionally developing hundreds of managers and thousands of sales people. His performance earned him "Coordinator of the Year" honors.

Joe resides with his wife, Diane, and son, Joseph Ralph Calhoon IV, in Clovis, New Mexico.

Joe and his wife have volunteered their time and efforts to such organizations as Faith America, Youth Employment Service, and Western Goals.

17

Divine Communication:
The Keys to Prosperity
and Success
by Joe Calhoon

"Then thou shalt have good success."
—*Joshua 1:8*

A New Definition for Prosperity and Success

Prosperity and success are two conditions we desire above all others. However, too few of us can say we truly possess either. Webster defines prosperity as financial success; success, as the gaining of wealth.

When we examine the lives of many wealthy individuals, we are inclined to question such simplified definitions. When we consider the effects of success and prosperity, as defined by Webster, on an individual such as Howard Hughes, for example, it becomes apparent that a re-evaluation of our priorities is in order. Despite all of his material acquisitions, Hughes led a lonely and desperate existence.

These Webster definitions can only provide limited internal fulfillment, but outlined in the Bible are the steps to true "prosperity and success." Joshua 1:8 (KJV) directs, "This book of the law shall not depart out of thy mouth; but thou shalt meditate therein day and night, that thou mayest observe to do according to all that is written therein: for then thou shalt make thy way prosperous, and then thou shalt have good success."

This secret to prosperity and success was revealed several thousand years ago. We simply read, meditate and do the Word of God—loving the Lord above all else and our neighbors as ourselves.

"Prosperity and success" redefined means having enough to spiritually and financially give to others, as we strive to achieve God-intended goals.

Experience in family living, aside from the spiritual blessings in life, are among the most fulfilling, loving and nurturing ones. Early in my life, as I pursued short-sighted definitions of prosperity and success, I faced problems. I was carrying guilt from a childhood experience. Rather than confront the problem directly, I took what I thought to be the best method for attaining happiness. I put all my God-given resources in the direction of having fun and accumulating wealth; instead of seeking the Lord—the true provider of love, contentment and joy.

Words and Actions Cannot be Recaptured

As one of seven brothers and sisters, sibling rivalry was a way of life. On the day of my biggest tragedy, I had been arguing and fighting intensely with my brother of whom I was most jealous. Jeff was tall, strong, and handsome; I had buck teeth, big ears, and wet the bed. That's not so bad but I was in the sixth grade! I was extremely cruel to my brother, because of my psychological problems. I was running a private advertising campaign to improve my own weak self-image. My behavior consisted of:

1. Arrogance (anxiously grasping for power when I felt weak);
2. Boastfulness (trying to look good when I suspected I wasn't); and

3. Rudeness (putting others down to hold myself up).

Our ability to use our tongues can either uplift people or devastate them. Blessing and cursing are in the power of the tongue. I now realize we have to take care in what we say, or it can often return to haunt us.

I verbally put Jeff down. Even though I eventually realized that what I actually said wasn't as severe as I believed at the time, nevertheless, the guilt that I ultimately assumed as a result of my careless words was severe. On this tragic day, my brother David and I had gone downtown. As a result of our conversation, I realized how cruel I had been to Jeff. I decided to apologize, then felt much better! I could not wait to go home and ask Jeff for forgiveness. I ran into the house, seeking Jeff but he had been struck by a careless driver in front of our house at lunch time. I got down on my knees and prayed, "God (if there is a God) let him live!" He was already dead. I assumed it was God's way of telling me that He did not exist. I was not really an atheist. I was mad at God. My alienation from God and my family left me pursuing Webster's definition of prosperity and success.

If That's All There Is, I Don't Want to Play That Game

A common conception about prosperity and success,

is that accumulation of material things is primary.

After graduating from high school I accepted a summer job to finance college, selling encyclopedias door to door. Within six weeks I was earning $3,000 per month, driving a company car, managing a crew of sales people, and receiving plenty of recognition. I was on the stair steps to prosperity and success . . . or was I? Peace of mind and inner fulfillment eluded me.

Attaining the material goal of a new Cadillac left me unsatisfied. My next goal was the "American dream" of owning my own home. But despite the extravagance of my home, I was still unsatisfied. The house, in fact, made the car less satisfying. I wanted more prosperity and success. So a cabin nestled in the majestic mountains of Colorado was the last in a series of unfulfilling acquisitions. As I walked up those materialistic stairs, each proceeding step was less meaningful. Eventually, I discovered that neither the car, the house, nor the cabin could provide happiness.

Ralph Waldo Emerson said, "Hitch your wagon to a star." I gradually discovered that in order to achieve true contentment, we must re-evaluate what kind of star our happiness relies on. I had chosen a vision which was distorted. It excluded a moral code which I now realize is the only factor in determining our contribution in life.

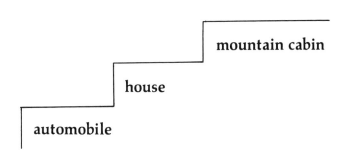

We Often Get What We Pay For With Free Advice

An advisor once told me, "To be prosperous and successful financially, you have to do one of two things: either get in deep financial debt or pay for everything with cash." He seemed to have it well calculated, playing the leverage game with his corporations. Unlimited gain and limited risks. Personally, he owned everything free and clear. Consequently, I went personally in debt up to my neck, "going for it." I further pursued prosperity and success. It is hard to see the picture when you're inside the frame.

My life was full of anxiety and fast-lane action. In pressure situations I drank heavily.

I was not doing well; my life was pretense. I had not emotionally matured, was still arrogant, boastful, and rude. (At least I no longer wet the bed.)

I falsely told people how great I was doing. I believe people are more deceitful than honest when it comes to discussing money matters. I was not honest with myself or others about my wealth. I exaggerated to make myself appear successful. Others, it seems, who have truly attained "prosperity and success" humbly joke about how little they have.

The company which employed me went bankrupt. My income plummeted to zero. My monthly obligations, though, included first mortgages, second mortgages, lines of credit, credit cards, and scores of other fast-lane habits which were very costly.

My economic plight indicated liquidation or bankruptcy. My thinking had become so narrow, I could no longer entertain the scores of alternatives that were actually available. I was also struggling with drug as well as alcohol abuse. It was the bottom of the barrel. It was at this time in my life that my lifelong spiritual vacuum was becoming dramatically apparent.

Getting Out of Myself and Into Someone Else

I was alone and depressed one evening, so I called my Dad and told him my sad story.

I asked Dad for advice on my options—bankruptcy or liquidation. He was recovering from painful disc surgery on his lower back. He told me that he wished he could DIE!

Talking with my father, large tears rolled down my face. Then I hung up and said, "World, you can mess with me, but don't mess with my Dad!" This was the turning point in my life. I was truly ready to assert my manhood, to strive for the maximum potential God had placed within me. After years of personal pity, for the first time someone else's problem was more important than mine! I got out of myself and into someone else. I was now ready to give and serve.

The pursuit of prosperity and success had left me frustrated. I wanted a new basis for life, one that would be positive and exhilarating. I was tired of superficiality and emptiness.

My fast-lane was a road that had led me directly to hell. I was destined for an eternity of misery if I did not change. I turned around and got back on the path going the other way. I realized that if you have never run head on with the devil, you are probably running the same direction he is. I realized it was going to be a challenging and difficult path and would take all the discipline I could muster. But I also realized obstacles develop character and a sense of personal integrity. These I had never previously known. As Dottie Walters, my publisher, says, "Keep your eyes open. The road to success may require a you-turn!"

I now devote my life to sharing truths of the Divine oracles in a simple, straightforward way. Nobody has all the answers, and I cannot tell you how to live or think. But I hope you will realize some of the wisdom which I gained as I moved from drug and alcohol addiction to true "prosperity and success."

Looking for God or Man

Rosie Grier, the former professional football great, delivered a moving speech in Phoenix. He explained how people let us down. Rosie said the family of President Kennedy took him in as their own. He would do anything for John and Bobby. He was there when Bobby was assassinated. "People will always let us down. They go and die, or something," Rosie said. "Only One has never let me down."

God's nature is difficult to understand. Impossible to comprehend. He sent us His Son Jesus Christ so that we might understand His nature. Jesus is the only way I could grasp the meaning of God. I had to have faith in Jesus, repent my sins, confess Jesus Christ as the Son of God and be baptized for the remission of my sins. Then God began to work in my life.

U.S. Senator Strom Thurmond said, "The

concept of serving one's fellow man made a profound impact in my life. After examining the ministry of Jesus Christ, as described in the Scriptures, I found that Christ's formula for an abundant life—namely following Him and serving others—was true."

God's Formula for Prosperity and Success

God's instruction provides us with the requirements for the true definition of "prosperity and success." Read the Word, meditate on the Word, and do all that is written in the Word. Then you will truly be prosperous and successful.

$$\text{Read} + \text{Meditate} + \text{Do} = \text{Prosperity and Success}$$

Here are the basic requirements. Einstein said, "If you can't explain it simply, you don't understand it well enough."

The Promise and The Price

The definition becomes an equation; read, meditate, and do. Then receive the benefits. Easy to understand but requiring discipline.

Life is conditional. There is the promise and the price. Nationally acclaimed speaker Jim Rohn told me, "If you want things to get better for you, you have to get better."

1. If you do this—you get this.
2. If you drink too much—you will be hungover. (Believe me, I know.)
3. If you are loving to others they will be loving to you.
4. If you misbehave—you will miss your opportunity.
5. Find the truth—the truth will set you free.

Zig Ziglar shared with me his formula for personal development.

$$\text{Positive Input} + \text{Positive Thinking} + \text{Positive Activities} = \text{Positive Results}$$

The opposite is also true. Negative input leads to negative thinking. Negative activities lead to negative results. If we want to change our results (the promise), we need to change the input positively (the price).

Take a long look at the promise and the price:

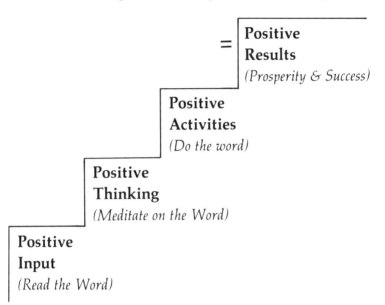

$=$ **Positive Results**
(Prosperity & Success)

Positive Activities
(Do the word)

Positive Thinking
(Meditate on the Word)

Positive Input
(Read the Word)

The price is always easier to pay if we have a goal or purpose.

What Is the Point?

There is a purpose for our "prosperity and success." We are meant to give to others. Andrew Carnegie kept a note in his top desk drawer as a reminder of his lifelong purpose. It said, "I'll work the first half of my life making a fortune and spend the last half of my life giving it away." I am not so sure of when my time is up, so I spend part of my week making money and part of my week giving it away. The first big word I ever learned was philanthropy. A philanthropist is simply anyone who strives to improve and promote the welfare of the human community. All of us have the potential to be philanthropic. When we give to others we are rewarded ten fold in spiritual, physical, and intellectual abundance. The time had arrived to implement God's requirements for my "prosperity and success."

Charles "Tremendous" Jones said, "You will be the same person you are today ten years from now, except for the people you meet and the books you read." That is why I have read the Bible from cover to cover and I love my best friend, Jesus Christ.

I also read *Living Positively One Day at a Time* by Robert Schuller. I wanted some new stair steps that would direct me to "prosperity and success." I found them in these three great virtues—faith, hope, love. These steps are built of substance and integrity. Love for others—not my own lust for merely a car, home, and cabin.

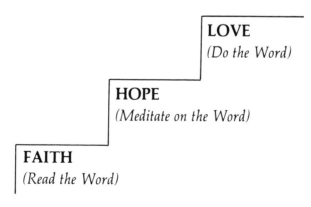

LOVE
(Do the Word)

HOPE
(Meditate on the Word)

FAITH
(Read the Word)

These virtues are not in our intellect. They come from the heart. Cavett Robert said, "Listen to your heart, it has knowledge your mind will never comprehend."

1. Faith comes from reading the Word.
2. Hope comes from meditating on the Word.
3. Love is demonstrated in doing the Word.

Faith Changed My Life

As I developed faith in God my life changed. I began to have hope. Hope does not mean a wish or a dream. Hope is assurance. When I began developing hope, as a result of faith, I *knew* my life was going to get better.

My faith rejected the habits of drugs, alcohol and all my fast-lane life for something far better. I knew there was something better—for me! I had hope! And when I found hope, I could really love others! Faith led me to hope. Hope led me to love. Each of these virtues fortifies and enhances the others.

Obedience in All Things—Love or Lust

My character continued to strengthen. My friend, Iggy Vargas, once told me, "If it does not kill you, it will strengthen you." I was getting strong! I felt I could really love, so it was not surprising that at 31 years old the woman who was to become my wife came into my life.

I always dreamed about a woman who would be attractive, bright, talented, funny, kind, a good housekeeper, a good cook, sensitive, intelligent, have a loving heart and a good figure, too. My wife has all of that and more. She loves the Lord!

I love my wife! Love is for others at the expense of self—it's the desire to give. Lust is for self at the expense of others—it's the desire to get.

Learn by My Example

I've told you my story and the fact that I took the wrong path in aiming specifically for prosperity and success. They say that everyone serves a purpose in life, if only to exist as a "horrible example." If you want to use me as your "horrible example" in life, by all means, be my guest. But please—I ask you to consider combining some of the major points that I found out the hard way, to make your own path to happiness more direct, less thorny and perhaps speedier.

NUMBER ONE: Read the Word, the Bible, and you can't help but improve your positive input.

NUMBER TWO: Meditate on the Word . . . that means more than just thinking about its ideas and truths. Discuss them; research them; speak them; memorize them. Fashion them into a Plan that becomes a part of you because God knows what is best for you.

NUMBER THREE: DO the Word. Participate in charitable activities. Work for the poor, the aged, the hungry, the mentally impaired. Volunteer for your church activities. *Give something back!* We should live our lives exactly as His Word tells us to live them. We should know His Word so well that we conduct our lives "according to all that is written therein."

You have been blessed in life—because you took the opportunity to hear this message. Not that MY words are a blessing in themselves . . . but HIS Words ARE!

I can promise you as He promised you. The results of these Promises and Prices will be Positive Results, True "Prosperity and Success." The Promises are real. The Prices are small for what lies at the end . . . because what lies at the end is SO VERY WORTHWHILE—that you'll wonder what took you so long to get there, and why you didn't start on this path sooner.

BILL OBERG, Consultant
Healthcare Communications
426 Howard Street
Wheaton, IL 60187
(312) 690-7887 • Res. (312) 668-0201

Bill Oberg

Bill Oberg is a nationally recognized speaker and consultant on communications, specializing in the healthcare field. He has addressed various healthcare audiences on doctor-patient relationships, practice management, medical listening techniques, getting and keeping patients, motivation for patient compliance and how to effectively use educational materials in healthcare settings.

Bill received both undergraduate and graduate degrees in communications, with concentrations in radio-TV and drug abuse education.

Bill's professional and business experience has included being Director of the Instructional Media Center at Wheaton (Illinois) College and educational materials development manager for the American Dental Association. He has presented communications skills seminars for national, regional, state and local healthcare meetings. He has consulted with numerous organizations on such diverse topics as health museum development, innovative audiovisuals for patient and professional motivation, health services marketing and World's Fair health exhibit planning. He has also distinguished himself as a professional magician in both stage and close-up settings.

Bill's memberships include the National Speaker's Association, the World Future Society, the National Association of Professional Consultants, the Society of American Magicians and the International Brotherhood of Magicians.

18

Doctor-Patient Communication: "What Was That About My Interproximal Surfaces???"
by Bill Oberg

"When anything fails today, usually nobody is at fault and the cause seems to be communication."
—Donald F. Bowers, D.D.S.

In 1971, when I began conducting patient education seminars for a national dental organization, there was a burning question which I heard from dental professionals wherever I went: WHAT

IS THE KEY TO ATTRACTING AND KEEPING PATIENTS IN OUR PRACTICES?

The question emerged out of the needs of that day: to know how to relate to patients so that preventive dentistry philosophies and practices could be effectively presented to patients.

In the 1980's, this time out of the context of consumer advocacy, institutional advertising, dental/ medical malpractice and competition for each and every consumer dollar, the question of a decade ago is still with us. I believe the answer to that question is the same today as it was in 1971 . . . and will remain the same for some time to come: TO ATTRACT AND KEEP PATIENTS, WE MUST TREAT THEM LIKE PEOPLE!

The late Dr. Bob Barkley once reflected, "Few things affect the attitude and educational capacity of a patient as much as the manner in which he or she is received in a dental office or a clinic *as a person.*" This is probably true of physicians' offices and other healthcare settings, too, hence the applicability of most principles discussed in this chapter to any healthcare providers.

Ms. Erma Angevine, former director of the Consumer Federation of America, told an American Dental Association Dental Health Conference some years ago, "People want *people* dentists, not *tooth* dentists. One consumer told me, 'My dentist only talks to my teeth!'"

How Well Are We Communicating with Patients?

Consider what some surveys tell us:

> *The number of patients who say they will leave a physician if dissatisfied jumped from 38 to 59 per cent in the last 20 years. Over two-thirds of the patients who switched cited this primary reason: the doctor was cold, abrupt and impersonal.*

—Medical Economics: May 30, 1983

According to a 1983 *Dental Economics* survey, the major reason patients leave their dentists is roughness and inadequately-explained treatment.

> *Up to 70 per cent of all recommendations for medication, home care, exercise and diet are not followed by patients.*

—**B. Ingersoll,**
Behavioral Aspects in Dentistry

> *When mothers were sent to the (pediatric) clinic, they expected the physicians to be warm and sympathetic to them as well as their children . . . but only 5 per cent of doctors' conversations were classified as being personal or friendly to the mother.*

—Medical World News:
January 19, 1973.

What Can We Do to Improve Doctor/Patient Communication?

Communication is a natural skill but like all of the other health skills, it is best when practiced and honed to its art. This chapter will focus on four key issues. Your "lab" work on your communications skills can direct your practice into a new dimension. Consider these important questions:

1. **How do you see your patients?**
2. **Do you and your patients talk the same language?**
3. **How well do you listen to your patients?**
4. **How do you come across to your patients?**

How Do You See Your Patients?

Beyond the Medical History Form. Most medical/ dental offices will ask a new patient to fill out a personal and/or a medical history form when he or she visits the office for the first time. The information gathered through these forms gives the medical/dental team basic medical and biographical information about the patient and his/her family to help the doctor with the patient's diagnosis and treatment. With a strong health data and health attitude profile, your practice can have a valuable tool for patient information, communication, therapy compliance and patient rapport.

In many offices there is no personal interview

of a patient after he/she fills out the requested forms. *This is unfortunate.* Even the briefest of personal interviews, preferably conducted by the doctor, can cause the patient to feel more comfortable and relaxed. In *Communication in the Dental Office,* Froelich, Bishop and Dworkin[1] explain basic interviewing techniques for the office.

The point is, you need to know more about a person than just the data gathered from the forms the patient fills out. Psychological profiles and questionnaires are available to probe how patients feel about their health. The doctor can ask the patients about their health IQ (not just dental health), health values, interests, personal details about family members and other personal matters which can be used in subsequent visits to show the patient that the doctor and the office staff have an ongoing and *growing* interest in the patients' total health and welfare *as persons.*

The Sweetest Sound in the World. Someone has said that the sound of one's name being spoken is the sweetest sound in the world. One's name is the essence of one's *person.* That's why it is important that on initial contact with patients, whether it be on the telephone or in person, that each patient's name be noted, correctly spelled, and correctly pronounced. Even if you *think* you know how it's spelled, ask anyway. You may find a Mr.

Smith is really a Mr. *Smyth*. And use the name often in conversation with the patient—especially at the beginning and closing of office visits.

It is a good idea to ask the patient upon his/her initial visit what name he/she would prefer to be called by. Some may prefer "Mrs. Jones" at first, then will become comfortable with "Mary" at a later visit. Other patients may suggest a nickname. The important thing is that you cared enough to ask about this personal matter.

One dentist received a rude awakening when a female patient who, after having been called by her first name in an office where all patients were spoken to on a first-name basis, finally confided to the dentist the anger she felt about this "too familiar" treatment.

If you're worried about remembering a patient's name, frequent spoken use of the name will help you remember. There is no such thing as a "bad memory." Memory is *learned*. Harry Lorayne's book, *How to Develop a Super-Power Memory*[2] and other publications of its kind, can help you learn simple steps to remember names. The most important key is to *want* to know and remember the name of each *person* who is your patient. It can be done!

Reading between the Lines. People frequently bring hidden agendas to their medical or dental office visit. What they tell you is their problem may

346 / The Great Communicators

not be the real problem at all! Questions about loose teeth may hide a concern about having to get complete dentures or what such treatment might cost. Questions about changing skin conditions might hide the real problem: fear of skin cancer. You need to observe and listen to each patient carefully to find these hidden agendas and cut through to the patient's real needs as quickly as possible.

Observe your whole patient—how he or she holds the body, walks, how the face looks (worried? tense? absorbed with other matters?), what objects they carry, signs of wariness, and the like. There are several ways that such reading of patients' non-verbal messages will help you in the medical/dental office.

1. **You will have a more accurate understanding of what the patient means when he/she is talking.** (And if the non-verbal messages are at odds with the verbal messages, believe the non-verbal messages!)
2. **You will get instantaneous information** about how the patient "feels."
3. **If your reading of the non-verbal cues tells you whether the patient is mad, sad, glad or scared, your response to the patient can be appropriate.** Your response to a sad patient might differ greatly from your response to a mad patient!

The text, *How to Read a Person Like a Book,* by Gerard I. Nierenberg and Henry Calero[3], and Gary Kreps' *Nonverbal Communication in Dentistry* in the January-February 1981 issue of *The Dental Assistant*[4] will introduce you to the basics of non-verbal communication. *Irresistible Communications: Creative Skills for the Health Professional* by Mark King, et. al.[5], presents a more sophisticated analysis of non-verbal cues. These and other texts such as *Body Language* by Julius Fast[6], Edwin T. Hall's *The Silent Language*[7], and *Kinesics: The Power of Silent Command* by M. Cundiff[8], can help you and your staff become more at ease with and adept at observing patients' behavior and using what you observe in your treatment plans.

Do You and Your Patients Talk the Same Language?

Healthcare professionals live in two worlds: *the world of things* (of *streptococcus mutans* and interproximal surfaces . . . of atrial fibrillations and amalgams and radiographs . . .) and the *world of language* (in which we try to talk with our patients about these "things.") We are successful communicators to the degree that we can manage to put these two worlds together in such a way that we can understand each other . . .

"The greatest problem in communication is the illusion that it has been achieved.'

—Anomymous

Putting the two "worlds" together is sort of like making a differential diagnosis in communication, looking at all the little parts of the whole, then determining how best to talk with those *"persons* who are our patients." *Let's look at a few examples.*

Pulling Is Better Than Extraction. A dentist acquaintance of mine was trying to explain to a dental school clinic adult patient why it was important to save one of her teeth. The dentist said, "Whatever we do, we must not *extract* the tooth. I'm going to suggest that we do a root canal treatment on the tooth." To which the patient replied, ". . . and if that doesn't work, you can just pull it, can't you?"

Here was a technical term (extraction) which had no meaning (or possibly the wrong meaning) to the patient.

Where Did Mr. Jones Go? Mr. Jones had come to the office for a dental procedure which had to be done in two parts at the same visit. After completing part one, the dentist said to Mr. Jones, "Why don't you go outside for just a few minutes. I'll call you when I'm ready to finish the procedure." The dentist fully expected the man to go back to the reception area where he had been reading a magazine before treatment. When it came time to complete the treatment, however, Mr. Jones was nowhere to be found! An exasperated but relieved dental assistant finally found Mr. Jones sitting *outside* the building, on the front steps, and returned him to the operatory. Mr. Jones said shyly to the dentist, "You told me to go *outside* for a few minutes . . ."

In this case there was an *easy* word (outside) which had a different meaning to the doctor and the patient.   That reminds me of another "easy" word—the four-letter word *"fast"*. If I use that word in reference to a racehorse, a *"fast"* racehorse is one which runs very rapidly: it is a good horse on which to invest a couple of bucks.

That is, unless the *"fast"* racehorse has been tied *"fast"*, in which case he is no longer *"fast"*, because he is *"fast."*

Let's take that same word *"fast"*—and our *"fast"* racehorse ran very rapidly—and use it in reference to a color. If it is a *"fast"* color it doesn't run at all! Or take the same word in a religious context. When we *"fast"*,.we abstain from something. But that same "easy" word, at least in an older generation, used in reference to a young lady, meant a young lady who abstained from virtually nothing! ("Fast" story, courtesy of Dr. Warren Guthrie, Western Reserve University.)

Conclusion: "easy" words do not necessarily make for "easy" communication!

Who Do You Think You're Talking To? A dentist was explaining periodontal disease to a woman in her forties. He told her that if her hands bled when she washed them, she would be very concerned. Why then shouldn't she be concerned about her bleeding gums when she brushed her teeth? The patient stiffened up and exclaimed, *"Who do you think you are talking to?"* The title of the dentist's article reporting the foregoing story gives the moral: "Keeping It 'Simple' May Mean You're Talking Down to Patients!"[9] The dentist in question was made painfully aware that he should never underestimate his patients . . . they are often smarter than he thought. The doctor, by the way, never did regain the patient's confidence in him, or her proposed dental treatment! Even "easy" words can be insulting!

A New York Plumber Speaks Out. Dr. Jerome Mittleman, in his *Once Daily* newsletter[10] tells the story of the New York plumber who once wrote to the city research bureau pointing out that he had used hydrochloric acid to clean out sewer pipes and inquired whether there was any possible harm. The first written reply read,

> *"The efficacy of hydrochloric acid is indis-*

putable but the corrosive residue is incompatible
with metallic permanence."

The plumber then thanked them for this information approving his procedure! The dismayed research bureau wrote again, this time,

"We cannot assume responsibility for the production of toxic and noxious residue with hydrochloric acid and suggest you use an alternative procedure."

Again the plumber thanked them for their approval. Finally, the bureau chief, worried about the New York sewers, called in a third scientist (a *good* communicator) who wrote:

"Don't use hydrochloric acid! It eats hell out of the pipes!"

Here is **plain speaking** at its best! Plain speaking to the audience works!

Here's a summary of some of the points we have made about talking with your patients (or even with your office staff, family members, or others!):

1. **Watch your use of jargon** (technical terms). Such jargon may have no meaning for your patients.
2. **Watch "easy words", too.** They may have different meanings to you and your patients. And they might be "insulting" to some.
3. **"Plain speaking" to the audience works.** If

352 / The Great Communicators

you know your patients' "word world" and address it thoughtfully!

Our final suggestion: get in the habit of talking "benefits" to patients in all your case presentations. Everything you do *for* and *to* the *persons* who are your patients has a benefit for them. (Better health, improved appearance, money saved, greater comfort are but a few.)

How Well Do You Listen to Your Patients?

Listening—a new way of caring for your patients as persons. Have you ever thought of why God has given man two ears and only one mouth? Some have suggested that the two-ears-to-one-mouth ratio tells us of the relative importance of listening over speaking in the communication mix. (Others have suggested that man's two-*eyes*-to-one-mouth ratio suggests the importance of observation in the communication mix, too!)

"No man would listen to you talk if he didn't know it was his turn next!"

—Edgar W. Howe

Dr. Ken Olsen, a clinical psychologist friend of mine, tells of sitting at breakfast during a dental meeting. He listened to a group of salespersons talking. As the conversation continued he became aware that none of the persons was really listening to anyone else—each was simply waiting his turn to speak!

When you listen to your patients, you must *want* to understand them and how they feel.

There is a difference between *hearing* and *listening.* Hearing is an acoustical phenomenon. Listening is an interpersonal skill. And like CPR or Heimlich *skills* in the medical/dental office, the skill of listening can save many potentially-deteriorating relationships. Here are some simplified tips about listening:

1. **Take time to listen.** You must *want* to be a good listener!
2. **Give your undivided attention.** Don't be distracted.
3. **Increase your listening span.** Don't interrupt the patient.
4. **Avoid overreaction to delivery or content.** Keep calm!
5. **Make the environment conducive to listening.** (QUIET!)
6. **Use reinforcing verbal or non-verbal signs.** "I understand . . ." or "What I think you're saying is . . ."
7. **Ask for feedback!** Encourage patients to talk even more! "If I use terms you don't understand, tell me . . ."

> *"A good listener is not only popular everywhere, but after a while he knows something.'*
>
> —**Wilson Mizner**

How Do You Come Across to Your Patients?

The One-Day Self Audit—Grading Yourself. Do you know if you communicate well with your patients (or staff)? Why not audit your communication skills? It could revolutionize your practice![11-14]

Here's a quick audit for starters:

1. **Record patient conversations on audio tape or video tape.**

   Most patients will give you permission to do so when you tell them it is for the personal growth of you and your staff. Play tapes back privately, for personal critiquing. Discuss selected tapes in staff meetings.

2. **Conduct patient surveys.**

   Ask your patients in a mail survey what they like or dislike about your practice. Be sure to enclose a stamped, self-addressed envelope! Sample survey questions can be found in the April, 1976, and the April, 1983 issues of *Dental Economics,* also in the June, 1980 *Dentalpractice.* [12-13]

3. **Start "rap sessions" with groups of your patients.**

   Begin by inviting patients you feel will be the most open and articulate with you. Read the book *How to Choose and Use Your Doctor*[14] for direction and encouragement.

Postscript

Remember where we began?—stressing the importance of treating patients as *persons,* and in so doing attracting and keeping them as patients for as long as you both agree to! It means treating them, listening to them, speaking to them as people and *most of all,* giving them more than what they expected, more than what they've paid for. (They don't even "owe you" referrals!) As professional consultant Bob Levoy has said so often, "We must strive for the bonus of patient enthusiasm, not just the adequacy of patient satisfaction."

Then your patients will become your friends and the best promoters of you and your practice!

References

1. Froelich, Robert, et. al., *Communication in the Dental Office,* (St. Louis: C.V. Mosby Co.), 1976.

2. Lorayne, Harry, *How to Develop a Super-Power Memory,* (New York: New American Library/Signet Books), 1974.

3. Nierenberg, Gerard I., and Calero, Henry, *How to Read a Person Like a Book,* (New York: Cornerstone), 1972.

4. Kreps, Gary, "Nonverbal Communication in Dentistry," *The Dental Assistant,* Vol. 50, No. 1, Jan-Feb, 1981.

5. King, Mark et. al., *Irresistible Communication: Creative Skills for the Health Professional,* (Philadelphia: W. B. Saunders Co.), 1983.

6. Fast, Julius, *Body Language,* (New York: Pocket Books), 1984.

7. Hall, Edwin T., *The Silent Language,* (New York: Doubleday & Co.), 1973.

8. Cundiff M., *Kinesics: The Power of Silent Command,* (Englewood Cliffs, N.J.: Prentice Hall), 1972.

9. Klarfeld, Nathan, "Keeping It 'Simple' May Mean You're Talking Down to Patients," *Dental Student,* October 1978.

10. Mittleman, Jerome, *The Once Daily, Inc.,* 263 West End Avenue, New York, N.Y. 10023.

11. Kress, Gerry and Silversin, Jack, "Patient Feedback Project Provides Real Measure of Patient Satisfaction," *Dental Economics,* April 1983.

12. Wilson, Richard S., "Let Your Patients Tell You What They Want," *Dentalpractice,* June 1980.

13. Morabito, Peter, "What Do Your Patients Think of You? Just Ask Them!", *Dental Economics,* April 1976.

14. Belsky, Marvin S. and Gross, Leonard, *How to Choose and Use Your Doctor* (Greenwich, CT: Fawcett Publications), 1975.

The secret of the man who is universally interesting is that he is universally interested.

—William Dean Howells

DANIEL E. PENDLEY
S.ales C.ommunication I.nstitute
824 Camino Real, Suite 206
Redondo Beach, CA 90277
(213) 543-4650

Daniel E. Pendley

Daniel E. Pendley is a dynamic speaker who has taught thousands of sales people how to open doors and close sales. Because of Daniel's burning desire to deliver the best sales training, he is often referred to others and is asked back again and again.

Daniel's excitement and energy, blended with inspiration and education, give his listeners a "How To" approach they can use immediately. His goalsetting and psychological insights show his audience how to open opportunities and overcome obstacles.

Daniel is a nationally recognized speaker, sales trainer and communicator. He is President and Founder of Sales Communication Institute (SCI). Based in Redondo Beach, California, he holds a Real Estate License in both California and Ohio. In 1983 Daniel co-founded Heritage Limousines in Los Angeles. He is a Certified Instructor for Jerry Bresser's "List More, Sell More" workshops.

Born in West Carrollton, Ohio, Daniel began his real education at the age of 17. He was newly married with a growing family. From that time in his life he progressed from selling shoes, working in steel foundries selling direct, retail, in real estate to owning several companies. He is an entrepreneur and world reknowned sales trainer and business executive.

Daniel has numerous sales awards. Among these are "The Professional Sales Master Award," "New and Used Car Salesman of the Year," "1981-82 Realtor Top 1% Club." Nominated "Ohio Professional of the Year," "Top Sales Lister." He has listed over 100 For Sale By Owner private sellers.

Daniel has earned the right through his own hard work, perserverence and determination to teach others how to develop their ability. He communicates on a "We" rather than "I" level. His topic is: LIVE AND PROSPER THROUGH EFFECTIVE COMMUNICATION.

Daniel has a complete cassette tape series, "How To" workshops and enjoys constant speaking engagements all over the United States.

19

GIVE MORE, GET MORE
Through Effective Communication
by Daniel E. Pendley

"If you think you can, or if you think you can't . . . You are right."

—Henry Ford

We were so young. My sweetheart was only 16, I was 17, both of us students in high school. We had pleaded our case to the Montgomery County Courts. The judge granted us the right to be married. We found a one bedroom apartment on

Elm Street in my home town, West Carrollton, Ohio. I was determined to support my wife and the baby on the way, while I continued to finish school. I had only one coat, a blue blazer. I put it on and set out to find a job. At our local Mall there were 26 shoe stores. I figured someone must need a worker, so I would call on them one by one. The first shop was Butler Shoes. I told the manager I would do anything; sweep up, stock boxes, wash windows, anything. I was a good worker who would show up every day.

The manager grinned and said he could see I was a good salesman! He gave me a job. Wow! $1.60 an hour for 30 hours a week, plus a commission. I could go to school and work over the weekends and evenings. It sounded like a lot of money until I tried to pay the rent, groceries, insurance, gas, electricity and doctor bills. The money soon ran out. Despite my constant hard work we were forced to go on welfare. Then our baby boy was born. We were officially a family, but a very poor one.

When school was over I got a job working for my electrician uncle digging ditches and hanging dry wall in the construction field. In the mornings before I went to that job, I had another early bird one loading aluminum siding on trucks. I worked 14 hours a day with my back and my hands, but it was still not enough to feed my family. I finally found a job paying $5 an hour in a hot steel foundry. It was hard labor in every sense of the word. But it was just enough more to let us buy a TV, a car and a better place to live. However, we barely paid the bills each payday. Looking back now, I realize I might have stayed at that level forever. "If you have to stand in garbage you eventually get comfortable and don't mind it." But I dreamed of selling real estate.

When I told my foundry co-workers then that I would someday be a successful, professional, serving-people type real estate broker and I would become rich, they laughed at me. "Sure you will," they teased me. "And we will all be movie stars and go to Hollywood."

Anything You Can Conceive and Believe, You Can Achieve—*Marcus Aurelius*

John, a friend of mine, suggested I try Direct Sales. What an eye opener. My friend was making more money in one day than I was in a week of blood, sweat and tears. He trained me and I went to work for him. This job enabled me to have the time and money to take the real estate classes I had hoped for. I learned enough about sales to look for even higher paying sales jobs. I applied and was hired as an automobile salesman.

The same ideas my friend had taught me

worked equally as well in this field. I was named "Rookie of the Year" by my dealership, then "Used Car Salesman of the Year" and finally "New and Used Car Salesman of the Year." I combined the hard work, drive and persistence of the physical work with the sales information my friend had given me in his training.

When I passed my real estate test I was 24 years old. Everyone seemed surprised when I sold a million three hundred in properties in my first six months. But I had discovered something. No one sells cars, or products, or property. There is only one thing to "sell"—people. Successful selling is service. When I applied my serving principles to this new field, they worked exactly as well as they had elsewhere.

Soon I was awarded the top "FSBO" lister ("For Sale By Owner") award in my company and received numerous other awards and titles. It took seven years to fulfill the dream I had seen while the sweat was rolling into my eyes in the Steel Foundry.

Those foundry workers are still where they were. They had no vision, no dream to hitch their hearts to.

Anything You Can Dream

Next I bought all the tapes and books I could find

on success. I memorized the materials of Earl Nightengale, Cavett Robert, Zig Ziglar, Ty Boyd, Art Linkletter, Dr. Robert Schuller. I listened to them and read their ideas every single day. Their ideas gave me strength. They confirmed what I had learned. "Anything you desire and can see yourself accomplishing can become a reality if you are willing to pay the price."

I could hardly wait to teach what I had learned to others who might still be standing in the garbage. The opportunity came through the internationally famous speaker and sales trainer Jerry Bresser and his real estate seminars, "LIST MORE, SELL MORE." Zig Ziglar had taught me "If you help enough people get what they want, you'll get what you want." I had proved it. To give is to receive. By giving what I knew, I would receive the fulfillment of my new dreams—to become a national sales speaker. Here are my principals of success through communication which I teach to my students:

1. **List the problem.** You have to be able to see what is wrong to be able to fix it.
2. **Show people you care.** They don't care how much you know until they know how much you care. Show caring in every gesture, every word you say, every action you take. Think of the other guy.

3. **Ask Questions.** When you ask your clients questions you can see how to better understand their problems and represent to them the solutions. 95% of the solution is the understanding of the problem.

A Good Communicator Acts in the Best Interest of His Client

Professional communicators give their clients enough good information so that they can make positive sales decisions. Good communicators never pressure clients into bad decisions. That is the difference between a sharp professional sales person and a "con" man. A "con" man does not believe in what he is doing for the client. He believes only in himself. He is thinking of his own good.

The professional communicator is genuinely concerned about helping the customers to achieve their goals.

A Good Rule in Communicating

Obtain a tentative commitment. Here is an example. My brother who is a psychologist in Ohio once had a young man come to his door who was the best communicator he had ever met.

As the young man walked up to the front door he saw my brother's name on the mail box. The salesman said, "How do you do, Dr. Pendley. My name is John. I am selling the finest cleaning products available. This is a beautiful home. I know you do not have anything dirty in your home, Dr. Pendley, but if you did, these cleaning products would prove to be miracle workers. They can clean up any problem. Even though I know you probably do not have a cleaning problem, I wanted to let you know what I have while I am in your beautiful neighborhood. I would be glad to demonstrate by cleaning anything with a stain or spot in your home, to show you how good these products are!"

My brother laughed and said, "Sure, come on in. I do have something dirty you can clean." He walked the boy through the house and out to the garage. There lay a disreputable green mat from an old MG my brother was restoring. It dripped with grease. He looked at the boy. "Here son, clean that mat. That's pretty dirty." "Yes Sir! Dr. Pendley," the boy said. He took the bag off his shoulders, put it down beside the mat, pulled a big brush out of his back pocket, squirted a little cleaning fluid on it and knelt down.

Just at that point he stood back up and asked, "Dr. Pendley, before I clean that mat, if I can get the spots out, will you buy my cleaning product?" Larry said, "We'll see."

The boy said, "O.K." He got down and started scrubbing and rubbing. In a minute and a half, sure enough, a bright green area appeared. He then looked at Larry and said, "Dr. Pendley, I know you don't have anything really dirty in your home, but maybe there are some lime deposits in your bathroom. This stuff works wonders on lime deposits. Could I take a look?" They proceeded into the bathroom. Sure enough, there were lime deposits. He looked at the long line down the side of the shower, pulled out his brush and said, "Let me see if this will work. But before I do Dr. Pendley, if I can clean this lime deposit off your bathroom wall will you buy my cleaning product?" Larry said, "Sure!"

"Yes sir, Dr. Pendley!' The boy cleaned off the whole strip of lime deposits. Then he packed everything up and said, "Dr. Pendley, would you like two or three of my cleaning products?"

How It Works

That approach was a simple "bridge" called a "Sharp Angle Close." It is used by all top communicators and sales people. If you will do something I will do something. A bi-lateral agreement. Then all you have to do is "show me." It's a terrific technique. Works fantastically. The key is to get the commitment before you give them the solution.

After asking that question, "If I do this, will you do that?", you only receive a tentative commitment, you need to give more information so

368 / The Great Communicators

that the client can make a decision. The boy with the cleaning products did not get a definite commitment after the first demonstration, so he gave Larry more information by cleaning something else in the house, the lime deposits in the bathroom.

OUR JOB AS PROFESSIONAL COMMUNICATORS IS TO GIVE ENOUGH INFORMATION TO OUR CLIENTS FOR THEM TO MAKE A DECISION. THE CLIENT'S JOB IS TO MAKE THE DECISION. WOULD YOU AGREE WITH THAT BASIC STATEMENT? SAY YES.

To make sure the client understands he has a problem, use question techniques. Depict exactly what the problem is. Simply repeat the problem back to the client as a question. "May I ask what your advantage is?" Always answer a question with a question. Then give all the informative reasons why he would benefit by having you as a professional represent him in whatever his situation might be.

Use Your Client's Eyes

Visual Aids are used by top professionals. They communicate visually with full color photographs or drawings which outline problems, solutions and benefits. Visual aids have a hypnotizing effect on the client. The visual aid gets their undivided attention. Visual aids focus all of their energies into exactly what is being said, hearing the tone of your voice. Point with a pen to the visual aid. Show and help. Once the client understands there is a problem, he is ready to open up the door to the solution. Show him how you will solve the problem. Give him all the reasons he will benefit, by having you represent him or by purchasing your service or product.

Ben Franklin's Advice

One good way to help the client understand all the reasons they will benefit is by using the popular "Benjamin Franklin Close." Ben Franklin was a wise man who made his decisions based on logic. Ben took a sheet of paper, drew a line down the center. On the left side he wrote all the reasons for, on the right side he put all the reasons against. If the reasons for were more than against, he took action. Try this the next time you have a disagreement with spouse or friend.

Reach the Adult

Each of us has a parent/child/adult personality within us. The parent tells us what to do. The child bases decisions on feelings rather than fact.

The adult personality decision is based on factual information. Our job is to give factual information to help clients make good decisions.

Once you have helped your client to understand and qualify his problem, you will have obtained a tentative commitment. Use the pre-memorized logic statement:

"If I can show you . . . or help you, will you then?" This is called a tentative commitment. With this method you explain the problem thoroughly then give the client all the solutions. Then you simply let the client make the best decision.

- The logical approach makes it easier to help more clients make quicker decisions and have fewer problems in making decisions.
- Logic helps predetermine the problem.
- You control the situation by answering a question with a question.
- When communicating becomes a procedure, it ceases to be a problem.
- Help others to get what they need and want and you will get what you want.
- **If you give more, you will get more.**

You will always be glad you used these techniques. I know you want more success with your clients, family, neighbors, fellow workers. Help them solve their problems. Communicate with them. Isn't that right? Say yes!

Doors of the Mind

Communicating is like going down a long corridor of doors. Let's imagine you have thirteen doors in a hallway. Six doors on each side with one large door at the end. The hallway is smoked-filled. Every time you ask your client a question and get a response, you close a door and fan away smoke or objection. Once you've closed six doors on the left side and six doors on the right side, you have twelve fact responses. Watch how difficult it is for the client to say "no" after saying "yes" twelve times. The trick is not to leave any of the doors open. When the client asks you a question, you must ask a question back. Realize that 50% of all objections are invalid. Your question back invites the client to think of the real reason he is asking.

"Life Is Terrific, Business Is Great, and People Are Wonderful." —*Daniel Pendley*

Fantastic thoughts, but attitude alone is not enough to communicate. You need three basic elements to accomplish your goal.

1. **Desire.** A burning desire. Know exactly what you want.
2. **Positive self image.** Believe that you can obtain that which you desire. See yourself as already receiving your goal.
3. **Obtain the knowledge you need to succeed.**

With the burning desire, specific knowledge and a positive self image anything is obtainable. All three are equal key elements in success. The #1 reason is desire because you must desire FIRST. You must know what you want and have an unshakable belief that it is what you want. #2 Crystalize. See yourself having your goal. Know that you are worthy. You can obtain and maintain that which you desire. #3 Go out and get the details out of the way, the paper work. Get the knowledge. You can if you believe you can, don't you agree? Say yes!

Everyone Is Someone Special

One of the most difficult tasks for a top level communicator-producer is to be humble. "Dear God, it's hard to be humble when you are great!" That'a a common attitude among top sales producers.

I once attended a banquet where there were several important business associates and V.I.P.'s A gentleman was to be the featured speaker who was a well known coach. We were first served our drinks, salad, then our bread. The waiter was called to the table by the featured speaker. He said, "Son, may I please have another pat of butter?" The young man replied, "Sir, I'm sorry, I can only give each person one pat of butter." The speaker then turned and looked at the rest of the table and then looked back at the waiter and said, "Son, do you know who I am? I am the guest of honor. The featured speaker. In a few moments I am going to get up from the table and go up on the stage. I will motivate, stimulate and inspire these 500 guests who are with us today. Now, son, I would like to have another pat of butter."

I'll never forget the look on this young waiter's face. He took two steps back, he looked the coach right in the eyes and said, "Sir, do you know who I am?? I am the man in charge of the butter!"

Anytime I feel like putting myself on a pedestal I think of this story. *Everyone is someone special.* You are not your clothes, you are not your car, you are not the stack of bills on your table, you are not your home, you are not any of those things. You are your ability to love, communicate and help other people. When someone says, "I think you're a bum, I do not like sales people, I don't like your clothes, I don't like your car, I think that you are obnoxious," Great Communicators simply acknowledge, not contest. Simply say, "I understand how you feel, I appreciate you and your opinion." Then move on, give them more information so they can make a good decision.

When people seem to attack you as a person they are really saying, "I don't like what has happened to me from past experience," or they may be simply putting out a smoke screen to cover up the real reason. So simply acknowledge and move on, give them more positive information to make a decision.

Use Appreciation

The perfect example of this is when I made an appointment to list a "for sale by owner" home for $350,000.00. In Dayton, Ohio in 1979 a $350,000.00 home was 6,000 square feet on 2 acres of land with a four car garage, next to the Wright Brothers' home! I'll never forget knocking on the front door. When the door opened an elderly gentleman in a white suit said, "You must be Mr. Pendley, come on in. I am Mr. Klint."

He took four steps backwards in his thirty foot entry, then crossed his arms and said, "I'm sorry Mr. Pendley, I cannot stand the way you smell." I immediately replied with, "I can appreciate that," realizing this was a smoke screen. I turned to Mrs. Klint and asked if she would mind giving me a tour of their beautiful home. After I toured the home with Mrs. Klint and qualified their motive to sell, I decided I would take the listing. We proceeded back to the forty foot living room where Mr. Klint sat at one end of the room and I at the other. I continued to qualify Mrs. Klint by asking questions. "May I ask what you do for a living, Mr. Klint?" He replied, "You may ask what I do for a living, Mr.

Pendley," but he did not answer me. He tested me by insulting my clothes, the way I spoke and by saying my car was "German Junk." Each time I acknowledged and said, "I can appreciate how you feel."

Then in the same breath I gave him more information as to why he would benefit by having me represent him. I helped him understand his problem and gave him solutions.

I used many "stall and objection techniques" and at least 30 different types of closes. But, after 2½ hours I listed the property. After he signed the listing he confessed to me that he had gotten rid of 24 sales people at the front door with "I'm sorry, I cannot stand the way you smell." You see I had an unshakable belief. I clearly understood his problems. I had all the solutions. Every time that he attacked me personally I would fan away the smoke-objection and ask a question, closing the door. I used prememorized language techniques as a script. I realized that some people need more information than others to make a decision. The result was real communication.

50% of All Objections Are Invalid

We must believe with an unshakable belief that no matter what people say to us, our job is to communicate enough information to make a decision. The client makes the final decision. *"If you want something you must give it away,"* if you want love you must give love. If you want a friend you must give your friendship. If you want money you must invest. If you want a crop, you must plant seeds, water, weed and harvest. Whatever it is you desire you must give FIRST.

You may not receive directly from the person you give to, or from the institution in which you give of yourself. But your giving will come back to you. Not once but ten times. Give without anticipation of receiving back. Give wholeheartedly with a genuine concern for the other person. In the giving itself we receive. You feel good when you give to someone else. You receive when you give. Help your clients prosper and you cannot escape your own prosperity.

Life Is Terrific! Business Is Great! People Are Wonderful!

Every morning, get up and say, "Today is going to be fantastic." It is going to be a good day. You might have to grit your teeth in the morning to say that. When someone asks how you are doing at 10:30, you might have to say "fantastic" through gritted teeth. Then at about 11:30 when somebody asks how you're doing you might be able to loosen up your jaw a little bit and say, "Doing terrific."

Later on in the day, by 2:00 p.m. when someone asks you "How's it going?" you'll say, "Fantastic! but I'll get better."

Watch what your mouth says. We have a tendency to believe what we say when we say it to others. While I believe in honesty, I have found it an invaluable tool never to accept my own or someone else's negative judgment. I haven't had a cold because of this simple rule in the last 8 years. I refused to acknowledge a negative thought, feeling or illness. Make every day a great day.

Achieve Anything You Want and Desire in Life

Financially, spiritually, mentally, physically, socially, and in your family life just take three very basic steps:

1. **Write it down.** Know exactly what you want. Be very specific.
2. **Put a time limit** on when you will achieve or receive that goal. Be specific.
3. **Express it.** Tell everyone that you are going to get this, or achieve this, or receive this within your time period.

Writing it down will help you to crystalize what you want. Take it one step further. Take a poster size piece of paper. Label the different aspects of your life, *spiritual, social, mental, physical, financial,* and *family.* Place a picture representing each category of your goal. For example if your goal is to have a perfect body, cut out a picture of someone who looks perfect to you. Place it under physical and so on. Do you get the idea? The picture will help you to crystalize your goal. Be careful what you place on your goal poster *because you are going to get it.*

Put a time limit on it. This makes it specific, know when you will achieve or receive that goal. A goal without a time limit is of no value. A time limit separates fact from fantasy. Expressing it is vitally important because it tells others when you are going to do this and it helps you to crystalize. Expressing puts you in a position to achieve your goal, because you want to make sure you maintain your word, your credibility. You do your best.

"What the Mind Can Conceive and Believe, It Can Achieve."—*Marcus Aurelius*

The keys are burning desire, positive self image and the knowledge that we can obtain any goal we set for ourselves. The only limits that we have are the limits that we place upon ourselves. I believe that you can move mountains if you truly desire to do so. Have a positive self image of believing that, then find the knowledge to move the mountain. Anyone can move a mountain, regardless of its size. Dream your dreams and set your plans. Don't let anyone tell you that your dreams cannot come true. Just build a fire deep in your soul, persist and follow through. Become the person that God intended you to be when He created you.

Anyone can move a mountain, regardless of its size. *Anyone means you.*

Those who bring sunshine to the lives of others cannot keep it from themselves.
—Sir James Barrie

JERALD H. RECKNER
Reckner & Company
4124 N. Colgate Circle
Milwaukee, WI 53222
(414) 464-0683 • Res. (414) 464-5553

Jerald H. Reckner

Dreams do come true! In the last 20 years, Jerry's childhood dream never left him. His solid determination to be the best he could be carried him through several career changes, loss of a thriving business, and the death of his 15-year-old son.

It was a wobbly ladder to climb, but Jerry made it—and he keeps reaching for the stars.

Jerry co-owns one of the largest insurance marketing firms in the country. He travels 43 states training salespeople in the 3300 agencies his company has contracted.

With his dynamic presentation and warm, friendly manner, he motivates and inspires his audiences to new heights of realization for their inner potential.

His speeches can be targeted for any audience. The continuous theme he conveys is "if you believe in yourself as you really are, you can be what you want to be."

His seminars, workshops and keynotes are: "As We Really Are," "To Be, To Do and To Have," and "Is It You Or Is It the Product?"

Jerry is also the president of Reckner and Company which specializes in motivational speaking, sales training and promotions consulting.

20

Communicating As We Really Are: Who Is That Face in the Mirror?
by Jerald H. Reckner

"Some men see things as they are and say 'Why?' I dream things that never were and say 'Why not?'""
—George Bernard Shaw

You're standing in the express lane of your favorite grocery store. There are ten people behind you and it's already been a *long* day! The only items you have are a pack of gum, two cans of tomato sauce (for your favorite spaghetti recipe), a 12-pack of soda pop and deodorant (so you don't offend your fellow office workers tomorrow...) The sign says: "No More Than 12 Items—Cash Only." That's when you notice that the lady writing a check in front of you has enough groceries to feed half a continent! What is the probability that you will turn to the complete stranger behind you and either verbally or non-verbally communicate your frustration?

Oddly enough, earlier, you passed that person in the frozen foods aisle without so much as a smile or acknowledgement. Different situations cause people to communicate—there are no strangers in broken elevators.

The reasons people choose to communicate or ignore one another are various and sundry. People do not communicate well because they do not *believe* they *can*. From the beginning of their lives, they are told what they "can't" do rather than what they *can*. They do not believe in themselves.

In my life of ups and downs, searching for something better, I found and discovered the real me. I discovered that having a good self image is imperative to becoming a good communicator.

The following are seven guidelines to help you develop the kind of self image you want in order to communicate as effectively as possible.

Seven Secrets for a Super Self Image

1. Become aware and accept.
2. Pinpoint goals and a purpose today.
3. Feel good with enthusiasm.
4. Learn from listening.
5. Smile and laugh frequently.
6. Do something for someone else.
7. Have faith.

Become Aware and Accept

Reacquaint Yourself With You.

Before you can communicate effectively with others, you must get to know that person in the mirror...accept who you are.

I was at the lowest ebb of my life—out of work, heavily in debt, and grief-stricken at the death of my 15-year-old son. My life had turned to one of bitterness, where I no longer cared about anything or anybody. One morning, I awoke from the most restful sleep I'd had in months. I bolted out of bed and nearly *ran* to the bathroom. I stood glued to the bathroom mirror for a full twenty minutes, staring unbelievably at what I had become. I vowed then that I would pay the price to become a success—the very best I could be.

The key to good communications with those around you begins with discovering an under-standing and acceptance of yourself. It is a difficult task. I was afraid of the face that stared back at me...afraid of the person I had become. But after I accepted who I was, as I really was, wonderful things began to happen.

Pinpoint Goals and a Purpose Today

Tomorrow Is A Dream

Once you accept who you are, you begin to take inventory of your qualities, good and bad. By taking stock of your qualities, you get a complete view of the total picture...you begin to map out a long range game plan for your life.

It's amazing how much time people spend planning vacations, weekends, weddings...they make lists for groceries, what to take on vacation, and to whom to send Christmas cards and graduation announcements. Yet they never take the time to PLAN THEIR OWN LIVES! Day after day, they keep putting off planning their goals until tomorrow. How many of us have said, "Tomorrow I'll start that diet, that exercise plan...Tomorrow I'll stop smoking..." Tomorrow....

There are no guarantees that there *is* a tomorrow. At a National Marriage Encounter Convention a couple of years ago, keynote speaker Jim Kern related this story: A little boy asked his father to build him a fort. The father said that would be fine, but not *today*. Days passed until one day, the father said to his son: "You come right home after school and we'll build that fort for you." The little boy couldn't think of anything else that day in school. And when the dismissal bell rang, he flew out of the school thinking: "It's only seven blocks, I can run all the way!" So he ran as fast as he could, because Dad was going to build him that fort. He was so entranced that he did not see the car that hit his body.

His father rushed to the hospital as fast as he could, and as he held the fragile little hand, his son spoke his last words: "I guess you won't have to build that fort for me after all, Dad..."

Yesterday is a memory, tomorrow is a dream, today is reality—squeeze every bit of life that you can out of today!

...'Till You Find Your Dream

Those words from the song *Climb Every Mountain* are the foundation for your life's game plan. We shape our own destiny. If you can dream it then you can be it. You project your image and you project your future. My dream began when I was a young boy on a dairy farm in Central Wisconsin. At that young age, I made a very important discovery—cows don't give milk...you have to take it! I did not mind farming, but I sure hated milking those cows! I decided then that I was going to get rich in the big city, because the city was where you could get rich. Yes, I was going to get rich in the big city so I could drive that Cadillac back home and say, "Look, Mom and Dad, I made it!"

Without a dream you have no focal point. Without a focal point, you are a fish out of the midstream of life, flopping around on the beach of despair. Eventually, you stop flopping and just rot. You don't want to be a rotten fish.

Start *today* writing down your dreams; what you want, where you want to go, and the reasons why. Then decide how you are going to achieve those goals—WRITE IT DOWN—study it! Write it on several pieces of paper and put them in strategic places where you will be constantly reminded of the direction in which you want to move.

Keep pounding your goals into your subconscious, and soon, everything you do in life will bring you one step closer to your goals and dreams. Never lose sight of your goals. Obstacles are those frightful things you see when you take your eyes off your goals.

Dream what you dare to dream. Go where you want to go. Be what you want to be.

"Make no little plans; they have no magic to stir men's blood and probably will not be realized. Make big plans; aim high in hope and work, remembering that a noble logical diagram once recorded will not die."

—*Daniel H. Burnham*

The Challenge of the Salmon

As a general rule, fish do not swim upstream... unless you are a salmon in the spawning season. Salmon instinctively know that they have a certain amount of time to accomplish their goals (spawning) before they die. Humans also have an alloted time on earth before they die. Yet, we approach each day as if we were immortal.

The most contemptuous force that we must deal with daily is the negative environment in which we live. We have grown up with it and subconsciously pass that negativism on to our children. At one point or another, we have all said things like: "You'll never amount to anything... What makes you so stupid?...I had a terrible day!" Every day is a great day; if you don't believe it, try missing one! We were not born negative—someone had to teach us.

But nobody ever told the salmon he couldn't swim upstream. You must recondition your mind to look at the positive side of any situation. We choose and we can condition our minds to be whatever we want to be, to do whatever we want to do.

So remember the salmon when you start to

encounter difficulties on your journey to success...
no matter what, that salmon keeps swimming
upstream until he reaches his goal.

"A great pleasure in life is doing what
people say you cannot do."

—*Walter Gagehot*

Feel Good With Enthusiasm

The Wonder Of Water

How many times have you awakened and said,
"I don't want to get up today!" or "Oh no, another
morning..."—Just a couple more examples of
negative forces in our lives. GET RID of those
negative thoughts!

The next time you roll out of bed onto the
floor, crawl into the bathroom, turn on the shower
and topple into the bathtub... That's right, the first
secret of enthusiasm is being coherent enough to
realize you are alive and you *need* enthusiasm!

Take your shower time to wake up, to think
through the tasks of the day and *get excited* about
them! Even if you can't sing, think of a song that
fires up and gets the adrenalin flowing...and sing
it! The acoustics of the shower always make you
sound good—at least in the bathroom.

Look Good To Feel Good

Remember Mother always saying: "Wear clean

underwear, you never know what will happen to you!" Let me make some adjustments to that piece of advice: *Always* look your best—you never know *who* you will run into! You'll also *feel* as good as you *look*. The dress code for all students at the Arthur Andersen Center for Professional Education is suits and ties. The philosophy seems obvious—if they dress professionally, they will act, feel and learn accordingly.

After you have dressed up, look at yourself in the mirror and compliment yourself. Take a quick inventory of all those wonderful qualities you possess. Then smile at yourself and go into your day radiating positivism.

Be Good To Yourself

We all hear our bodies when they are hungry, or when they are stuffed, or when we are sick. But how many of us listen to our bodies when we are healthy?

Smokers with a cigarette cough say, "It's just a tickle in my throat"—For the last 10 years?! Overweight people say, "My knees and feet must be hurting from that new exercise program..." They are not listening to what their bodies are saying: "There's too much smoke in my lungs or too much weight for my knees and feet to carry."

Listen to and *be good* to your body—it will

return the favor in numerous ways. It is just another way to feel good about you so you can feel good about others.

Synergize!

The advertisement for Eveready batteries screams, "Energize me!" Our bodies and attitudes work like a machine that needs a battery. But the energy we gain is with other high-energy enthusiastic people.

Negative people are always tired. It's no wonder—negativity expends volumes of energy. It takes fewer muscles to smile than to frown. It *feels* better to smile and be positive.

Surround yourself with positive, energetic, enthusiastic people. The energy flow between you will rejuvenate each of you. People like to communicate with positive people. You will find it easier to talk to others because you feel good about you!

Learn from Listening

Listening is a critical part of good communications. When you are talking to someone, give them your undivided attention. Never mind who is in the corridor, at the next table, or the incredibly gorgeous brunette that just passed you and smiled. If you are a clock watcher, break that habit when you are talking to someone. When you look at your watch, that is a departure signal—it conveys to the other person that there is some place else you have to go or would rather be. By paying attention to the person you are conversing with, you non-verbally tell them that you care about them.

Because someone is different is no reason to tune out what they are saying. Yes, there are people who talk just to hear themselves. But maybe they do that because that is a check-point for them to reassure themselves that they are alive. They approached you because they needed someone and you looked like you might listen. A friend of mine worked the midnight shift at a radio station. As most radio personalities do, he received all types of strange calls. One particular caller kept calling all week. She had a peculiar voice and said some very strange things. The last night she called, she thanked my friend for listening. Knowing that she possessed an unusual voice, she told my friend that she was a student doing a paper on listening. She had been afflicted with a stroke that paralyzed her right side and had affected her speech. At the prime age of 33, she had had to give up a promising radio career (she was one of the top disc jockeys in the city) because of the stroke. Very simply, read the book *then* judge the cover.

While you are listening, ask pertinent questions. Again, this will reinforce the fact that you are listening and interested in what that person has to say. Suppress the urge to constantly interject. How many of us have learned something from someone else while we were talking? If you give the other person the courtesy of hearing them out, they will do the same for you.

Laugh and Smile...Frequently!

I could have included this with the section on enthusiasm, but I felt it important enough to warrant its own section.

Laughing and smiling are *FUN!* And it is *extremely* contagious. I was at a baseball game and two girls started to laugh. No one else in that section of the stadium knew *what* was funny, but within minutes, all those within earshot of the laughter were turning around and either smiling or laughing with the girls. At the end of the game, our team had lost. But I heard one fan say to the girls as he was leaving: "Thanks to you two, I've had the most fun I've ever had at a baseball game..." I had to admit, my face hurt from all the laughter!

Smiling makes people wonder what you are up to. A friend of mine was walking into a shopping mall with an ear-to-ear grin. A very handsome man had just paid her a *very* nice compliment. She was amused that a complete stranger would do that. As she strode through the mall, a smile on her face and bounce in every step, people stopped and stared. One man even stopped her to inquire about her happy countenance. She left him smiling as she walked away. Smiles act as a magnet—they draw people to you. It has been said that the smile is the international language.

Smiling and laughing relieves stress. Look for the humor in any given situation. It even makes you sound good! Try reading the funnies or seeing a comical movie. You will find that you are relaxed. You may even catch yourself chuckling out loud! There is one Pepsi commercial that makes me smile and chuckle every time I think of it. The commercial that comes to mind is the little boy giggling hysterically because he is being inundated with a litter of overly-affectionate (is there such a thing?) puppies.

"Make good habits, and they will make you."

—*Parks Cousins*

Do Something For Someone Else

My father taught me three things in life: 1) Work hard, 2) Be honest, and 3) What you give out will come back to you. For years, I kept wondering when it was going to come back. Well, it *has* come back to me in *multitudes*.

Giving gives you a sense of accomplishment

and reward. When giving comes from the heart, the receiver knows it and it means so much more.

In order to give love, you must first love yourself. We frequently get so caught up in the trap of society's daily demands that we forget to stop and enjoy a beautiful sunrise, sunset, the magic of a child's smile or the giving and receiving of the seven secrets of a super self image.

Have Faith

Once you discover you as you really are, have faith and believe you *can* be the *best* you can be. Review your own affirmations and believe you can change your world. Everything happens for a reason. Believe only the best can happen and it will.

Tape a picture of you, smiling, on to your mirror in the bathroom. Every morning, look into that mirror and see if the face in the mirror matches the one in the picture. Before you leave the house, make sure the faces match.

Reach out and touch someone you care for. Feel the positive energy exchange and smile. Don't look back. Keep going. Whatever you do, DON'T QUIT!

> "The difference between a successful person and others is not a lack of strength, not a lack of knowledge, but rather in a lack of will."
> —*Vincent T. Lombardi*

"TO BE, TO DO, AND TO HAVE"

"TO BE"..........is looking in the mirror, seeing yourself as you really are. It is projecting your image to be whatever you want to be.

"TO DO".........is climbing the highest mountain, walking the lowest valley, weathering any storm and never looking back.

"TO HAVE" ......is living today, never quitting, reaching out to discover your highest potential and helping others to help themselves.

—Jerald H. Reckner

It is our hearts that make us eloquent.
—Quintillian

JOSEPH C. BAUER
Walters' International Speakers' Bureau
P.O. Box 1120
Glendora, CA 91740
(800) 438-1242

Joseph C. Bauer

Joseph C. Bauer is a dynamic, creative innovator, experienced in all phases of communication, promotion and marketing with a wealth of specialized training, history of academic achievement, and a solid record of accomplishment in professional responsibilities. Producer, director, narrator and master of ceremonies, equally at home in front of a microphone or behind a camera—creating an extravaganza or starring in one, few people are as experienced in so many diversified areas of Mass Media/Communications.

Dubbed "The Voice" by his peers, he is heard on national commercials, film and tape, radio/TV shows and has "Voiced" special productions such as "Get High on Life" and the "Music Hall of Fame" series. He produced, directed and narrated the official National Speakers Association documentary.

As Executive Director of advertising, public relations and special events for Caesar's Palace he's master minded novel concepts and creative appraches to complex advertising campaigns and multi-million dollar promotions. His voice welcomes you in the world famous Omnimax Theatre.

With unique expertise in Mass Media, he trains, advises and represents top executives in press inter-views. As Senior Vice President for the Las Vegas Entertainment Network and President of Creative Media International, he works with the world's top entertainers in many exciting productions.

Creator and director of seminars and conventions for many prestigious organizations, he delivers keynote speeches at international conferences, and M.C.'s numerous events. His popular cassette tapes cover every aspect of communications.

Joseph C. Bauer shares the inside secrets of sorting through the mass of misinformation to under-stand the complex process of communicating. Apply his suggestions and you will become better at putting your ideas in "their" minds.

21

Everything You Always Wanted to Know About Communication (But Were Afraid to Ask)
by Joseph C. Bauer

"Trifles make perfection,
and perfection is no trifle."
—Michelangelo

Communication begins by transmitting thoughts. Good communication will transmit a thought from sender to receiver, from speaker to listener, and implant that thought in the listener's mind.

Billions are spent each year on advertising in the hope of moving the listener to action—to buy a product. A tremendous amount of money is spent to improve the way advertising affects behavior. Advertisers know it is important to describe the benefits of their product. How well do you describe the benefits of your product?

Most people cannot name their senator, or explain a single crucial issue, but almost everyone knows what is meant when they hear, "You deserve a break today," or, "Reach out and touch someone." Communicators must use the research, the breakthroughs of intelligent advertising, to reach listeners. Study and use the newest knowledge to affect your audience, and bring about a positive response.

The Purpose of Communication Is Persuasion

Communication, when effective, will cause a response. Some speakers feel they communicate to inform or entertain, as well as persuade. But whatever your theory, we all communicate in order to influence—to persuade . . . and we expect a response.

Just as success is a journey, not a destination, communication is a process. It is dynamic, alive and exciting. Communication does not happen when you preach or scream at the listener. Communication is a two way process and the listener must be part of it. The listener must interact with the speaker.

Speaking-communicating is also a mixing process carefully blending together different elements. Consider the ingredients of a scrumptious cake. Sugar, flour, butter, etc. These ingredients will not make a cake until the exact amount of each is properly blended. Then energy (in the form of heat), and a certain amount of time is applied to the final mixture. If the energy is kept long enough, and if the recipe is followed, the cake is a masterpiece, devoured and enjoyed by everyone. But if even one ingredient is wrong, or the mix slightly off, disaster results.

My sister, an excellent cook, once baked an angel food cake that smelled and looked suspiciously like she used overripe eggs. So she baked another one, with the same repugnant result! My mother, in carefully reading the recipe, discovered that in her haste my sister had used baking soda instead of baking powder. For years, we called it Pauline's egg soda surprise! Every ingredient must be right to produce a perfect product.

The basic ingredients of any communication process are speaker or sender, a message, and a listener or receiver. (I would add feedback is very necessary to being a successful communicator.)

The average American spends about 70% of waking time communicating verbally. That's more than ten hours a day speaking or listening. The television is on eight hours a day, and you are bombarded with billboards, magazine ads, radio commercials. To maintain sanity—you must learn the skills of communication, and realize how much time and effort advertisers spend trying to manipulate listeners.

You have read the necessary ingredients for communication, but what are the essential ingredients for a good communicator? I will summarize them as (1) attitude, (2) purpose, (3) skill. In this chapter are many positive suggestions about improving attitude and skills, and getting involved in the communication process, with a purpose!

Whatever You Do . . . Do With Your Might

I've spent many years in the communication business, training announcers, teaching students, coaching well known speakers, from politicians to actors. I'm convinced the most important aspect of a good communicator is *attitude*.

Attitude is the critical ingredient of all great speakers. Your attitude dictates your selection and use of material in any conversation or speech. I cover this in greater detail on my cassette training tapes.

Breaking Through

Communication is a combination of verbal and nonverbal skills, but attitude is all important. It affects the way you stand, the way you move, the way you speak to the audience. Showing respect and concern has a great bearing on whether anyone will listen. If you are interested in developing the ability to break through, to communicate with others, you must be concerned first and foremost with attitude, and your reason for speaking, as much as your ability and speaking skills.

In every communication consider the listener, the place, the time, the subject. Are you interested in your image . . . or in breaking through to the listener? Are you pumping up your own ego . . . or educating the listener? (All communication is learning.) Are you "speeching," or are you communicating?

The Average Speaker, When Preparing, Thinks More About Himself Than About the Listener.

Respect and concern for the audience will always show in the long run, and lack of it will show much sooner.

Again, I stress, the successful communicator must have the right attitude, followed by a positive purpose in speaking. Do you have a burning desire?

Are you committed? Do you feel you were born to speak? Are you involved in learning more about speaking? Do you want to improve your presentation? What is your purpose in speaking?

Your image of "self" is developed through communication. Your concept of self is changed and shaped and formed through the communication process, and the feedback from others. It makes sense to improve your communication "every day in every way," to improve your self image.

As speakers, we must be sensitive not only to our growth but to other people's as well. If you're not interested in human kind, it will show. Your communication will become less effective. Listeners instinctively know when a speaker is interested in their well being, their thoughts and ideas.

Every Audience Should be One Person

Attitude is the foundation upon which all great speakers build their career. Part of that attitude is focusing on one listener at a time. Your message must have meaning and clarity to one single listener. Every audience that you address should be viewed as one person.

You cannot concentrate on the listener if you are all wrapped up in yourself, and impressed by addressing a group. Ego and vanity have no place in the middle of important communication.

408 / The Great Communicators

As you shift your gaze to one person, then another, you establish eye contact each time. You cannot look at several people at the same time, and establish personal contact. Focus on each listener one by one to make your message effective.

I teach video technique—how to be a super effective communicator on television. The first nervous habit I help to eliminate is "shifty eyes." Nothing destroys credibility faster than a person whose eyes are constantly darting around the set and all over the studio.

There is a tremendous advantage in television, you can focus on one spot, the lens, and establish eye contact with the entire viewing audience. A good television commentator looks directly into the camera, as if he is speaking to you and you alone. Indeed, the viewers at home feel like the news reporter is speaking directly to them.

Part of the charisma of Walter Cronkite, who according to surveys, is the most believable person in America, was the comfortable "one to one" way he spoke to millions at the same time.

Communicating Is More Than Speaking... Listening Is More Than Hearing

A great deal of communication must take place in the listener's mind. Listening takes energy and concentration. Listening is active involvement. The listener must be interested and stay interested in what you have to say. Your communication or speech therefore, must have a reason for the listener to spend his time and energy. Do you focus the audience on your meaning? Do you help them concentrate? Do you get them to listen behind your words?

An audience watches your body language, they watch your facial expression, and many times those things carry more meaning than the words you're saying.

Audience attention and interest will vary throughout the speech. Therefore, you must consider their attention span from the opening statement to the conclusion. It will change, it will rise and fall. Use this information to your advantage. Build high points, emotional spots in your speech, bring that audience to full attention again, and again.

Check yourself and find how many times you jump to conclusions. See how often your mind wanders and you tend to tune out when listening to someone else. How often do you make assumptions and misjudge the intent of the communication? Do you allow distractions to pull your attention away from someone you're listening to? Expect your listeners to have the same problems and prejudices. So work hard to reduce or eliminate these communication problems.

Billboard the Benefits

How do you get others to listen? It's important to feature the benefits. Ask stimulating questions which demand attention or reaction, then make the benefits measurable.

Show them why you're asking them to do something, and how it will benefit their own self interest, give some method to actually measure the benefit. Get the other person to ask for more information, more ideas, more communication. Stimulate the listener to seek deeper understanding and they will give you feedback, which will indicate if you're getting through.

Communication depends upon a sender and receiver. How much (and what) does the listener understand? Information must flow both directions if communication is to take place.

Listening takes time and effort, it is work. What are you giving the audience in exchange for the work they've invested in listening to your message? Every speaking occasion should be a "value for value" exchange with your listeners.

Your Audience Controls Your Future

The audience influences and even exerts control over your future communication. The response and feedback they give you will, to a large extent, shape and form your future messages.

Strive for a deeper level of interaction between speaker and listener. Work for a merging of you and your audience. A good speaker learns from every talk and from every listener, IF (big if) he wants to become a great communicator. When I lecture or teach or coach, I learn a great deal from every single individual, every audience, every class. Each person I've ever spoken with has had something of value to give me regarding my presentation. Feedback is essential, it is the life blood of improving your communication.

Bigger or Better?

As the size of the audience increases, interaction becomes more difficult, distractions enter in, and effective communicating demands more skill on your part.

The audience reacts to the speaker, the occasion, the message, even the surroundings. The listener shares responsibility for the success of the speech. Most people have incredibly poor listening habits. Listening demands active involvement.

Too much comfort may hinder listening. I enjoy going to the MGM theatre, in Las Vegas, to watch classic movies. They have large, overstuffed couches so you can really relax while watching classic films. They'll even bring you a bit of liquid refreshment if requested. I have never yet made it through one complete movie without dozing for a few moments. It is just too comfortable to focus on even the greatest movies ever made, and maintain mental involvement for an hour or two.

Does The Listener Ever "Get It"

Engrave this in your mind . . . no one can *ever be* completely objective! A part of our meaning in every communication, whether personal, business or professional speaking, stems from our personal opinion. No listener will ever "get it" exactly the way we mean it.

With this in mind it is extremely important to eliminate as much clutter and static as possible. At least we can strive to help the listener "get it" as close to our meaning as possible.

Accurate communication is an amazing achievement because most often the message received is not the message sent.

Good communication is a skill of the highest order, it takes a tremendous amount of work and a lifelong commitment. Daily effort is necessary to improve communication.

To be more effective as communicators we must reduce the effort required by the listeners to understand and respond.

Good Communication Brings a Response

Direct mail is a good example of making response

easier for the receiver. Direct mail experts constantly strive and test to make the receiver respond immediately. They include a self addressed stamped envelope. They keep the response form short so that you only need to initial or checkmark. They make it as easy as possible to respond.

Good speakers should use the same methods to get a response from their audience, adapting new research to become better communicators.

What Is the Listener's Reward?

Benefits to the listener must be enticing or they will not act. What benefit does the listener get from following the course you advise?

When the listener feels an immediate response is in his own self interest, he will act. As negative factors decrease and positive factors increase our message becomes more effective and the response will improve.

Five Skills in Communication

There are five skills in communicating, two of them deal with sending (speaking and writing) two of them deal with receiving (listening and reading) and the fifth deals with both . . . the thinking process— the thought that goes into communication.

And through it all, I emphasize attitude! Your attitude is paramount. When thinking of it as a

414 / The Great Communicators

skill, remember attitude involves:

1. Yourself
2. Your listener
3. Your subject.

Your ability to communicate has a critical effect on the way you impact your audience. As you speak, the words you use, the way you move, the sound of your voice, the way you blend these ingredients, affect the listener in ways you do not even realize.

Words, and how you use them, show your thinking process. How you think, what you think about, and if you think at all. Vocabulary is extremely important, and has actually been used to predict future success. Do you strive to improve your vocabulary each day? Do you *at least* work through the Reader's Digest list of words that appear each month in "It Pays to Enrich Your Word Power"? Have you ever taken a vocabulary test? Bought a simple paperback book such as "Thirty Days To A More Powerful Vocabulary"?

Words are the tools a communicator uses, they need to be sharp, clean, sturdy, useful . . . the very best.

The Most Important Element in Communication

The only justification for communicating at all is to

make contact. To interact with the one at whom
everything is aimed . . . the listener. Therefore the
most important element in real communication is
the listener.

Why work to be a great communicator? The
best possible reason is because you want to reach
out to listeners and influence them. The greatest
skill a speaker must learn is forget the self, and
focus on the receiver. Your aim must be to impact
the listener in a positive way.

Seek improvement one day at a time—every
day. Too many people concentrate on speaking well
when they're in front of an audience or being paid,
and forget all about it the days in between. Always
strive to improve your delivery on the phone, in the
office, in personal communication. Keep at it. Make
it a permanent part of your daily routine.

It is a wonderful skill to get to the point
quickly, in anecdotes and stories. In jokes and
humor, nothing bores a listener more than long
laborious stories with too much detail and not
enough punch. Eliminate obfuscation in daily communication, it will have an amazingly good effect
on your public communication and speeches.
Cultivate colorful language, be clear and concise,
use short sentences that pack a punch, keep your
communication moving. Listeners will bless you for
it and you will stand out as a marvelous and
entertaining speaker.

Regular, systematic and purposeful rehearsal will improve every speaker. Rehearse in a realistic and goal oriented manner. I stress the need for creative communication every waking moment, and structured rehearsal. The regular use of good training tapes is a must!

Qualities of a Good Speaker

Audiences have a right to expect a speaker to have these qualities:

1. Sincerity and conviction
2. Directness of manner
3. Pleasant expressive voice
4. Pleasing personality
5. Sense of humor
6. Well organized material
7. Applicable topic and purpose

They Shall Know You by Your Style

What to say and how to say it, to be convincing, to hold the listener's attention, to speak with confidence, to develop rapport are a few goals of a good speech. Every speaker has a different style to accomplish these objectives.

Style is important. You set the tone (and often the audience reaction) by your style. Take the focus off yourself and concentrate on sending your message with the greatest clarity.

Three important ingredients in every speaker's style are:

1. Eye contact
2. Facial expression
3. Physical movement.

Every speaker develops a different style of using the face, but all the great ones are expressive. They smile when appropriate, always radiate warmth and enthusiasm, and even frown if the story calls for that.

Speakers develop a style of movement around the stage. If you've seen Cavette Robert in his boxing stance, you never forget his physical style, his movement.

A great speaker will not try to use one set style for all occasions. Make sure the style fits the purpose. Show an understanding of the event, do not get up and cheerlead at a wake. Use showmanship, make every audience feel it's the first time you've given that speech.

Words Paint Pictures

No matter what your style, it is extremely important for an effective communicator to paint word pictures. The brain can only think about things it can picture. Listeners can only think about things that they can identify or name.

If I say, "See it, taste it, smell it, feel it," you

don't know how to do those things unless first I tell you what "it" is. If I say, "See, taste, smell, feel *a lemon*," everything falls into place. The brain instantly sees a picture, sends info to the salivary glands and you may find yourself puckering from the mere thought of a lemon.

Pictures are the way we communicate; paint your pictures with colorful words, powerful vocabulary. Be sure the listener has a clear image of your idea.

Feel it, see it, describe it, make the listener see it with you. We communicate only when our mind can see the subject. Make sure your subject, your purpose, your ideas are absolutely clear. Describe ideas in the most colorful terms possible, and use humor.

The mind must work with names and words to form pictures. When you're working with minds be sure you're using colorful, descriptive, exact terminology.

In sports broadcasting the color commentator uses descriptive word pictures, phrases, humorous stories. He conveys the excitement, the details of the sport. We all enjoy broadcasts a great deal more because of the excellent descriptions of the "color commentator." Have you noticed how much you enjoy his personality, and feel you know him based upon his observations and ability to describe complex situations?

Care About Sharing

Great communicators share feelings with listeners. If you're angry or sad, find ways to use that emotion constructively. Feel the emotion of sorrow when the occasion demands it. Great speeches have been remembered for centuries because of emotion.

Don't be afraid to share your joy. *Most of all* share the joy! Relive experiences in your speeches each and every time. As a great actor uses previous events to interpret a role, make your stories and your communication live with graphic, meaningful, reliving of experiences. Share with your audience.

Emotion is one of the tools many speakers are afraid to use. That's one reason I call this, "Everything you always wanted to know about communicating, but were *afraid* to ask." I can teach anyone to improve their speaking skills, but they must have the *emotion*, and the desire to share with an audience.

Do you have the desire to be a great speaker? Is it a burning emotional desire? Do you have the right purpose in wanting to share yourself, your life, your emotions with an audience?

It is extremely important to be aware of your purpose, attitude, and desire when communicating and speaking professionally.

Sit down and decide what it is you want from your speaking career and how much of *yourself* you're willing to invest. Hundreds of professional speakers share these ideas through the National Speakers Association and our conventions and workshops.

Emotions are at the same time necessary and dangerous to proper communication. We all have knee jerk reactions to things with which we do not agree. Personal views are often difficult to explain. You must be willing to *"hear"* reaction and feedback. If you learn to listen, I guarantee it will change your view of yourself, your neighbors and the world. That's one of the best reasons to become a great communicator.

You must not be afraid of change, because communication will change you. It will change your views and your attitude. It will improve you. Therefore, resist the temptation to be the final expert in all things. Always be open for new information and change.

Look Before You Lip

I believe many speakers have a problem with eye contact because that is one of the most personal ways to interact with an audience.

Study a lawyer in a court room. He learns to get close to the jury. To transmit his emotions he must look each juror straight in the eye. Watch a great lawyer at work and he will lean into each individual in the jury one by one, speak emotional-ly, sincerely, and convincingly with a steady gaze deep into their eyes. He must convince them to believe him, and bring in the verdict he wants.

It always worked for Perry Mason, make it work for you.

Why do newsmen and politicians use invisible teleprompters? Again, the purpose is to make the audience believe they're talking from the heart.

That figure speaking on television looks directly into the camera through the reflective glass of the teleprompter. Viewers do not want to watch a commentator looking down, reading a script. Viewers look for that steady gaze so they may judge the credibility of the reporter. Sincere eye contact convinces your listeners of your credibility.

Your Sound . . . It's You

Once you have your purpose for speaking clear, your attitude is right, your desire is high, eye contact, emotion, facial expression, all perfectly in tune, it comes time to develop the most important part of a speaker's physical attributes, your *voice*. The speaking profession constantly deals with sound. Audience comes from the root word of audio. The listener is someone who will hear what you have to say by interpreting sounds coming from the mechanism in your throat. How is your sound?

I train and voicecoach the world's most beautiful models in Hollywood and Las Vegas. Their first
contact with a prospective producer or agent is
usually on the telephone. So we work on creating a
warm, pleasant voice. It doesn't matter how perfect
their make-up, or how beautifully they're dressed,
how gorgeous their figure or face, if their voice on
the telephone doesn't come across with warmth,
quality, and sincerity, they will never even get an
appointment to show the rest of their talents.

The telephone is not a high fidelity instrument,
therefore your voice must be better than good to
impress listeners on the other end of Ma Bell's
wire.

When you do radio interviews the *sound* of your
voice could mean a constantly improving career, or
it could cause the listeners to tune out before they
ever have a chance to hear your speech or see you
in person.

You must sound natural and at ease. Learn to
use your voice in every way possible. I teach voice
personality to many celebrities, executives, politicians, and actors. They never stop learning to
improve their voice.

Actors change voices to fit new characters they
are creating. Each new role demands anything from
foreign accents to a gruff harsh voice. They must
do it all, for these people use their voice as an
instrument. It's their most important asset, and

they learn to play their instrument well.

When talkies took over the movies, many major stars could not make the transition because they had neglected to work on the *sound* of their voice. They thought that looks, or talent, or image, would carry them through the "fad" of sound and they rapidly sank into oblivion. Their voices just didn't please the audience.

You could be the most sincere, honest, reliable, friendly person in the world but if you sound jittery, nervous, or have an unpleasant voice—an audience will turn off. People will not listen to you.

If you have annoying speech habits, strange sounds, odd or irritating vocal patterns, all your other fabulous qualities will never be known, because people will not listen through the static to hear the real you.

Sound . . . Vocal Quality

Your voice is more important and vital to your success than you can possibly imagine. Work on your sound and vocal quality. I have created a series of exercises available on cassette tape. Many people use these tapes to wake up, to go to sleep, and throughout the day as they travel from one appointment to another. They report fantastic results. They get a big kick out of hearing their voice improve, and getting compliments on how much better their communication has become.

Sounds Have Meaning

Human beings learn meanings for sound first. Much later they learn written words. But the majority of the people in the world never learn the meaning of the written word. Our responsibility as speakers is great, for speakers must communicate with oral sounds, in the clearest, most direct, meaningful way possible. The *sound* of your voice is critical to your success.

There are seven areas that define a good voice. How well do you score in them?

A good voice

1. Must be heard, it must be loud enough
2. It must be clear, not slurred or mumbled
3. Must be pleasant, not scratchy or harsh or whiney
4. Must be flexible, change pitch and speed, and use vocal variety, be able to use different voices in a story
5. Be unaffected with no annoying accents of poor diction or sloppy enunciation
6. Be warm, friendly, interested, involved— with a pleasant smiling sound
7. Be enthusiastic, you must have life and energy, and most of all *joy*.

How many of these areas do you work on each

day? I encourage you to make a check list, have a good friend give you feedback. You can improve in all of these areas. The rewards will be enormous.

Now that you know the ingredients of a good communicator, (1) attitude, (2) purpose, (3) skill, continue to build upon that foundation. The basis of all interesting communication is the experience of the speaker. The better able you are to share your experiences, your knowledge, your travels, your education, the better the audience will understand and enjoy you and your message.

All motion is relative, when you stand still you are going to fall behind, because life is constantly changing and moving forward. Picture running up the down escalator—if you stop running . . . .

A Word Fitly Spoken Is Like Apples of Gold In Frames of Silver

Your personal views on subjects of importance must be tempered with wisdom and knowledge. Therefore, resist always the temptation to use careless information. If you care LESS about an accurate, positive message and its impact, than you do about your own personal opinions, you will never make a great communicator.

Communicate Good Will

When it comes to achieving communication, the

426 / The Great Communicators

speaker must not only be a person of good will but must communicate that attitude to the audience. I give you . . . four important principles.

1. **Know your audience, be able to read their reactions.** Make your speech conform to the needs and desires of that audience. Give them something they can really use. Help them to respond to your suggestions.

2. **Give evidence of your knowledge of the subject.** Demonstrate your ability in this field. Know your material, and present it with honesty and credibility.

3. **Demonstrate through your record of achievement that you are a leader.** If you solicit support from others you must indicate that you know how to lead. Use your record of accomplishment without conceit.

4. **Your audience is influenced by your character.** How well do you live the virtues you espouse? The audience expects you to practice what you preach. When character is in doubt, other qualities of personality become questionable.

In today's world with most values being questioned, and many destroyed, it is imperative for those in the speaking profession, who shape public opinion, to establish and uphold positive values.

Study and Use My "Big 10"

1. Talk with one person, make your thoughts clear as if speaking to a friend.
2. Believe in your message. Transmit the emotion of sincere, solid belief. If you don't believe what you're saying totally and completely, with dedication and emotion, how can you expect the audience to believe it?
3. Visualize the response you want. See each person taking the desired action. Believe that every one you talk to will heed your words and be a better person because of it.
4. Speak in colorful, exciting word pictures. The mind can only grasp a concept if it is described clearly.
5. Relax and be natural. Let go of stress and pressure, ego and nervousness. Enjoy what you're doing. Smile and show you're a warm friendly person. The audience will be delighted and react positively.
6. Use clean, crisp enunciation. Don't rush and don't slur. Change the pace in your presentation. Pronounce your words properly, with ease. Work for perfection with naturalness.
7. Build your confidence through professionalism. Concentrate on doing it right . . . and then do it better. Don't be overly harsh or severe in criticizing your own learning

process. Build upon the right things you do.

8. Use every proven technique, and try new ones all the time. The greatest slogan of advertising is "new and improved." Use pauses, change the pitch, vary the speed, and stretch the range of your voice. From a shout to a whisper keep the audience always moving forward and interested. Move fast and then slow across the stage. Strike a pose and then break it. Lean into your audience. Get them involved.

9. Share your story with sincerity, warmth, emotion and humor. Be involved in what you say. Inspire and uplift each listener every time.

10. Be prepared. Use every experience in life to understand the needs and desires of your listeners. "There is no substitute for preparation."

Use every moment of every day to prepare for tomorrow and your next communication.

Let me hear from you. I care about the quality of your communication! Contact me through the Publisher if I can be of further help.

Warmest personal wishes for great success and joy.

*Let your speech be always with grace,
seasoned with salt.*

—Colossians, IV, 6

ETIENNE ANTHONY GIBBS, MSW
Executive and Group Development
P.O. Box 1508, 2 Nye Gade
St. Thomas, VI 00801-1508
(809) 776-1927

Etienne Anthony Gibbs, MSW

Etienne A. Gibbs is no stranger to Royal Publishing's Anthologies. His chapter, "How to Motivate Yourself When Obstacles Knock You Down . . ." was featured in The Magnificent Motivators.

Etienne, a native of St. Thomas, U.S. Virgin Islands, has more than 20 years experience in teaching, training, and traveling.

As a Clinical Social Worker who graduated from California State University, Sacramento, Etienne pursued a minor career change and became a certified Human Resources Development Consultant. "In working as a psychotherapist with people and their problems, I had taught them to maximize their potential AFTER they had developed a psychopathology. I decided to direct my energies to the other side of the coin; to teach them to maximize their potential BEFORE problems arise."

A frequent writer of articles, Etienne consistently motivates readers to maximize their potential. He counsels Vietnam Veterans as a Readjustment Counselor in the VA's Vet Center. His private practice, a consulting firm, conducts lectures, seminars, and training sessions.

A devoted father and husband, Etienne is a dynamic speaker and trainer active in community activities.

He was honored by being the first male auxiliary member of CEWN (Caribbean Executive Women's Network), was Administrative Vice-President of V.I. Toastmasters Club 4040U; Vice-President of St. Thomas/ St. John Mental Health Association; President of V.I. Association for Counseling and Development. He and his wife, Gisela, are the proud parents of daughter Stefanie Angelika. A son, D'apres-Etienne, resides in California.

22

Avoid Communication's Stumbling Blocks
by Etienne A. Gibbs, MSW

"There's no problem so big that it cannot be solved by means of communicating."
—Mr. Edwino Rivera
Vietnam Veterans Outreach Center
San Juan, Puerto Rico

"Now son, don't ever let me catch you smoking," states the father while puffing on a cigar.

Does it sound like this father is communicating effectively with his teenage son? I'll say not! The only thing that the father is doing drastically is giving his son a double, or mixed message.

The message his son inadvertently receives is, "Smoking is OK; just don't let Dad catch you doing it." However, the message that Dad intends to convey is, "Son, I don't believe that smoking is what you should be doing at this point of your life."

Doing something (nonverbally communicating) while, at the same time, instructing (verbally communicating) someone NOT to do as he sees you doing is a confusing, mixed message. It is guaranteed to produce the opposite results of what you intend.

To avoid this type of communication stumbling block, always give clear and consistent messages. In the case of our dear old Dad, he would have been more effective in this communication to his son if he had not smoked and if he had given a clear message.

Dad could have prevented undue stress and conflicts with his son by giving a simple message such as:

- "You are not to smoke in this house." (a command)
- "Your mother and I prefer that you not take up the habit of smoking." (a request). Followed by, "Would you honor our request?"
- "So, you want to start smoking? How do you plan to support your habit?" (an inquiry)

Mixed Messages Are Stumbling Blocks

Giving mixed messages is the most common stumbling block to effective communication that I've observed in my professional experience as a psychotherapist and consultant. Sending mixed messages is only one of several stumbling blocks that we'll look at in this chapter.

The art of communicating includes the co-existing skills of speaking, listening, interpreting (comprehending) and responding. We often take these skills for granted. Unless we pay attention to and sharpen these skills, we run the risk of developing lazy habits, and, consequently, stumbling blocks to effective communication.

Consider this: If we're communicating effectively to our family members, to our employees, to our students, how come they respond to us with comments like these:

- "Oh, I'm sorry, dear, I thought you wanted fish for dinner tonight," Or,
- "Yes, sir, I understood you to say that you wanted me to turn in the report next month." Or,
- "But Professor, I'm sure you said that we only had to study the first four chapters for the exam."

Apparently, communication between the speakers and their listeners in the above examples had broken down to the point that each mis-understood the *intended* message and assumed an *interpreted* message.

To communicate effectively, ask yourself:

- Is the *intended* message that I am conveying the same as the *interpreted* message that my listener is receiving?
- Is my nonverbal communication (attire, appearance, gesture, and mannerisms) consistent with my verbal communication?

A negative reply to either of these questions means the communication is not effective. Put it to a test! Before going any further, ask your listener for immediate feedback. I often use this question, "Am I making sense to you?" You may wish to ask your listener to restate your comments or to rephrase it in his own words.

Wait! I'm Coming To My Point!

Have you ever had the experience where someone, in attempting to ask a question, rambled on and on before getting to the point? I have experienced this time and time again. I particularly notice this during the question-and-answer period of my lectures and seminars.

Someone raises his hand, prefaces his question with a statement, and in what seems like hours later, eventually gets to his question. Sometimes I get a member from the audience who rambles on so long he forgets his question.

Whenever I sense a rambler, I interrupt him tactfully. After taking a moment or two to sense what he's trying to say, I ask this simple question:

"Are you making a statement or asking a question?" Believe it or not, this short, simple question helps to bring him back into focus. He gets to his point, and we move on to the next topic while preventing communication stumbling blocks and avoiding hurt feelings.

Am I Distracting My Message?

I was not aware of how many unnecessary and distracting mannerisms I used while speaking. I still vividly remember the first night at a Toastmasters meeting in which I was asked to count the number of *ah's, you know's,* and other distractions used by Toastmasters in their prepared speeches. After giving my report, I was informed by Mrs. Toya Andrew, then-President of the Virgin Islands Toastmasters Club 4040U, that I managed to rattle off 43 *ah's* and *you know's* within my three minute report.

Wow! Was I shocked! Forty-three times I had used unnecessary expressions that distracted from my message. Until it was pointed out to me, I always thought I communicated effectively. My

Toastmasters experience taught me to pay attention to my distracting verbal and nonverbal mannerisms. By practice, practice, and more practice, I was able to rid myself of these distractions.

Some of my noted nonverbal mannerisms included rocking, swaying, and pacing. Instead of conveying my message, I succeeded in frustrating my audience. They reported to me that they were distracted by my bouncing and swaying. I reminded them, they said, of the white bouncing ball in the old sing-along movies.

Such unnecessary and distracting mannerisms frequently occur to everyone. They are the results of simple nervousness. They occur unconsciously.

The first step to eliminating any superfluous behavior is to obtain an accurate perception of your communication mannerisms. Taping yourself on audio or video cassettes are excellent ways to learn about your mannerisms.

Other excellent sources for instant and constructive feedback are speech clubs in high schools or colleges or at Toastmasters clubs. The key element to your effective communication, of course, is gaining and using the priceless feedback.

I Hear You (But Am I Actually Listening To What You're Saying?)

To maintain a satisfying relationship with others at home, work, or school, we must learn to communicate effectively. To make it easier for others to communicate with us, our communication with them must convince them that we care enough to listen.

Do you talk to, at, or with others? Does your "talking to" include nagging, reminding, criticizing, threatening, lecturing, probing, and ridiculing? Such unnecessary tactics distract, rather than improve, communication. They put a strain on your relationships.

Becoming an effective listener requires concentration. It involves establishing eye contact and a posture that says, "I'm listening." Sometimes listening requires you to be silent or sometimes requires you to respond. Listening also requires letting your speaker know that you recognize the feelings behind what he is saying and what he is not saying.

Dr. Don Dinkmeyer and Dr. Gary McKay, creators of the STEP (Systematic Training for Effective Parenting) Program, teach parents *reflective listening*. Here, parents learn to separate the deed from the doer. They learn to give "I-messages" in which they acknowledge their child's feelings behind what he's saying, or not saying.

I-messages demonstrate that the listener is actually listening, understanding and responding to the speaker. I-messages, according to the STEP program, are usually constructed in three parts:

1. A description (without blaming the child), of the child's misbehavior that is interfering with the parent.
2. A statement of the parent's (speaker's) feelings about the consequences that the misbehavior produces for the parent.
3. A statement of consequence.

For example, by using reflective listening and an I-message, we can respond to our speaker with:

"When you speak so fast and use big words, I feel cheated because I cannot follow or understand the remainder of your discussion."

Try using I-messages in your communication at home, work, or school. I guarantee that you won't have the misunderstandings, communication stumbling blocks, we cited earlier.

Additionally, you can take several steps to increase the likelihood of your listener listening to, retaining, and comprehending the information you wish to convey.

• Set a good example at home, at work, or at school. The more effectively you listen and respond to your speaker, the more likely he will listen carefully when you speak.
• Encourage your listener to ask questions and take notes when you speak.
• Motivate your listener by emphasizing why the message is important.

Air Force supervisors reported to me in training programs I conducted with them that the principles of reflective listening were helpful to them in becoming effective supervisors. Parents in my STEP group have often indicated to me that their skills in constructing reflective listening and I-messages have improved their relationships with their children and spouses.

Am I Wording My Communication Correctly?

Productivity in communication refers to two things. First, communication, by its very nature, is intended to produce results. Second, effective communication is presented in the shortest manner possible.

Do you sometimes create stumbling blocks in your communication? Do these stumbling blocks prevent you from being understood and from moving others to action or reaction? Have you ever given a speech, presented a live commercial, or told a joke that got a poor response? Could the negative response be a result of your choice of wording? Perhaps you said, "Those of you who are driving to work . . ." or, ". . . are within the sound of my voice . . ." How much more effective and personal would you have been with a statement addressed directly *to* the listener rather than *about* the listener. Try these on for size:

"If *you* are driving to work, I caution you to drive carefully."

"If you can hear me, *you* are wide awake!"

Consider how effective and popular these proverbs would have become if they were to exist in this form:

- Avoid calculating the possible number of your infantile poultry before the usual period of incubation has been completed. *(Don't count your chickens before they're hatched.)*

- A canine that gives vent to its sentiment by a series of vocal effects seldom finds use for its bicuspids. *(A dog's bark is worse than its bite.)*

- Each mass of vaporous substance suspended in the firmament has an interior decoration of metallic hue. *(Each cloud has a silver lining.)*

- Refrain from traversing a structure erected to afford passage over a waterway prior to the time of your arrival at its location. *(Don't cross your bridge until you come to it.)*

- Persons of exiguous intellectual power project themselves precipitately into situations in which the winged, ethered likeness of man hesitates to perambulate. *(Fools go where angels fear to thread.)*

How many did you understand at the first reading? To avoid the stumbling block of superfluous wording, follow these three rules developed by author George ("1984") Orwell:

- Never use a long word where a short one will do.
- If it is possible to omit a word, always leave it out.
- Never use a foreign phrase, a scientific word, or jargon if you can use its everyday English equivalent. (Jargon is defined as any specialized or technical language used by a group or profession.)

I Have Something To Say But My Emotions Get in the Way

Psychology teaches us that a person who is angry, worried, depressed, or frustrated tends to lose his perspective. Such a person becomes ineffective at communicating.

Remember the time you laughed so hard that tears came to your eyes? In fact, as you laughed and cried, it became increasingly difficult to hold a conversation or to attempt to communicate. Other emotions have a similar affect on our ability to communicate.

Have you ever noticed how difficult it is to get your point across while you were in the midst of a heated argument? Have you ever been victorious in any argument where you were so mad that you could blow your top? I'll say not!

If you ever experienced severe depression (a normal reaction in most cases of mourning and bereavement), then you're the first to realize how emotions (as well as the lack of them) hamper the ability to communicate. Although a depressed person seldom loses the ability to communicate, he communicates minimally or not at all.

Regardless of the level of emotion, we hold control of the final outcome.

"How so?" you say.

"Well," I'll reply, "It's all a matter of pursuing an appropriate attitude." "Attitude," according to my Webster dictionary is defined as "position or bearing as indicating action, feeling, mood."

Our attitude makes a positive impact on our lives. It seems to control nearly everything we choose to do. Attitude can help us achieve better grades in school, increased productivity in the work place, and, naturally, improved and effective communication wherever we go.

Psychology has also taught us that people with a positive attitude about themselves and their environment tend to work better and communicate more productively than those with a negative attitude, or poor control of their emotions.

What type of attitude-bearer are you? Take a serious look at your attitude and the manner that it is affecting your life. Gather feedback, then take appropriate steps to improve your communicating skills and personal goals.

Sorry! I Don't Know What I'm Saying

Sometimes our communicating skills are hampered by physical impairment, but most of the time they are hampered by self-imposed stumbling blocks.

How effective is the town drunk in communicating to his listener his request to be assisted across the street or directed to the closest toilet? Not too effective!

How effective is our communication with our loved ones after we've deprived ourselves of sleep for several nights? In my case, just one night of sleep deprivation turns me into a human bear. I become irritable, impatient, and a poor listener. While driving in this condition, if I were to be stopped by the Highway Patrol, I'm sure I would fail the psychomotor-coordination tests used for drunk drivers. I am virtually useless as a parent, husband, and wage-earner when I'm sleep-deprived. My ability to communicate effectively is severely hampered. I know this, so I avoid depriving myself of sleep.

I recall another situation that severely hampered my communicating ability. I was giving a luncheon presentation at St. Thomas Rotary. Prior to going on the platform, I took two antihistamine tablets.

Combined with my ever-increasing anxiety, my medication caused a devastating side-effect that I had never experienced. Not only did it exacerbate my nervousness, it triggered a disturbance in my coordination causing confusion, forgetfulness, and disorientation. I became dry-mouthed and unable to carry out the remainder of my well-rehearsed presentation.

Motivating Techniques That Work

My good friend, Terry Robinson, a Rotarian and current President of the V.I. Toastmasters Club 4040U, was in the audience. His constructive feedback, along with my first-hand experience, will help to maximize your effectiveness, especially in high-stress situation:

- Stick to a minimum of audio-visual media. In my case I was using an overhead projector, a flip chart, and a tape recorder for my 10 minute talk.
- Pay particular attention to taking medication and drinking alcohol. Avoid medication, if possible, that can cause adverse reactions.
- Avoid full meals. Eat lightly, but nutritiously.
- Be prepared, well rehearsed and relaxed by getting there early.

Wrapping-Up Your Stumbling Blocks

Now that we've had the opportunity to look at several Stumbling Blocks to Effective Communication, wrap them up and throw them away. You don't need MIXED MESSAGES any more. So, put them in a box. In the same box you are invited to place RAMBLING and UNNECESSARY MANNER-ISMS. Before you tie a ribbon on the box and throw away your Stumbling Blocks, take a moment to listen to your LISTENING SKILLS. Are you listening to what's going on around you?

Let's resume packing your throw-away box. Next, add a hefty dose of SUPERFLUOUS WORDING. Tie a ribbon of your favorite color around the box and prepare to discard it along with all your Stumbling Blocks to Effective Communication. Take the box out back and bury it.

Check your EMOTIONS and other SELF-IMPOSED Stumbling Blocks. Congratulate yourself! Celebrate your victory! You are now a person free of Stumbling Blocks. Your effective communication is at the tip of your tongue.

> "Do not say things. What you are stands over you the while, and thunders so that I cannot hear what you say to the contrary."

—From Emerson's Letters and Social Aims, 1875

A fool may talk, but a wise one speaks.
—Benjamin Franklin

PAUL DONNER
Bonaventure Group
255 North El Cielo, Suite 480
Palm Springs, CA 92262
(619) 320-4440

Paul Donner

Paul Donner is founder of the Bonaventure Group, an international network of professionals dedicated to the advancement of human potential and the development of OPTIMAL PERFORMANCE TECHNOLOGIES.

He has received international acclaim as a distinguished communications consultant to major corporations in the United States and abroad. He has 10 years experience leading seminars for executives in business and government.

His business background includes the creation of several companies and the developing and refining of communication skills in Telemarketing.

Paul is consultant to the DAWN Show (Dynamic Achievers World Network) in Dallas, Texas, seen all over the world. The TV show, hosted by National Speakers Association's Past President Ty Boyd, has featured Cavett Robert, Founder and Chairman Emeritus of NSA; Zig Ziglar, author of "See You at the Top;" Joe Batten, author of "Tough Minded Management" and featured in "Here Come the Sales Trainers;" Victor Kiam, President of the Remington Shaver Company; Kenneth Blanchard, author of "The One Minute Manager;" and Publisher Dottie Walters.

23

You Are What You Communicate
by Paul Donner

"The most immutable barrier in nature is between one man's thoughts and another's."
—William James

"The meaning of your communication is the response you get. If you are not getting the response you want, change what you are doing."

Personal Power!

What does it mean to you?—Money? Freedom? The skill to command people and things? The ability to direct your life exactly as you want?

How much power do you have in your life right now? What would you change in your life if you knew you had the power to do so? What is your definition of success? Do you really desire it? Is it worth the effort? What makes some people succeed while others of seemingly greater intelligence fail? What is the essential foundation to all success?

My first answer was knowledge. Surely those who succeed have the information that those who fail do not, right? This is the key ingredient that sets them apart. Wrong! My initial presumption couldn't have been farther from the truth. While it's true that knowledge is a key factor in one's ability to succeed, it isn't the essential foundation of all success.

My answer is PERSONAL POWER—the ability to take action. Successful people may not possess outstanding knowledge or talent, but they are able to take action and use the resources they have at their disposal. They are able to communicate effectively and develop the sensory acuity to read other people.

Experts from various disciplines in the past few

years have described a radical shift from an age dominated by industry to an age dominated by information. Entry into the information age has altered the nature of strategic resources. A shift of focus has taken place. Capital was once the hallmark of wealth and could even buy information. The systematic growth of knowledge is becoming the driving force in today's advanced economies, worldwide.

Now, communication is taking center stage in all social transactions. Communication affects the way we run our lives, from our business to our families. But unless it can be communicated, information is worthless. If you can't communicate, you can't command.

Great Persuaders

Observing people who seem to have a natural talent for effective communication, experts have concluded that these people's strength is not *what* they say (content), but *how* they say it (process). Great communicators have in common positive skills of persuasion. The acknowledgement and use of these tools lead to better decisions and better choices.

Most of us rarely think about communication. Talking (just one form of communication) is like breathing, it seems so natural. Essentially words surface, turn into sentences, and conversation happens. But words are only seven percent of the communication process, tonality of voice is twenty-eight percent and physiology, at fifty-five percent, is the majority of the communication process.

Effective communication begins with the acknowledgement that each of us is unique. Sometimes we do not speak the same language although we may use the same words. Effective communication skills bridge these differences. Bridging skills are persuasion skills: they increase understanding and improve the quality of the communication process. These powerful tools of persuasion are the result of a new technology, Neuro-Linguistic Programming (NLP), combining psychology and linguistics. Neuro-Linguistic Programming is the process of how communication, both verbal and non-verbal, affects our nervous system and the resulting behavior.

Focus on the Big Picture

The first step toward communication excellence is to know what you want. Once you know your desired outcome, you need three skills to get there.

1. **SENSORY ACUITY**—The ability to gather accurate information by means of the senses.
2. **FLEXIBILITY**—If you are not getting the response you want when you communicate,

you need to be able to change your behavior until you do by having additional choices.

3. **CONGRUENCY**—The alignment of all your subpersonalities in agreeing on what you want.

Knowing specifically what you want in any situation, how you want things to turn out in the end, keeps you from wandering aimlessly or getting bogged down in the mechanism of what is happening at any given moment. You already possess these skills. Some of you have developed these skills more than others.

Have you ever tried to put together a jigsaw puzzle without having seen the picture of what it represents? That's what happens when you try to put your life together without knowing your outcomes. Like pieces of a puzzle, you have abilities, experiences and situations in your life, but no idea of how the pieces are going to fit in the overall picture. Without the picture you might throw out a piece that you think doesn't fit or get so frustrated that you make no attempt at fitting them together.

Knowing what you want is like having that big picture. You can see how it all fits together. You see the patterns of how people and experiences fit in your life, and you can operate more effectively.

Knowing what you want allows you to be focused. The sharper you are about your desire, the more motivated you will be to tap your skill and energy. Be specific. Clarify your outcomes.

Well defined achievable outcomes:

- are stated in the positive
- are sensory specific
- have an evidence procedure
- are congruently desirable
- are self initiated and maintained.

Engage Your Senses

Use your senses to detect the mood, feeling and direction of an outcome. The more specific you are, the easier it is for your brain to activate the resources it needs to achieve it. Engaging your senses allows your mind to make distinctions about what resources will be most effective for achievement of your outcomes.

Know how you will look, how you will feel and what you will see and hear in your world when you have achieved your outcome. Project yourself forward into the experience of your achieved outcome. Let yourself actually be there in your mind. Sense every aspect of your accomplishment and know this is how it will be, how it will sound, how it will feel.

Your outcome must be one that benefits you and other people, it must have integrity. Verify that your outcome is congruent with you as a person, that it is what you truly want and are committed to achieving. If it is not congruent and desirable, you can not mobilize your full resources to achieve it.

Define Your Target

The ability to channel your energy and skills requires a target. Our minds operate as servo-mechanisms. In his best selling book, Maxwell Maltz calls this psycho-cybernetics. When the mind has a defined target it can focus and direct and refocus and redirect until it reaches its intended outcome.

In an attempt to understand the amazing ability of the brain to create sensory specific images, with our eyes closed, the realities we see with our eyes open, we have modeled the brain on the latest technology available. Dr. Karl Pribram, a Stanford University neurosurgeon and psychologist, often referred to as the "Einstein of brain research," believes that the hologram (a three dimensional image projected into space re-created from inter-ference patterns of laser light) provides the long sought after model of how visual and sensory information is received, stored and recalled by the brain.

A three-dimensional holographic image repre-senting an object cannot be visually distinguished from the real object. A holographic image is a by-product of an electrical and chemical process.

Visual images and sensory impressions generated by the brain are holographic in nature. Every
image and impression is composed of electro-
magnetic energy that consists of matter. Vividness
and sensory detail increase the energy and power of
the visualized image. Essentially, what one visualizes
is real. The body and mind interprets visual images
and sensory impressions as reality and reacts to
them accordingly.

Electromagnetically charged visual images produce a magnetic field that attracts to you those
things that you vividly sense and visualize. This
attraction is what gives you power to control your
life and environment for success.

You have an exact sequence of pictures, sounds
and feelings that you use to motivate yourself. If
you probe your mind you will discover a very
specific strategy that you do consistently. This
process is like the function of a computer.

If someone gives you information in a way that
does not fit your strategy, it would be like trying to
retrieve information from a computer without
processing the correct program. You won't get it.
To operate a computer you must type in the proper
digits in the proper sequence. Your mind works in a
similar way. Correct mental strategies give you the
ability to input vital information in a way that frees
the brain to create new patterns.

458 / The Great Communicators

Watch the Eyes

An important means of eliciting strategies—your own and others—is to understand the effect of eye movements and how they reveal your ability to tap different portions of your brain.

How can an understanding of the meaning of eye movements be of value to you? Wouldn't it be valuable to be able to look into someone's eyes and know if he was remembering or creating, visualizing or feeling? What would happen if you could observe a person's eyes and ask, "What feelings do you have?" or "What were you asking yourself?" If you were exact each time and knew what those thought experiences were, you would have an advantage in communicating few have ever achieved.

The value of this skill in terms of mental strategies is even greater. If you are in sales, you can use this to elicit a prospect's buying strategy, which will give you a definite advantage. So as you're beginning to note, each of us has a specific strategy for everything we do. We even have a strategy for feeling wanted, loved or needed. Through our eyes, the mind reveals the exact sequence of those pictures, sounds and feelings that move us to action or derive pleasure.

When the NLP technology was being developed, it was discovered that in order to access memory in

Eye movements show whether someone is making pictures, or listening to sounds, or aware of feelings to make sense of their communication.

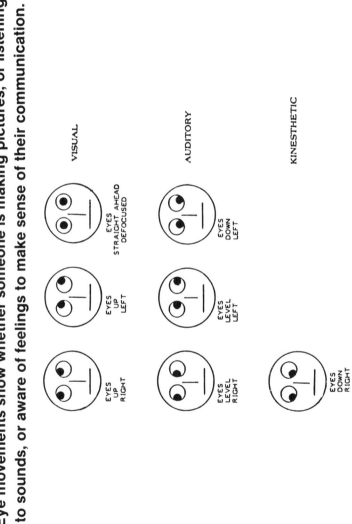

a normal right-handed individual, it was essential to watch the eyes. A person's eyes may move to the right side or to the left side, up or down, depending on what the mind was searching to answer. When an individual is constructing or creating in his/her mind, he/she usually looks to his/her dominant side (the side of the dominant hand). To visualize, the eyes go up and to the left or non-dominant side. The only other way an individual can do this is by defocusing the eyes or dilating the pupils.

When individuals look to their right, or dominant side, they are in an auditory state, creating sounds. When they look down to their dominant side, it is called auditory digital or internal dialogue. They are talking to themselves. If they look down to their left or non-dominant side, it is called kinesthetic (body sensations, feelings or emotions). The only exceptions occur in left-handed people, who often reverse the normal eye movements, and ambidextrous people, who also have a tendency to manifest the reverse patterns.

The Power of Rapport

By understanding people's strategies, you can learn to present information in a manner that is appealing, making you a powerful communicator.

Have you ever been in an encounter with a stranger and thought, "I really like that person, and

I don't know why. There was just something about him I could relate to."? You've just experienced rapport—that mysterious something that makes you feel aligned with another human being.

In a study of super successful people, it was discovered that all of them had a remarkable ability to establish an almost immediate bond of commonality with others, which gave them influence with the people around them.

These successful people managed to put themselves on a level that induced others to accept them, giving them a great advantage in achieving their outcome. The majority did this unconsciously, intuitively acting in a way that inspired confidence and trust.

These intuitive patterns were identified and broken down into skills that could be employed consciously. They are:

- Matching and mirroring people's physiologies (by becoming like the person we are communicating with we develop a bond at an unconscious level).
- Matching speech patterns. (By matching the tonality, tempo and volume of someone you are communicating with, you will actually begin to think more like the other person than you did before).

It is a fact that when we alter our physiology—

voice and posture—we alter our mental and emotional patterns as well. You can literally "get into someone's mind" by aligning your body exactly with them.

Life is like a dance. If you're doing an animated mambo and your partner has a waltz in mind, you're not going to be in rapport. Exercise your flexibility and learn to develop the distinctions that will permit you to understand others and respect their thinking and behavior. Use that understanding to develop a wide range of behaviors so that you can have rapport with the greatest number of people. You will then be able to establish rapport with almost everyone. Rapport is power.

The more flexible you are, the wider your range of behaviors, the more you're likely to succeed in any situation. This is known as the law of requisite variety, which is: In any system, all other things being equal, the individual with the widest range of responses will control the system. The truth is, there is no such thing as resistance, there are only inflexible communicators.

There are three distinct behavior patterns present in every successful communicator.

1. Good communicators continually set explicit outcomes.
2. Good communicators have sensory aware-ness and observational skills that provide

them with feedback about their progress toward those outcomes.

3. Good communicators have flexible behavior and continually adjust their communication and activities to achieve their outcomes. If one method of communication doesn't work, they try another approach.

Among all the differing theories of science, one thing is agreed, that there is no limit to the potential of the human mind. You have enormous untapped power. You need only recognize it to burst its bonds and put it to use to achieve what you desire in life. That is personal power.

The Quality of Your Life
Depends on the
Quality of Your Communication!

H.I. SONNY BLOCH
The Action Line Group
1410 15th Street N.W.
Washington, DC 20005
(202) 483-2314 • Res. (305) 644-4200

H.I. "Sonny" Bloch

As host of the nationally syndicated Action Line TV and Radio series, Sonny Bloch is fed by satellite each day to millions of American homes on PBS UHF, VHF and cable networks—in fact, Action is what Sonny is all about!

Born in Chicago, he attended the University of Miami from 1954-58, and for the next 20 years developed and marketed 36 Real Estate communities. He retired for two years, and then started a new career in the satellite communications industry.

Sonny shared his ideas on real estate and development through a magazine column and a call-in radio program. This led to a television program, the beginning of the Action Line series.

The Action Line Group, based in Washington, D.C., features Real Estate Action Line, Investors' Action Line, Pet Action Line and The Weekend Business Report—all hosted by the energetic Mr. Bloch.

These syndicated programs have been seen on **PBS, Financial News Network (FNN), Satellite Program Network (SPN),** and the **Satellite Business Network (SBN).** Featured guests have included former President Gerald Ford, columnist Jack Anderson and U.S. Treasurer Katherine Ortega. Mr. Bloch has a cumulative weekly viewing audience of more than 100 million homes.

Sonny Bloch is the recipient of numerous national awards including the American Society of Appraisers' award for journalistic excellence.

In addition to his own television shows, Mr. Bloch appears on **ABC's Nightline** and **PBS's Late Night America,** as well as hundreds of radio and television stations across the country.

Each week Mr. Bloch broadcasts his radio program coast to coast live for two hours from ABC News headquarters in Washington, D.C. The show is also carried on the AP Wide World Network.

24

Communicating Via Television and Radio to Make Money
by H.I. "Sonny" Bloch

"We have now entered the age of the satellite communications explosion."
—Ronald Reagan
President of the United States

Welcome to the communications explosion. As communicators, we must examine every aspect of the art of communication. Especially satellites and broadcasting, keeping in mind that the year 2000 approaches quickly. I will share with you on these pages my personal experiences in the world of electronic communication including narrowcasting on radio and television, teleconferencing, and the art of making public speeches via satellite worldwide. Using the electronic media available to you today, you can reach more people for less money more quickly than ever before.

The Birth of a Communicator

My mother, in her youth, was a singer and an actress in Dayton, Ohio. When I arrived on the scene she projected her enthusiasm for communicating and entertaining to me. And, I must admit from the very beginning, I loved every minute of it! Mother would "showoff' her children's talents at the mere arrival of a guest in the house and as we grew into our teen years, she would constantly encourage us to perform whenever possible. By the time I was in high school, I was excelling in public speaking, music, singing and acting. My father taught me the art of selling myself first. "What a great start!"

By the time I was a junior in high school, I was a member of the American Federation of musicians and was earning money for something I would have gladly done for free. I arrived at the Univerity of Miami with my automobile full of instruments. My decision was to major in speech and to use music as an advocation, a way to earn extra money while I was in college. I pursued my music career with gusto and since the University of Miami was located so close to Miami Beach, getting work as an entertainer-musician was not hard to do. My speech courses in college were a breeze, simply because I had overcome that initial fear of speaking in front of an audience and I was performing almost every night as an entertainer-musician. By the time I reached my junior year in college I had a hit record plus lots of publicity and recognition. Somehow, my parents instilled in me that without your audience, you are nothing. Back then, and even to this day, whenever a person applauds one of my performances, or tells me in writing or in person that they have enjoyed what I did, I am *truly* thankful.

Let your audience know how much you appreciate them. Do not forget to return the love that they are giving to you. After four years in college, I decided to hit the road and become a full-time entertainer. The life was fast and furious. (A little bit too fast for me.) At the ripe old age of 23 years, I decided to withdraw from the business of performing and jump head first into the wonderful world of business. For seventeen years, I toiled in the business world (not happily) with a constant yearning to return to the stage. In 1977, I decided to call my business career quits, and move to Palm Beach, Florida, to spend some time determining what I was going to do with the rest of my life. And then the communications explosion hit me.

First, in my ears, while listening to a talk show in Palm Beach, Florida. I said to myself, why not take your theatrical and performing background and tell people on the radio what you have learned in the past seventeen years about the world of real estate. I went to the local radio station, they said yes, and thus, my first electronic show was born, Real Estate Action Line, October 6, 1979 in Palm Beach. The show was a smashing success from the first day. Shortly thereafter we took the show to television at the local level, and by July of 1980, Real Estate Action Line was being fed via satellite to over 15 million American homes.

The thrill of communicating via television and radio is sometimes frightening, like the time I was in a little town in Colorado (population 620). I stopped for a quick libation at the local bar. An older gentleman came over to me and said, "We just saw you on television yesterday." That's the kind of thing that brings the power of electronic com- munication home! As of this writing, I am doing three nationally syndicated television shows plus a live two-way talk radio show fed via satellite to 2500 stations from New York City to the nation. We also have five shows on the drawing board.

I must share with you one of the most thrilling moments in my career thus far. I received a call from ABC in Washington, D.C. to appear on a national program, Nightline, which I watch constantly. I did not ask to be on the show, the invitation came as a result of my broadcast efforts during the past several years. I found myself in the ABC studio at 10:00 at night face-to-face with Ted Koppel, who happens to be my favorite broadcast journalist. All I could say to Ted was, "I love your program," and in a sincere humble fashion Ted Koppel said to me, "I *really* appreciate that Sonny." The point: no matter how big you are you appreciate your audience.

Radio Is the Spark Plug

No matter how large or small your town is, if you are a speaker, if you plan to be a speaker, or a seminar giver, or if you even imagine the possibility of being a broadcast journalist, there is no better way to start than on radio. There are over 10,500 radio stations in this country and there are thousands of radio stations looking for programming if you can talk and if you have interesting things to say, go to your radio station and tell them you are interested in putting a special program on the air. The usual time for programs of this type is on the weekends. You must first go to your news-talk radio stations. If you are turned down, go to your MOR—"middle of the road" or variety stations. Then check into your local public radio stations. The best way to approach the radio station is to have a sponsor prior to arriving. In the case of commercial stations, they are always looking for revenue. And, in the case of public radio, they are always looking for underwriters. You will be surprised how little it costs to put your name in front of the public on a regular basis, via radio.

Before going on radio, ask for permission to watch radio talk show hosts in operation. There are a lot of things to know and of course you can attend a college course or even a seminar. There are several excellent seminars on how to be a radio host available in this country. Of all the various ways I communicate, I consider two-way talk radio to be my favorite, simply because you get immediate feedback from the audience, and as a person who loves to wear jeans and dress in a comfortable fashion, I can do my communicating with a very large audience without having to put on a suit and tie. However, I cannot deny that the live audience with the applause, smiles and pats on the back, still makes me feel great.

If your subject is pets, then get a local pet store to sponsor you; if your subject is real estate, get a real estate company or bank to sponsor you; if your subject is insurance, get an insurance company to sponsor you. There are plenty of sponsors out there, who are willing to put their money on the line if you'll talk about their company to an audience that is going to be buying their product. This is called NARROWCASTING, which I will explain in more detail at the end of this chapter.

Is Television for You?

Television is the least favorite of the ways in which I communicate. However, television is the most lucrative media. Television requires very special skills. Within the three ways I communicate to the masses, I utilize *different* skills in each media. Public speaking requires a special separate set of skills as do radio appearances and television appearances. In television, you are dealing with a highly restricted, small area. Television requires you to wear the proper make-up (yes, that includes you men too). It requires the proper clothing colors; stay away from loud, brash colors, stay away from white. Look into the eye of the camera as if you were making love to it. Your spirit and energy leaps from your eyes into the camera lens and thus into the living rooms and bedrooms of the people who are watching you. Television is a very intimate media. Communicating on television is the most difficult task in the electronic media.

The quickest and least expensive way to break into television these days is through the local access channels of the cable system in your area. The cost is usually free or extremely cheap. Using the local access channel will give you an opportunity to see how you look on television and it will also give some of the local people a chance to watch your work. The key to commercial television or public television is teaming up with a superb producer. My partner and executive producer, Gale Nemec, and I have been together for six years and our programs only look as good or sound as good as she can make them. The people behind the scenes make the difference for you. Find a producer that believes in what you're doing. Start your team and go forward on television.

After you make your decision use the same technique that you used for radio for finding a sponsor, approaching first the local UHF independent station. The network affiliate probably will not listen to your presentation. Therefore, go to those who have the greatest need: the small stations in your market place. Remember, I started in a little market place, which was the spring board for my nationally syndicated programs. Do not be discouraged with your first turn-downs. Ask the station why they have turned you down and then re-work your presentation. Go back time and again until the answer is yes. If there is a small radio or television station starting up in a town near you, go there before they even build the station and start to make your deal. The Federal Communications Commission has approved the licensing of four thousand *new television stations* in our country which are now being built. There are presently 500 low power television stations on the air. What a great opportunity for you to begin your electronic communication career in the field of television. There has never been a better time for anyone interested to break into the radio and television field.

Speak to the World from Your Living Room

Video teleconferencing has come of age. It costs less money now that the technology has made it easy for you to beam yourself from anywhere in the world to anywhere in the world. I recently performed a three-day 18-hour video television conference to 36 colleges and universities throughout America. The purpose of the teleconference was to introduce seniors in college to various employers who were interested in hiring them. We had major employers such as NASA, Sperry-Rand Techtronics, and the Secret Service, with us in the studio talking to college students at the various locations. The students had a telephone in each room and were able to go to the phone and talk to us live via satellite.

Video teleconferencing could do the following

for you as a speaker or communicator. If you wanted to give a speech to New York City and lived in California you could do so simply by going to a studio, talking to the camera and having yourself beamed live to New York City. While your audience is listening and watching you they can in fact come to the microphone and speak to you.

I host a program which is called, "Beam Me Up." Recently, when I was in Denver, Colorado, I was invited to speak to the American Land Development Association in New Orleans, Louisiana. While I was giving the speech in Denver it was being beamed via satellite, live, to New Orleans, where a 25 foot television screen had been set up at the front of the room. I had asked someone at the New Orleans meeting to relay to my producer via phone what the people were wearing as they walked up to the microphone to ask me questions. The producer then relayed this information to me through a device in my ear; thus I was able to compliment the lady in the yellow dress, even though I could not see her. The reaction was phenomenal. It was amusing and entertaining because the audience had no idea that someone was telling me what they were wearing.

As a speaker you can speak to ten different organizations in ten different cities simultaneously. That's right, there will come a day when speakers will do less traveling via airplane and more traveling via satellite. Just think about saving the wear and tear on your body, your mind and your family! I have made many personal appearances and speeches via satellite live and it is fully my intention to cut down on my travel time and do more speeches in this manner. Another item which is of extreme importance to speakers is, if you have the need to audition, via tapes or brochures, why not do it via satellite? You could call meeting planners and organizations in various parts of the country and let them know that at the Holiday Inn (most have satellite dishes) at a particular time on a particular day, you will be giving them a sample of your work via satellite and an opportunity for them to talk to you two-way. The total cost of such an operation is a small percentage of the cost of travel to each one of these places for an in-person presentation.

Recently, I did a teleconference from Washington D.C. to San Diego, and my entire cost was less than $2000.00. I spoke to more than 2000 potential clients at a cost of less than $1.00 per client. The most wonderful thing about the electronic communications system is that as technology improves, the costs go down. I have had a truck pull up in front of my office while I was unable to make a trip, bring a camera in to the room and actually feed the signal from the truck to the satellite. Yes, speakers, the day has come when you can make your speeches from your living room or even less formally from the side of your swimming pool.

Narrowcasting: Now Let's Sell It!

Major corporations and small businesses alike are quickly discovering the best-kept secret in the marketing world: satellite-fed television, or narrowcasting. The new communications explosion and high-tech satellite and cable television capabilities are providing the business world with a way to instantly reach more people for less money than ever before in the history of communication.

Narrowcasting can best be defined as television programming designed especially for a specific viewing audience. Sponsors like Proctor & Gamble, General Foods, Mazda, Campbell Soup and others, produce their own television show in which they advertise and promote their products. And instead of trying to jam their message into a 30- or 60-second advertisement, the sponsors have a full half-hour to develop their ideas and demonstrate their products. Although the show itself utilizes the sponsor's products, traditional commercials are part of the programming as well, and the sponsor can present its product in this conventional manner too.

For example, General Foods produces *Woman's Day USA,* a program for housewives. As part of the program format, recipes are prepared and of course the ingredients used in those recipes are General Foods' brand name products. Since few women uninterested in cooking would be likely to tune in to the show, the sponsor has a prime audience of individuals who are likely to go out and purchase the products used in the preparation of the various recipes on the program.

More people are turning to television than to any other medium for the news, entertainment and information. A few years ago it was simply too expensive for smaller businesses to use television in their marketing campaigns. Not so today.

The picture has changed dramatically within the past five years and today cable and satellite television programming provide an alternative that blows conventional advertising out of the water. Television has literally become an audio-visual magazine with the ability to meet the needs and requirements of even the most discriminating special interest groups. From real estate to choice vacation spots, investments, medicine, sports and even pets, the range of effective, narrowcast television shows is limitless.

Producing top quality television shows that feature a sponsor's products and are, at the same time, entertaining, is not easy, but viewers who have grown up watching the three conventional broadcast networks will accept nothing less than excellence; if a sponsor-produced program is to be successful, excellence is mandatory.

At the same time, for narrowcasting to be cost-effective, it must be much less expensive than conventional television—and it is. The cost of making an average sitcom on ABC, CBS, or NBC is about $300,000, but top quality 30-minute narrow-cast programs are currently produced and distributed by us nationally for as little as $6,000.

According to ABC, CBS and NBC, 48% of their audience has been lured away to satellite-delivered television. Any industry (such as the satellite cable industry), in its infancy, has higher supply than demand. For example, many cable operators have large amounts of unsold time. This means that they are willing to sell that time at a reduced rate. For example, 30-minute programs are now being placed in select, major markets for as little as $125. In addition, 30- and 60-second advertising spots can be purchased in major markets for as little as $15 apiece. Prime time spots on the conventional networks average more than $83,000 for a 30-second ad.

In an era of highly competitive advertising and marketing campaigns and strategies, narrowcasting makes the nation's number one communications medium affordable and effective for businesses of every budget and size.

I have shared some very important information

with you on how to communicate electronically. Since communication is a sharing profession, I hope that you will share some of my ideas with the people you meet along the way. I really enjoy speaking to live audiences throughout the country, especially college students. Some of my themes are entrepreneuring, narrowcasting, the communications explosion, and how to appear on radio and television. There is however, *one major theme* in all of my speeches, and that is, IF YOU DON'T TAKE A CHANCE, YOU DON'T GET A CHANCE.

My life thus far has been an excellent example of a person who, in early, years, was fulfilled as a communicator and by taking a few wrong turns on the roadway of life, almost came to a dead end. It is never too late or too early, to follow that dream. As a youngster, I did all of the things to prepare me for a life as a communicator, but somehow, decided that if I was going to raise a family, it would be better for me to be in business. I could have stayed in that business for the rest of my life.

When I left the business world, after 17 years, I was well into my forties. Those closest to me thought I had lost my mind. When I made the decision to go back into the "show business" again those who loved me so dearly tried to discourage me. Each time I performed, whether it was a success or failure, I was still happy. It really isn't the money that makes you happy in life. If you do decide to continue as a professional communicator, or if you haven't yet begun your career as a professional communicator, make sure that you feel that you are being paid for something that you love to do. As long as that feeling continues to exist and you approach your career with enthusiasm and gusto, the money will come automatically. I have many friends, and I am sure you do, who are totally dissatisfied with their life, their work, and themselves. These are people who are not taking a chance, so they don't get a chance. We live in a country where opportunities are guaranteed, but success is not. Talent is a gift, not to use it is a sin. If we have a talent for communication and we don't use it, then shame on us. I have had the opportunity to share my thoughts personally with many of today's great communicators.

They have inspired me and encouraged me, including: Art Linkletter, Ty Boyd, Wayne Newton, Senator Paula Hawkins, Jack Anderson, Robert Allen, Dr. A.D. Kessler, Ted Koppel, Dick Clark, Sally Struthers, and Dr. Robert Schuller, plus hundreds of other communicators, who have touched my life. To those who encouraged me to go forward, I thank you. Remember, if you have a question or thought about the life of a communicator, ask one.

If you find that you are great on radio and not so good on television or vice versa, concentrate on the electronic media that is best suited for you. Let some professionals listen to your tapes and watch your shows . . . and like the proverbial diagnosis from the doctor, *always* get more than one opinion. I have started many people in this business. We were the first company to put the real estate program on the air and as you know, hundreds are now being shown each week across the country. Many of the people in other fields of expertise have taken our advice and have gone out into the world of electronics and are actually part of the new communications explosion. There is lots of room for more electronic communicators. Welcome to my world!

Great eloquence, like a flame, must have fuel to feed it, motion to excite it, and brightens by burning.

—*Tacitus*

LILLET WALTERS
Walters International Speakers' Bureau
P.O. Box 1120
Glendora, CA 91740
(818) 335-8069

Lillet Walters

Lillet, "Lilly" Walters began teaching the neighborhood children horsemanship when she was only 12. She organized classes, then held mini horse shows.

Today Lilly is the Vice President of Royal Publishing Inc. and Executive Director of Walters International Speakers Bureau. She sends speakers, trainers and consultants all over the world. In addition, Lilly gives seminars all across the country on how to hire speakers, and basic program planning.

Lilly obtained a Horsemaster degree when she was 18 and began a small training stable. One of the classes she offered was Vaulting, the art of gymnastics on the back of a moving horse. Within the first nine months her team became champions in regional and national competitions! The team consistently remained champions for 10 years.

Lilly has never had any gymnastic training, never vaulted herself, and has never been considered (even by the kindest of people) to be an athelete! Yet she consistently brought each team she taught to one and often several championships.

This is the story of how Lilly helped average people become champions year after year.

25

Championship Communication: Building A Winning Team
by Lillet Walters

"We never fall, we gracefully glide to the ground and roll!"
—Rainbow Vaulters

Over the past 10 years, I have taught the ancient sport of vaulting; the art of gymnastics on the back of a moving horse. Not the modern sport of "vaulting" that is done in a gymnasium on a "horse," but the original sport that is done on a real horse in a dirt arena! It was used to teach cavalry units how to ride.

My teams have brought home over 30 National and hundreds of Regional Championships. Yet, I myself have never vaulted, never had any gymnastic training, never been an athlete of any kind! My friends (and rivals!) always ask, "How can you do it? It's impossible, you're just lucky and get talented students year after year. " But any team leader can tell you, you don't just *happen* to attract winners to you.

Any time you bring more than one person together on a project, the wonderful power of synergy comes into play. Synergy is the extra-ordinary power of forces being combined together. Synergy is the total of those combined forces being much greater than they would have been if added up by themselves. The *potential* power for creativity and accomplishment is phenomenal! Unfortunately, power has the ability of going in any direction; up, down, right or left with equal force. Team projects will either be wonderful or a disaster! They are rarely mediocre!

Many leaders feel they must hire champions to achieve championship results. I've heard it said, "You can't take a turkey to eagle school!" But I've rarely been able to pick and choose. I had to use what was available. Most leaders are stuck in the same position. Once the team members are chosen and it's time to sink or swim, then it's time to look at the real reason your team is going to soar with those eagles or muddle around with the turkeys. That reason is YOU!

Communicate the Challenge!
(The Thrill of Victory)

Your team will never be greater than you envision them to be. You must want them to succeed desperately, then *live* the excitement and thrill. Lee Iacocca says, "By Monday morning I was ready to hit the ground running! I have found that the speed of the boss is the speed of the team!" In comparison, the attitude of the leader is the attitude of the team.

Even the most uninspiring project has thousands of inspirational aspects. True, some projects I've worked on took a lot of imagination and digging to find those aspects, but they are there! Be responsible for finding the keys that will kick each member of your team and yourself into high gear! Your attitude and emotions for a project will rule your actions. Your actions will communicate to your teams much more loudly and strongly than any words you can use.

Vaulting is the kind of sport where you hit the ground . . . a lot! When one of your team members lies in the dirt, looking up at you with pain and frustration, then you really have the ultimate test as a leader. The words I use to communicate at that point are unimportant. I feel with them. I cry when they hurt. But, *most importantly,* I find that part of the exercise that *did* go right. I get *very* excited over that (often tiny) successful part! Eventually they catch my excitement over the success and forget the pain of the fall.

Communicate Passion

Each team is made up of individuals. Those individuals will have individual keys to hidden passions. A team will never be greater than the weakest member of the team. So find out *which* key works for every member, *when* it works, and *how hard* you have to push to turn each one on!

Don't shy away from thoughts of *passion, devotion,* and *commitment.* The world could do with more of these emotions! Use them when you ponder the problems of the project in your mind. Then your mind will begin to communicate with their souls, what was formerly impossible for you to express. Performance levels *will* rise.

The desire to be totally involved and dedicated to *something* is in everyone. If you don't get them involved and stimulated about your project, they will give those private passions to another endeavor, like Little League, a bowling team, whatever. Give them a way to feel prideful and possessive about your project. They must feel that their commitment to the project will indeed make it *their* project and their project will have importance and meaning. Give that to them and they will give you results that you never dreamed them capable of giving!

As you set the challenge out for each member of the team, gauge how much pressure they can stand. Without a certain amount of pressure and stress, they will never grow. Give them enough to stretch them but not defeat them. As they grow, you must change the goals so they will continue to grow.

In the beginning, most team members will only want recognition and praise. As they become more advanced, a desire for fame and glory will develop. Many leaders are afraid of their members when they reach this point. They're afraid they'll lose control and be displaced if the members get too much glory. You won't get championship results if you can't offer them the glory deserved by *any* champion. It's part of that sweet thrill of victory. If you are afraid of their getting too much glory, get out of the leadership game, you don't deserve the title! A student that does not surpass his teacher, fails his teacher!

In the first stages with your new team, you will be the only one that will know just where you are all going. You can tell them about that thrill of victory, but they won't understand how much it is going to cost them in time, pain and sweat! But it's just as well, many of them would quit if they knew how much you needed to pull out of them to raise them to those championship levels. So, give them those parts of the dream they *can* relate to at their level. Change it as they progress. Once they have tasted victory themselves, they will become addicted. Your job will change from *pushing* for each new improvement, into *directing* them toward all the new schemes and dreams they will have themselves.

The Agony of Defeat!

On my team, members do not *fail* when they fall. Indeed, we do not fall! Now I know the more skeptical of you are thinking there is no way to teach hundreds of people how to do gymnastics on the back of a moving horse *without* falls. To be honest, we do come off the horse when the original intent is to stay on! That happens every few seconds . . . but we don't call it falling. "Fall? We never fall, we gracefully glide to the ground and roll!" Then they run like crazy to catch the horse and *get back on!* Calling it falling sounds too painful Falling is too essential to learning to allow them to be afraid of it. You don't fail when you fall, you fail when you don't get back on!

Be ready for the falls. Teach your team to fall as safely as possible. But know that falls are a mandatory part of the success pattern. They must fall again and again to make a worthwhile finished product. Jim Newman, world famous speaker says, "Anything worth doing, is worth doing badly!" As the movie "Fame" said, "You want to be a star? *Here is where you pay the price!*"

You can't let *your* fear of failure get in the way of your team's success. If you are too shocked over their hurts, and there will be *many* hurts, they will never rise over your fear and sympathy level. As you are stretching them out of their former comfort levels, make sure *you* are growing with them!

As they get more advanced, the situation reverses. They will come to you with ideas that seem crazy and outlandish! You are thinking inside, it's insane, it'll never work, it's way past their ability level, they'll get hurt! Stop yourself before you stop them. Is it really past *their* ability level or past yours?

It never fails, the question always comes up, "Lilly, do you think we'll win?" My answer is always the same. "Well, you have much less experience than anyone else out there (whenever possible I put them into the level above their expertise so they are the underdog!) You are going to have to put out more effort to win than anybody else. But I promise you, when you run back out of that arena, you will be filled with such a feeling of excitement that it won't matter what the judges think! You are going to give one of the best performances of your lives. All of your senses will be alive with an intense feeling of pride and success. When you have that, it won't matter if the judges like you or not! Let's not kid each other, I've won and lost. Winning is much better! But that will be our second goal. The first is being much better than you have ever *dreamed* you could be!"

When they get discouraged and say, "It's too hard," I answer, "Of course it's *hard*, thank heaven it's hard! If it was *easy* everyone would be doing it!" As you lie on the ground, trying to find the energy to get up, think of your arch rivals. Are they trying this project too? Did they *give up* at this point, or did they try it that final time that it *did* work?

There is a fine line between being reckless and being courageous. The main difference is that they call you courageous if you are reckless successfully! I am responsible for many new rules being added into the rule book. They called me innovative when they liked my ideas and eliminated us when they didn't! We were almost never in the middle, which is great by me! I hate to be thought of as average! If we had to lose, I wanted to go down with them all knowing that I at least had the courage to try something new!

These words of Teddy Roosevelt have always

summed up my attitude about "the agony of defeat"...

"It is not the critic who counts,
Not the one who points out how the strong fighter
  stumbled,
Or where the doer of deeds could have done them
  better.
The credit belongs to the one who is actually in the
  arena;
Whose face is marred by dust and sweat and blood;
Who strives valiantly;
Who errs and comes short again and again;
Who knows the great enthusiasms,
The great devotions;
And spends the whole heart in a worthy cause,
Who at the best
Knows in the end the triumph of high achievement;
And who at the worse, if failure comes,
At least fails while daring greatly,
So that this fighter's place
Shall never be with those cold and timid souls—
Who know neither victory nor defeat."

—**Teddy Roosevelt**

Louder Than Words.

The most important thing I have learned in coaching my champions, is that it is darn near impossible to tell anybody else *how* I do it! There are few knowledgeable reasons for me to set down. It has been the most magical, wonderful experience I have ever had. All other accomplishments in my life will be measured by the thrill of each championship performance we have had together.

The power that emits from the team is so intense, that I literally feel like fainting when we run back out of the arena. It isn't just the pride of a job well done, it is the hours of sweat in the heat and dirt, the tears, anger, love, frustration, devotion and bruises.

The hair is braided neatly with tidy little bows. The horses are scrubbed, washed, bleached, braided and groomed to perfection. Everything is clean and tidy, in harsh contrast to the dirt we put up with the rest of the time. The vaulters' delicate vaulting slippers are polished. They line up in height order, the tiny seven year old girl on one end, the 30 year old man on the other.

Everyone who has performed for large audiences knows that all-encompassing feeling of power that is communicated to you from an excited crowd. They don't have to say one audible word, but you can feel from the excited murmurs and pitch of the voices that they are *waiting* for you. They are excited that it's *you* that is coming up next! They know your reputation. Will you pull off something new and unique again? Or is it your turn to bomb?

As we are ready to run in, the vaulters and I are waiting outside the gate. Now is the time when the stress will *make* them or ruin them. I make a few jokes, "Gosh, I'm really hungry, you all go on without me, I'm running out for a pizza!" (When you're that nervous, anything seems funny!) But then I reach for their souls and let them know we're *going to be great.* "You know, I am *so* proud of you, you have come so far! I have never been more proud of anyone in my life." With each group, each year, I have felt that from the bottom of my heart and each person has known it. "Are we ready to go in?" Nervous smiles. "All right . . . dazzle!"

We run in to thunderous applause. A formal salute to the judges. The music starts. The first vaulter mounts right into a full split along the horse's back! Slowly and gracefully, she arches into a backbend over her leg, the arm extended in a delicate ballet pose. It looks so perfect, it seems effortless. Those of us on team in the arena can see the muscles bulge and the teeth grind behind the forced smile as the horse takes a wrong step and jars her. But she never gives any *obvious* signs, so the audience doesn't know, the judges don't know. But the *team* knows that she has just saved them from a terrible knock down in the score by keeping her composure and forcing herself to go on without any outward sign of pain. It sends such a surge of pride through the team that there are virtually no further mistakes in the rest of the routine. It lasts for five minutes. Building to three vaulters on at the same time and finishing with double and triple flips off the horse.

The crowd rises to their feet, we give the formal salute to the judge and composedly trot out of the arena. Then all the surpressed emotions break loose! They scream, cry, laugh, hug, fall on the ground. Scores of people run out of the stands to congratulate us, hug us, cry with us.

I saw the finished product in mind, they had caught the dream from me, we had communicated much louder than words ever could have. We reaped the glory of that ultimate form of communication.

Synergy . . . Control It . . . Use It

Because of the amazing power I feel at work in my teams, I did a study of how to utilize it. I am convinced that emotions, *any* emotion, will travel from one receptive mind to another. Anytime you put people together in a team situation, their minds will become receptive to each other's emotions. If the emotions are positive, they can bring you to the winners circle. If they are negative, they can drag you down in defeat. Call that kind of power whatever you want, I call it synergy.

I first saw it come into play when a vaulter was

having a "bad" day. Sometimes they'd let their emotions of frustration and fear of failure explode. Within 10 minutes the rest of the team was falling off, from standard exercises that were normally easy for them. The amazing part was that it visibly started with one vaulter and suddenly the whole team was crying in the dirt! *But,* it also worked in reverse. When a vaulter got thrilled over something they had accomplished, the whole team would start performing miracles!

Talk to them about how much their emotions will effect their work. Give them an object to lift, a heavy book, a brick, whatever. Ask them to close their eyes and visualize in their minds a moment of triumph and success. When they truly *feel* that moment, have them pick up the object, then set it back down. Now, have them visualize a moment of defeat, despair, unhappiness, when they feel the emotion, pick up the object again. It will be *much* heavier the second time!

Performance works the same way. If you allow yourself to dwell on negative thoughts, your performance level will fall. Your own temper tantrums may make you feel great as a method of venting your frustrations, but what did you do to the performance level of the rest of the team? Are they losing productivity because of your temporary loss of control?

When you are struggling with an intense

emotion, you can react in several ways. You can sit in the dirt and vent it orally by tears, yelling, etc. Or simply let it defeat you and walk away. Remember, that frustration that has formed inside you is a *power*. Use it! Don't let it use you. Let it get you mad enough to throw you back up into the fray again! When you want to cry out in pain, try yelling out a huge laugh! Sounds crazy, but you feel much better and the team will sense your determination and will become more determined themselves!

When one of my team members is at that point of breaking into a destructive emotional tantrum, I quickly find the part of what they are doing that *is* going right and praise them for that. If that doesn't work, I try being very calm and mildly humorous or motherly. I use my instincts to find what is going to work with that vaulter in that situation. I could be the nastiest witch in the world and bodily throw them out of a lesson if they need that. Destructive emotional tantrums must be stopped. But ecstatic emotions of success must be cherished, relished and relived!

Rising and Falling Stars

After you have brought your team to repeated success, a few will have a tendency to fall into a star syndrome. Rising stars are wonderful. They are hungry for success. They think nothing of repeated falls and bruises. They want more and more of that glory and fame! But some will change. If you can't find keys to keep them motivated, they will simply hang around the group to reap the glory of the "lesser beings" and receive some hero worship. Don't misunderstand me. Hero worship is part of being a champion. They deserve to be admired and honored. But when they reach a point when they feel they are not "on the way" anymore, that they have arrived, I don't have have use for them.

The newer members of the team will watch and emulate these so-called stars. They will think they can make it to the top by coasting too! They were not around when the star was still rising and struggling. Not only do these lackadaisical stars become a very heavy burden for any leader to carry, they can become destructive to the team!

My first year of coaching, I lost my first star of this type. I was devasted. How could we ever win again? Nobody on the team came near that person's ability! But, we went on. I discovered another of the most valuable lessons I've ever learned. We received *higher* scores and results *without* those so-called heroes than we did with them! Over 10 years it happened several times. I hated to give them up at first and tried to make them stay, in spite of the fact that they made the rest of us miserable!

When a "falling star" leaves your team, the rest

of the team will feel like a great weight has been lifted. They feel that they have a chance of winning now, and they start working harder. You lift that weight and misconception from them and they become rising stars themselves!

Don't mistake a falling star for a member whose time has come to move on. I hate to lose anyone for any reason. But they grow up, move, or just need to grow in another direction. Don't feel hurt when one of them leaves. It's your job to make them grow and change. If they change so much that they need to leave, then you've done your part! Don't be bitter, instead tell yourself . . . "Well done!"

Communicate from the Heart

When I was 10 years old, I was in an accident. We had rented a forklift to move hay. It flipped over on top of me. My left hand was pinned and acid dripped on my body. I went through 10 operations because of complications from the acid burns and gangrene. I don't remember much of those first few weeks in the hospital. But, events were happening that would shape the rest of my life.

My mother is an international speaker, president of four corporations and a famous success motivator. But when I got hurt, she couldn't even motivate herself to dry her eyes. She was struck so low, they almost had to hospitalize *her*.

I was always her star child. The one she hoped would go into business with her. She had just signed me up for piano lessons, she wanted me to learn to type. She thought all the special hopes she had for me were over. She was so low herself at that point, she couldn't envision my rise either.

One day in the hospital, a small black girl in the next bed stopped Mom as she came in. She said, "You put those things down, I have a job for you! The boy down the hall is sad, he thinks he is going to die. Now you go down there and cheer him up!" Mother was so shocked at the child's commanding way, she went. I think that was the turning point for her. She had a job to do that she was well suited to, giving hope and motivation to someone in need.

When she came back, she spoke to the girl, who told us all about her handicapped high school. Her best friend was the typing teacher. She taught the others with a wand in her teeth! She had no arms! IBM had developed a system for handicapped people, no matter how many fingers or hands they had!

That was it! Hope came back up in Mom. She literally ran down the hall and grabbed a social worker. "How do I get those typing charts from IBM?" The social worker said, "Why ever would she want to learn to type? It would never be of any use. It's too hard for handicapped people anyway."

Mom ignored him and grabbed a phone and called IBM. "I hear you have typing charts for people with one hand! My baby has lost her hand, I need them . . please!" and she broke down and cried. The woman on the other end at IBM must have been shocked. She stuttered, "Of course we have them, I'll go get them, I'll send them today, this morning, never mind, I'm going now!"

It took a leader that was 12 years old and crippled herself to give Mom that key to get back up again. Did that child see the depression in my mother and recognize her need for something constructive? I don't suppose I'll ever know for sure, but the results are surely the same.

It was by my family's constant love and devotion that I have never considered myself in the least handicapped. But, it was by the excitement my mother generated that I was able to achieve things that others thought "too hard" for me. She'd say, "Just think, you'll be the only seven-fingered guitarist in the country!" (An exaggeration I know now, but it certainly helped to keep me excited back then.) "You'll learn to ride and jump horses, not the easy way that any old person could do it, but you'll figure out a new way!" "You'll be the only one-handed typist in our city!"

At every tiny accomplishment, she'd rave and praise me. She'd call in newspaper reporters and we'd make scrap books of the articles. She showed me the glory was in the success! Not in staying down in the dirt, depression and pity where it was safe.

I wish I could say that I am successful today, because of my own courage or fortitude. But it isn't true. I am successful today in my own small way because there was a leader in my life who had the vision to see past the obvious setbacks that any idiot can see. She saw and felt the accomplishments with her heart . . . then simply communicated what she saw . . . to me!

By words the mind is excited and the spirit elated.

—Aristophanes

DR. DON BAGIN
Communication Briefings
806 Westminster Blvd.
Blackwood, NJ 08012
(609) 589-3503

Don Bagin

Don Bagin is Professor of Communications at Glassboro State College and Publisher of Communication Briefings, a newsletter going to more than 15,000 subscribers.

He has spoken to more than 100,000 people on the topic of communications. He has written seven books, including Communication Ideas That Work (McGraw-Hill) and School and Community Relations (Prentice-Hall). Don developed the country's first masters-degree program in school communications and has served as a public relations director for colleges, schools and the New Jersey Department of Education.

He has been President of the National School Public Relations Association and has delivered major addresses for the American Association of School Administrators, the National School Boards Association, the National Congress of Parents and Teachers and the National School Public Relations Association.

He has conducted extensive research in the area of staff morale and speaks on the topic of improving morale and productivity. He serves as a consultant to companies and associations helping them improve their public relations efforts.

Epilog

Communication in the Year 2000
by Dr. Don Bagin
Professor, Communications, Glassboro State College
and Publisher, Communication Briefings

How will communication in the year 2000 differ from the way we communicate now? What skills will we need to succeed as communicators?

Despite the presence of technological breakthroughs and the advent of voice-activated computers, here's a prediction that might startle some futurists and communicators.

We'll be using pretty much the same skills we use now to communicate in the year 2000. But the big news might be that more people will be expected to communicate effectively.

In many organizations, we have staff members designated as communicators, much like the designated hitter in the American League. Many other employees defer to the communicators and those employees mistakenly feel they don't have to communicate well.

As more and more computer communication takes place, employees at all levels will be expected to provide answers to questions and proposals instantly. This means that non-communicators will lose status in many organizations.

Another predictable change focuses on the personalization of entertainment and sales efforts. More direct mail efforts and more choices of television programming will encourage communicators to research narrowly defined audiences and prepare programs and persuasive messages for them.

What are the implications now for the challenges that await those who will be expected to communicate well in 2000?

The biggest challenge faces the schools that are preparing people to work in the year 2000. The next largest challenge falls to industry, which depends on its workforce to increase productivity.

Both educational and industrial leaders must place clear communication on the country's agenda. When Sputnik captured the world's attention, we quickly committed the country's resources to improved math and science programs.

As business leaders continue to complain about the inability of employees to write and speak well, we must put the importance of communication skills on the public agenda. If we don't do this soon—if we don't prepare people to communicate ideas as well as to generate them—the country will not be all that it can.

Solid Communication

For openers, we should insist on solid communication from all with whom we work. We should let our school leaders know that we expect high school and college graduates to write well and to speak well.

We need to teach interpersonal skills so people can get along with each other better. The best contributor to productivity is still a motivated staff. Too many schools continue to emphasize how to crunch numbers without teaching the ability to work with people to get the best from all. We need a commitment to communicate.

If we don't demand such a commitment, all kinds of chaos and mediocrity await us as we turn loose millions of non-communicators with computers that quickly display the fact that many people can't communicate very well.

SUCCESS SEMINAR SERIES
ANTHOLOGIES

#1: SUCCESS SECRETS! How 18 everyday women became builders and famous speakers! Role models! Beautiful hardback. Stimulating, inspirational, how to build your business and your life. ■ *$11.95*

#2: POSITIVE POWER PEOPLE. Men and women of achievement radiate positive attitudes, inspire readers to greater success. Foreword Cavett Robert. Book, hardback. ■ *$12.95*

#3. THE PEARL OF POTENTIALITY. Are you ready to catch it? An anthology of women of achievement from a woman. Train engineer to inventors, to speakers a wealth of inspiration! Hardback, beautiful gift for women beginning their careers. ■ *$11.95*

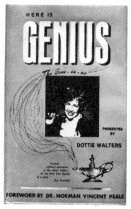

 # 4: HERE IS GENIUS. Men and women tell the stories of achievement and inspiration by opening the *genius channel.* Foreword by Dr. Norman Vincent Peale. Book, hardback. ■ *$11.95*

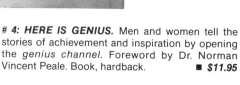

 # 5: THOSE MARVELOUS MENTORS. Amazing stories of the influences on their lives of top notch speakers and business people. Hardback. Foreword by former Arizona Congressman Somers White. Outstanding! ■ *$13.95*

#6: STAR SPANGLED SPEAKERS. Here are stories of the Space Shuttle, the Statue of Liberty, Americans who have overcome. Hardback. True stories of the people who won the battles of life. ■ *$13.95*

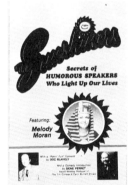

 # 7: THE SUNSHINERS. Secrets of humorous speakers. You'll laugh, you'll learn, you'll love them. Hardback. The speakers who light up your life. ■ *$13.95*

 # 8: THE GREAT PERSUADERS. Sales and sales management. The top managers in the United States give you their best information. Hardback. A treasure trove of how-to and when-to by the very top people. ■ *$16.95*

 # 9: *NEVER UNDERESTIMATE THE SELLING POWER OF A WOMAN by DOTTIE WALTERS, C.S.P.* The FAMOUS bestseller. The best sales book ever written by a woman for women in sales. Used as a textbook by many national sales firms. Easy to read, full of power. The classic! Hardback, book. ■ ***$13.95***

 # 10: *THE MAGNIFICENT MOTIVATORS.* Inspiring collection of motivational techniques revealed by some of the country's foremost speakers. Learn how these same methods can inspire you to greater achievement. Hardback ■***$14.95***

#11: *THE SYNERGISTS.* Exceptional achievers focus on qualities that help you develop a healthful, secure, successful lifestyle. ***$16.95***

#12: *THE MANAGEMENT TEAM*. Top rated management experts give an Encyclopedia of Management Tips, Systems and Advice. Foreword and Introduction by Joe Batten, C.P.A.E. and George Morrissey, C.P.A.E.

#13: *HERE COME THE SALES TRAINERS*. Here are the secrets of the best Sales-managers in the U.S. An exciting Anthology in which each Salesmanager offers the quintessence of great ideas in the field of Salestraining. ■ *$19.95*

ORDER FORM

BOOKS

No.	Quantity	Amt.	No.	Quantity	Amt.

NEWSLETTERS

No.	Quantity	Amt.

Check Enclosed

Master Charge _____

Bankamericard

VISA

Acct. No. _____

Expiration Date _____

Ship To:

Name _____

Address _____

City _____ State _____ Zip _____

Signature _____

Add 6½% sales tax in California.

Plus **$1.00 Shipping and handling per item.**

$2.00 out of the U.S.A.

American Currency only.

$20.00 Min. on charge card orders (M.C. or VISA)

Total _____